Working with Volunteers in Sport

Theory and practice

Graham Cuskelly, Russell Hoye
and Chris Auld

 Routledge
Taylor & Francis Group

LONDON AND NEW YORK

First published 2006
by Routledge
2 Park Square, Milton Park, Abingdon, Oxon OX14 4RN

Simultaneously published in the USA and Canada
by Routledge
270 Madison Ave, New York, NY 10016

Routledge is an imprint of the Taylor & Francis Group, an informa business

© 2006 Graham Cuskelly, Russell Hoye and Chris Auld

Typeset in Goudy by
Florence Production Ltd, Stoodleigh, Devon
Printed and bound in Great Britain by
Antony Rowe Ltd, Chippenham, Wiltshire

British Library Cataloguing in Publication Data
A catalogue record for this book is available
from the British Library

Library of Congress Cataloging in Publication Data
Cuskelly, Graham, 1958–
    Working with volunteers in sport : theory and practice /
    Graham Cuskelly, Russell Hoye, and Chris Auld. – 1st ed.
        p. cm.
    Includes bibliographical references and index.
    1. Sports – Management.   2. Volunteers – Management.   I. Hoye,
    Russell Stephen, 1966–   II. Auld, Christopher John.   III. Title.
    GV713.C87 2006
    796.06 – dc22   2006002915

ISBN10: 0–415–38452–4 (hbk)
ISBN10: 0–415–38453–2 (pbk)

ISBN13: 978–0–415–38452–0 (hbk)
ISBN13: 978–0–415–38453–7 (pbk)

Working with Volunteers in Sport

Working with Volunteers in Sport is a comprehensive guide to the issues surrounding the management of volunteers in sport organizations.

The contribution of volunteers at all levels – from local clubs to national governing bodies, right up to the Olympic Games – is at the heart of sport throughout the world. Yet changing policies and increasingly professionalized approaches to running sport are putting volunteer cultures at risk. Good management and a clear understanding of the way volunteers work in sport are essential to protect and develop the role of this core group of people.

This text covers the key issues, including:

- the nature and scope of sport volunteering
- sport development through volunteers
- recruiting, managing and developing volunteers
- specialists: coaches, officials, administrators and event volunteers
- legal issues.

Working with Volunteers in Sport links theory with research to provide clear guidelines for good volunteer management. For students, researchers and professionals working in sport management, sport development and sport policy, this book represents a valuable practical resource.

Graham Cuskelly is Professor of Sport Management in the Griffith University Business School, Brisbane. He is also Associate Editor of *Sport Management Review*.

Russell Hoye is a Senior Lecturer in Sport Management and Director of Postgraduate Studies in the School of Sport, Tourism and Hospitality Management at La Trobe University, Melbourne.

Chris Auld is Professor of Leisure Management in the Griffith University Business School, Brisbane.

Contents

Illustrations

Tables

Figures

Preface

The focus of this book is sport volunteers – their characteristics, contribution to the sustainability of sport, the settings and organizations in which they work, and issues associated with their management. Organized sport is an important arena for volunteering and in many countries sport volunteers represent the largest category of volunteers who contribute their time in formal organizational settings. Sport volunteers and voluntary sport organizations (VSOs) are the core of the club-based sport system in countries such as Australia, Canada, New Zealand and the UK. The substantial contribution of volunteers to sustaining and developing sport indicates that despite increasing trends in the employment of professional staff, volunteers are of central importance to the future of a number of national sport systems.

A prominent feature of VSOs and sport volunteering is diversity. The characteristics of volunteers, the organizations in which they participate, and the nature and degree of their involvement need to be understood in order to maximize the effectiveness, efficiency and satisfaction of sport volunteers in the planning, management and delivery of organized sport across thousands of communities. This book provides a comprehensive analysis of the issues associated with managing and working with volunteers in club-based sport systems. While sport volunteers are integral to the achievement of sport development outcomes, their capacity to do so is often constrained by a number of societal and institutional pressures that create barriers to volunteering. These include perceived time pressures, shifting demographic trends, changing community values and a more commercialized environment. VSOs also face an increasingly complex and dynamic legal environment, especially as sport club members and sport participants perceive that VSOs have become more professional and therefore should take more responsibility for their actions. Government also exerts pressure on VSOs and volunteers. The relationship between government and VSOs has now evolved towards contractual-based partnership arrangements that reflect the government view of sport funding as an investment and the sport system as a conduit for policy implementation and the achievement of broader social, economic and community development outcomes.

The success of government sport policies is largely dependent on the capacity of the voluntary sector and the motivation of volunteers to work within and, in some cases, take responsibility for implementing such policies.

VSOs and the volunteers and professional staff who work within them also face a range of internal organizational challenges. These include structural issues such as a need to manage changes in formalization and centralization, potential for conflict between volunteers and professionals, and an increasing emphasis on good governance and committee processes. In order to manage the impacts of these issues many VSOs have adopted more formalized structures and management practices, something that may not fit well with the expectations and motives of all sport volunteers. Much of the contemporary literature advocates the application of traditional human resource management (HRM) practices to managing and working with volunteers. This approach has several significant limitations including the assumptions underlying HRM practice, the lack of volunteer coordinators within VSOs, the complexity of volunteer roles and volunteers' perceived experiences in VSOs.

The book is written primarily for academics and individuals who wish to understand the characteristics of sport volunteers, the contribution they make to the sustainability of sport, the organizations in which they work and the issues associated with managing sport volunteers. Chapter 1 provides an introduction to the roles and impacts of volunteers and third sector organizations in sustaining and developing communities. Chapters 2 to 7 cover the scope and nature of sport in relation to other parts of the third sector, and explore recent trends in volunteer participation, the role of volunteers in sport development, the intentions and impacts of government policy, legal issues, the structure of VSOs, and the management of sport volunteers. Chapters 8 to 11 focus on specific issues and trends in four major areas of sport volunteering: administration, officiating, coaching and sport events. Chapter 12 discusses the future challenges for sport volunteers and their management.

We would like to thank Samantha Grant, Commissioning Editor at Routledge, for her continual support and Kate Manson for steering the book through the production process. Special thanks are due to Chris Smith for assisting with some of the research and administration tasks in the preparation of the manuscript. Finally, we would like to acknowledge the support and understanding for this endeavour provided by our families.

Graham Cuskelly
Russell Hoye
Chris Auld

Abbreviations

ABS	Australian Bureau of Statistics
AFL	Australian Football League
AIS	Australian Institute Sport
ARU	Australian Rugby Union
ASC	Australian Sports Commission
BASA	Backing Australia's Sporting Ability (sport policy)
CGF	Commonwealth Games Federation
CSP	Canadian Sport Policy
FA	Football Association
FIFA	Fédération Internationale de Football Association
HRM	human resource management
IFNA	International Netball Federation Limited
IOC	International Olympic Committee
IPC	International Paralympic Committee
ISF	International Sport Federation
LIRC	Leisure Industries Research Centre
NCAS	National Coaching Accreditation Scheme
NGB	national governing body
NOAS	National Officiating Accreditation Scheme
NSO	national sport organization
SPARC	Sport and Recreation New Zealand
TSPG	Targeted Sport Participation Growth (Program)
UNESCO	United Nations Educational, Scientific and Cultural Organization
VIP	Volunteer Investment Program
VMP	Volunteer Management Program
VPA	Volunteer Protection Act
VSO	voluntary sport organization

Chapter 1

The role of volunteers in sustaining communities

This book focuses on sport volunteers – their characteristics, contributions, the settings in which they work and the issues associated with managing them. However, in order to develop a comprehensive grasp of how to work effectively with sport volunteers, a broader contextual understanding of volunteering and the third sector is necessary. This chapter provides the background to and rationale for the remainder of the book. It outlines definitional issues related to volunteering, provides a brief historical overview of volunteering and describes how research in the area of volunteering has progressed in recent years. A variety of international data is utilized to describe volunteer trends and the nature and scope of the contributions made by volunteers before briefly concluding with an introduction to the importance of volunteers in community sport.

Although the United Nations designated 2001 as the 'International Year of the Volunteer', it would be difficult to argue that there has been a continuing sustained and widespread commitment by governments, peak organizations and communities to nurturing volunteerism. To the contrary, some evidence indicates that volunteering is in decline (Lyons and Fabiansson, 1998; Nichols *et al.*, 1998a; Gaskin, 1998; Davies, 1998; Daly, 1991). To therefore argue that the International Year of the Volunteer initiative has resulted in a sustained heightened consciousness about the importance of volunteering on the part of most citizens may also be optimistic. However, it is not unusual to hear and read statements by politicians and third sector administrators such as: 'Volunteers are the backbone of the community!'; 'Volunteers are the lifeblood of this organization!'; and 'Without volunteers this club could not survive!'. Despite these assertions, there is sufficient anecdotal and empirical evidence suggesting that volunteers are often taken for granted, not treated or managed well and are becoming increasingly difficult to retain especially in organizations that do not value volunteers. Hager and Brudney (2004) found that the more benefits an organization perceives it receives from volunteers then the better its volunteer retention rates. Somewhat surprisingly, they also reported that only one-third of organizations they studied had adopted the practice of public recognition of volunteer efforts.

Despite an apparent and perhaps superficial recognition of the critical role of volunteers by community leaders, it seems that more needs to be done to fully acknowledge the significance of volunteers in building and nurturing communities. Although Saxon-Harrold (2001) argued that the voluntary sector will not thrive without awareness of the importance of its many contributions, according to Oppenheimer and Warburton (2000) volunteering has long been under estimated, under researched and under valued, despite the objectively measured extent of its broader social and economic contributions.

The contribution of volunteers

To reinforce the importance of volunteering, a presentation at the 2004 World Leisure Congress began with the question: 'Can you imagine a world without volunteers?' (Thibault, 2004). Of course it would seem impossible to do so. Volunteers make substantial contributions to sustaining communities at many levels (e.g. from local community through to international organizations) via a wide array of often complex activities (e.g. reading programmes in schools, recreational activities in nursing homes, coaching kids in local sport clubs, support networks for the homeless, working in community radio, counselling, undertaking air and sea rescue patrols, and assisting with major sport events). Without a vibrant volunteer sector the quality of life enjoyed by most people living in developed countries would be substantially affected and/or they would have to pay considerably more to sustain their lifestyle. For example, if volunteer numbers declined significantly it is probable that government taxes as well as the direct costs of participating in a variety of everyday activities would increase. Perhaps more importantly, many attributes of community life usually taken for granted could disappear or be severely curtailed and consequently, perceptions of 'community' and the meanings associated with community life may also be adversely affected.

The available evidence reinforces the view that the social and economic consequences resulting from a stagnant volunteer sector would be alarming (Salamon and Anheier, 1998; Ironmonger, 2000; Saxon-Harrold, 2001). Despite differences in collection methods and definitional approaches to volunteerism, data from a wide array of countries reveal the significance and scope of the contribution by volunteers. For example, in a number of countries, the economic value of the voluntary sector is estimated at between 7 per cent and 14 per cent of gross domestic product (Ironmonger, 2000; Saxon-Harrold, 2001). In Australia in 2000, 32 per cent of the population aged 18 years and over performed voluntary work in the preceding 12 months contributing 704 million hours worth an estimated AUD$24–31 billion to the economy (ABS, 2002a). Ironmonger (2000), using slightly different techniques, estimated the total value of volunteering labour time for 1997 to be AUD$37 billion.

Statistics Canada (2000b) reported that the National Survey of Giving, Volunteering and Participating (NSGVP) found that more than 6.5 million (27 per cent) Canadians volunteered in 2000 contributing approximately 1.05 billion hours. These efforts accounted for the equivalent of 549,000 full-time jobs and more than CAN$17 billion in payroll costs (Statistics Canada, 2000b). According to the US Department of Labor (2004), 64.5 million Americans (28.8 per cent) volunteered in 2003/2004, averaging around 52 hours of voluntary work per annum. The Independent Sector (2004) estimated the value of volunteer time in the US in 2000 to be US$239 billion. In the UK the 1997 National Survey on Volunteering reported that 48 per cent of the population volunteered in 1997. The economic value of volunteer work in the UK was estimated at GB£41 billion in 1995.

While these data provide some indication of the scale and scope of volunteer work, they do little to reveal the nature or significance of the outcomes from those efforts. Of particular interest to researchers and policy makers are perceived social benefits such as the building of social capital and community cohesion derived from volunteer participation. Although social capital can be developed anywhere, its production is most commonly associated with the voluntary sector and when social capital stocks are high, it seems that communities are more resilient and better able to respond to adversity (Cox, 2000 cited by ABS, 2002a). After the 9/11 attacks on the World Trade Center and the Pentagon in the US, the number of people who contacted one online service to volunteer for different charities almost tripled. More people offered their service as volunteers than at any other time in the three-year history of the service (Penner, 2002). The SARS outbreak in Hong Kong in 2003 is another example in which there was a vigorous public response to actively engage in activities to combat the epidemic. Strong communities (i.e. those that have the capacity to help themselves) are, among other things, characterized by strong networks that are continually nurtured and developed (Department of Family and Community Services, 2001). Some studies have suggested that a society rich in social capital will tend to have lower crime rates, lower levels of school absenteeism and higher levels of economic growth, happiness and neighbourhood vitality (Johnson et al., 2005; Putnam, 2000). There is also evidence indicating that the extent and nature of social interaction (some of which could be facilitated through volunteering) contributes to satisfaction with community life (Lloyd, 1999).

Defining volunteering

While the evidence supporting the nature, scale and importance of volunteering to society is strong, there are a number of underlying and enduring questions concerning volunteer participation. The answers to these questions are becoming more important as the pressures of modern living make it increasingly difficult to initially commit to volunteering and to subsequently sustain involvement as a volunteer. Critical questions include: how is volunteering defined?; what initially motivates people to give their time to assist others?; and, what factors influence people to continue to volunteer?

Defining volunteering, something that on the surface appears to be relatively simple, is actually quite complex. Although the word volunteer may seem to have a common shared meaning, there is not universal consensus about the meaning of the term. Cnaan et al. (1996) suggested that this lack of shared understanding confuses would-be survey respondents, who when asked if they have ever volunteered, are unsure as to whether the work they were doing falls within the meaning of the term. Cnaan et al. (1996: 380) argued that it was critical to 'delineate the boundaries of the term volunteer' and thus focus its meaning rather than allow the term to remain 'a catchall for a wide range of non salaried activities' (Cnaan et al., 1996: 365). They identified four key dimensions of volunteerism definitions (see Table 1.1):

- free choice;
- remuneration;
- structure (the context within which the volunteer activity is performed);
- the beneficiaries.

These authors developed a continuum for each dimension in order to distinguish between what they termed 'pure' and broadly defined volunteers. Pure volunteers tend to be narrowly defined by these dimensions (e.g. free choice to engage in the activity; no reward or financial interest in the voluntary activity; conducted within a formal organization; no connection to those

Table 1.1 Dimensions of volunteer definitions

Dimension	Categories
Free choice	1 Free will (the ability to voluntarily choose)
	2 Relatively uncoerced
	3 Obligation to volunteer
Remuneration	1 None at all
	2 None expected
	3 Expenses reimbursed
	4 Stipend/low pay
Structure	1 Formal
	2 Informal
Intended beneficiaries	1 Benefit/help others/strangers
	2 Benefit/help friends or relatives
	3 Benefit oneself (as well)

Source: Cnaan et al. (1996). Copyright 1996 by Sage Publications Inc. Reprinted by permission of Sage Publications Inc.

benefiting from the voluntary activity). Such an approach suggests a dislocation with what many would consider to be volunteering. However, more recent work by Handy *et al.* (2000) concluded that public perceptions of what constitutes volunteering are strongly associated with the perceived costs and benefits that accrue to the volunteer. They found that when an individual can perform the same voluntary service with or without private monetary or social benefits, people regard the individual receiving the private benefit as less of a volunteer. Similarly, when the costs to the individual of volunteering are higher, the person is rated more of a volunteer.

In terms of the specific focus of this book, the definition developed by Volunteering Australia appears to encapsulate the key volunteer involvement dimensions relevant to the sport sector. Volunteering Australia (2005: no page) defined formal volunteering as 'an activity which takes place through not for profit organizations or projects and is undertaken: to be of benefit to the community and the volunteer; of the volunteer's own free will and without coercion; for no financial payment; and in designated volunteer positions only'.

Volunteer motivations

While the issue of volunteer motivation has been the focus of much research, according to Cuskelly and Harrington (1997) there appears to be little agreement about volunteer motives. There is more agreement, however, that volunteer motivation is complex and multifaceted (Winniford *et al.*, 1997). Different people may be engaged in the same volunteer activity/organization yet be pursuing different goals or participating in different volunteer activities/organizations for similar motivations. Noonan (1998: 124) concluded that 'there is little that is typical about these people who give so freely of their time'.

In terms of attempting to understand this complex phenomenon, much of the research has generally taken the approach of either simply listing reasons for volunteering or describing individuals by their motives. For example, Davies (1998) argued that a number of 'generic' motives had been identified including: social contact, to help others, fill time, gain recognition, meet the expectations of others, help achieve goals of organizations, personal enrichment, develop skills, fun and enjoyment, having a sense of accomplishment, self-expression and improving self-image. However, some authors have attempted to go beyond this level of analysis and develop more structured and theoretical approaches to understanding the multifaceted motives of volunteers.

Perhaps one of the most widely adopted of these is that of Clary and Snyder (1991) who used a functionalist perspective to understand volunteer motives. They argued that people act to satisfy important socio-psychological goals and, although individuals may be involved in similar voluntary activities, their goals can vary widely. They identified four distinct functions for volunteer service: expression of value – to act on the belief of the importance of helping others; understanding or knowledge – a need to understand others; social – to engage in volunteering to meet the normative expectations of salient others; and, ego-defensive or protective – to relieve negative feeling through service to others. After further research, Clary *et al.* (1996) expanded the number of functional categories to six by including: career – to enhance career opportunities or skills and/or facilitate the development of career related contacts; and, enhancement or self-esteem – to feel good about oneself or to feel needed or important. The functional approach emphasizes the diversity of motives that underlie volunteer behaviour and also contends that sustained volunteerism depends on the person-situation fit, suggesting that volunteer satisfaction will be enhanced if the roles of volunteers are congruent with their motives. Clary and Snyder (1999) later argued that motivation plays a role in three key stages of the volunteer process: initiation of volunteer service; satisfaction with the volunteer experience; and sustained volunteer service.

In order to further understand the volunteer phenomenon, the functional approach has been extended and elaborated by a number of others including most notably Penner and Finkelstein (1998), Penner (2002) and Davis *et al.* (2003). These researchers have incorporated indicators of pro-social personality, role identity and perceptions related to the organizations in which people volunteered (e.g. organizational commitment, managerial practices). Hager and Brudney (2004) underscored the importance of understanding the role of the organizational setting when they reported a 1998 study by the UPS Foundation in the US. The study found that 20 per cent of volunteers had stopped due to poor volunteer management practices and this factor was more critical in the decision to leave than changing personal or family needs. This finding reinforces those of Dorsch *et al.* (2002) who reported that factors such as satisfaction with organizational performance, organizational identity and organizational psychological climate were key predictors of volunteer commitment. Similarly, Grossman and Furano (2002: 15) concluded that despite the best intentions by volunteers, 'unless there is an infrastructure in place to support and direct their efforts, they will remain ineffective at best or, worse, become disenchanted and withdraw'.

This latter group of researchers focused on explaining why individuals continue volunteering for extended periods. Their work reflected the evolution of research efforts in volunteering from an initial somewhat atheoretical focus on describing why people get involved (see Lockstone *et al.*, 2002) to investigating variables associated with the mechanisms underlying why people stay involved and how to improve the capacity of organizations to work effectively with volunteers.

The development of volunteering

Most of the available information on volunteers has tended to describe their participation rates, motives and behaviours in organizational settings and reflects an historical shift in volunteering as it moved from an informal behaviour to one that increasingly occurred in formal organizational contexts. According to Rossides (1966, quoted in Arai, 1997: 19) 'volunteering is a specific form of voluntary action that is unique to Western democracies' that grew from democratic principles such as freedom of speech and assembly. This is a common view reinforced by earlier writers such as Tocqueville and Weber among others (Curtis *et al.*, 2001).

It seems almost self-evident that throughout history, societies, and especially rural societies, depended on a certain level of informal voluntary behaviour in order to survive (Gillette, 1999). This of course would still be the case in most contemporary Third World nations. The industrial revolution, however, was the catalyst for numerous changes in community structures and hence the nature of social interactions. Gillette (1999) observed that the increased use of money as a means of exchange, and the desocialization and anonymity as consequences of urbanization, undermined values such as solidarity and mutual assistance.

While it is clear that much informal volunteering still occurs, a manifestation of 'progress' in the nineteenth and twentieth centuries has been the rise of more formal volunteering in organizational settings. Arai (1997) argued that as various needs arose within society and government activity expanded into public service delivery, so too did the role of volunteering. An early example in the sport and leisure context included the 'sand garden' movement initially developed in Boston in 1855. Corrigan (2001) cited McCarthy (1982) who argued that in the US much of the early rise of volunteerism was 'fuelled' by the religious revivals in the 1820s due to very personal and religious reasons. However, the twentieth century witnessed the gradual professionalization and bureaucratization of the voluntary sector with the resulting withdrawal of the wealthy from direct involvement. Gillette (2001) also pointed to the response to the First World War resulting in the first modern international voluntary service movement, the Service Civil International. Gillette (2001) in summarizing the development of volunteering in the twentieth century indicated that other volunteer organizations soon appeared in the 1920s and 1930s and suggested that the economic crisis at this time acted as a further catalyst. He argued the trend continued during and after the Second World War when volunteers assisted in maintaining domestic infrastructure while soldiers were away and also in the reconstruction of Europe in the 1940s and 1950s culminating in the 1948 launch of the Coordinating Committee for International Voluntary Service created by the United Nations Educational, Scientific and Cultural Organization (UNESCO). Volunteering was given a further boost internationally as new movements grew in Asia, Africa and Latin America as they emerged from colonial control in the post-war period. The United Nations Volunteers Program began in the 1970s and reflected a strong commitment to enhancing quality of life in developing countries. Gillette (1999) argued that the beginning of the new millennium has witnessed two new developments in the history of volunteering. The first is the resurgence of volunteering in ex-socialist countries and second, the increasing numbers of retired professionals who are now offering their services as volunteers. Arai (1997) concluded that the nature and scope of volunteer work will continue to evolve as the relationship between government action and civil society, and between the structure of the economy and employment, also change.

Social capital and civil society

As suggested earlier, it is generally accepted that volunteering results in an improvement in communities. The community benefits derived from volunteers are often summarized in terms such as social capital, social cohesion and civil society. Although these terms are interrelated, social capital in particular is usually suggested as being one of the most important outcomes of volunteering and a strong voluntary sector. In general terms, the literature summarizes social capital as a contextual characteristic that describes patterns of civic engagement, trust and mutual obligation among individuals (Jarvie, 2003). The Organisation for Economic Co-operation and Development (2001: 41) described social capital as 'networks, together with shared norms, values and understandings which facilitate cooperation within or amongst groups'.

Key indicators of social capital include levels of membership in formal and informal groups, social participation and civic engagement. Volunteering is therefore instrumental in the development of social capital, contributes substantially to the proper functioning of civil society and is a means to evaluate community cohesiveness in terms of responsible citizenship based on mutual respect and trust (Putnam, 1993; Dekker and Halman, 2003; Jarvie, 2003). Reinforcing this perspective, Onyx and Leonard (2000: 113) argued that volunteering 'is at the heart of social capital'. Third sector organizations act as vehicles for individuals to connect with each other and display behaviour that often, but not always, incorporates elements of altruism and social responsibility. Badcock (2002) suggested that social capital is formed by informal networks and community support mechanisms found in a range of settings, including school committees, resident associations and sporting clubs. This suggests that the development of social capital, although frequently facilitated through formal organizations, has an immediacy and strong personal element rather than the more distant and formalized relationship formed with government institutions and policy (Onyx and Bullen, 1997). Onyx and Pullen (1997: 24) argued further that social capital is 'the raw material of civic society' and community development at the grass roots level. The development of social capital within a community requires 'dense, lateral networks involving voluntary engagement, trust, and mutual benefit' (Onyx and Bullen, 1997: 24). Therefore, social capital is considered to be the essence of community development. Community development implies the enhancement of the whole community and its citizens through social interaction, voluntary engagement and trust (Onyx and Bullen, 1997).

Similarly, the concept of civil society refers to grass roots level activities of citizens: organizations, social movements, unofficial groups and personal social networks (Cohen and Arato, 1992). Jarvie (2003: 141) suggested that civil society is 'an arena between the spheres of the state . . . and domestic or interpersonal relations' in which voluntary agencies, among others, 'actively hold the middle ground between government, the state and the individual' thus providing a system of checks and balances on the power of the state. Civil society has three distinct sectors, the public, private and the third sector, actively engaging its citizens and with each other in joint efforts for the public good (Independent Sector, 2004).

However, Putnam (2000) argued that social capital in the US was steadily declining with a resultant challenge to those organizations that rely on volunteers. Jarvie (2003: 139) similarly argued that in 'Britain there is a concern that communities have weakened and that civic culture is in decline'. Putnam and others (e.g. Badcock, 2002) suggested that the emerging focus on individual rights and self-reliance has resulted in the loss of social capital and subsequently a reduction in community cohesion. Furthermore, Putnam argued that secondary and tertiary social networks (e.g. attending community events) do not provide effective opportunities to build social capital. Conversely, others suggested that at least in the US, social capital may be moving into a new form as Americans turn to less intimate and more public locations to connect with each other (Wann *et al.*, 2001). This shift has been influenced by such factors as urbanization, technology, individualism and geographical mobility, which have reduced opportunities for traditional forms of sociability. While the broad relationships between volunteering, social capital and civil society are generally considered to be strong, the role of volunteerism in shaping the nature and mechanisms of social capital development and maintenance of civil society is under investigated.

Government policy impacts

Consistent with the emerging understanding of the importance of nurturing social capital and civil society, a number of national governments have concluded in recent years that they alone cannot and should not deliver all social and welfare related services and further, that citizen participation is important in the provision of many services. Hence, many governments have gradually scaled back their involvement in the direct delivery of welfare and social services and now rely more on nonprofit organizations and volunteers to deliver many services, maintain community cohesion, and build mutual trust and social solidarity (Hodgkinson, 2003). Subsequently there has been a gradual shift in responsibility for many community and welfare services to the third sector. These broad public policies have been given titles such as the 'third way' and 'social coalition'. For example, in 2000, the Australian Prime Minister John Howard proposed the idea of a social coalition in which rather than continually relying on government to solve social problems, a partnership, based on the concept of mutual obligation is established between different levels of government, business and the third sector (Oppenheimer and Warburton, 2000). Such efforts are 'seen as a means of sharing ownership of and responsibility for social outcomes' (Department of Family and Community Services, 2001: no page). The Blair government in Britain has placed a similar strong emphasis on volunteers and established the third way framework to guide the relationship between government and the voluntary sector (Dickson, 1999). In the 2002 State of the Union address, George W. Bush exhorted Americans to dedicate two years or 4,000 hours over the course of their lifetimes as volunteers (White House, 2002). Perhaps not surprisingly, Penner (2004) reported that there has been an increasing unwillingness by government in the US to provide goods and services to economically disadvantaged groups. These developments are not restricted to the Western context. In a policy address, Tung Chee-hwa (2004) the Chief Executive of Hong Kong strongly advocated the need for Hong Kong to become a more caring society and one means by which this could be achieved was for government to engage in tripartite partnerships between government, the business community and the third sector in order to meet increasing community needs.

A number of people have criticized third way and social coalition policies. Weaver (2001) reported that the National Council of Voluntary Organizations in the UK had expressed its concern about the implications of the increasing reliance by governments on charities to provide public services. Powell and Edwards (2002) argued that such policies represent a 'blaming approach' whereby the state places the onus of responsibility on individuals although the social problems are structural in nature. Some argue that government has simply recognized and grasped an opportunity to reduce its responsibilities and hence financial outlays. Powell and Edwards (2002: 3) suggested that citizens become 'portrayed as consumers of social services and the role of the state is but to facilitate this consumption preferably through the use of private providers'. It is perhaps telling that the Department of Family and Community Services (2001) in Australia argued that strengthening communities can result in reduced outlays for health and welfare support services as well as for the justice system. It has also been suggested that there has been no proportional transfer of resources to accommodate the needs of the third sector in fulfilling government agendas. Furthermore, where such resources have been made available they are increasingly in the form of contracts rather than grants with concomitant increased levels of accountability and other associated reporting requirements. For example, Statistics Canada (2000a) reported that more than two-thirds of organizations in a provincial level study indicated that they now spend significantly more time reporting to funding agencies. Statistics Canada also reported that voluntary agencies now find themselves in an increasingly competitive environment characterized by government cut-backs in which they compete for limited grants and contracts as well as for clients and volunteers.

Penner (2004) suggested that social coalition and third way policies reflect a process in which volunteerism may actually exacerbate or at least do little to alleviate social problems. He argued that these policies represent a situation where politicians advocated policies that perpetuate social inequities and then encourage people to volunteer to help victims of such inequities. Consequently volunteers tend to focus only on providing short-term solutions to symptoms of social malaise rather than addressing the root causes of such problems. Voluntary action thus reduces the perceived need to change those social structures that contribute to these problems. Furthermore, and perhaps of most significance, social coalition policy shifts have occurred at a time when the third sector is probably least prepared to cope with increased service delivery expectations as voluntary agencies face mounting pressures to attract and retain volunteers (Saxon-Harrold, 2001). Statistics Canada (2000a: 2) reported in a study of voluntary agencies in Ontario that most organizations in the study experienced a 'constant struggle to recruit a generally rare volunteer'. The problems of recruitment and retention of volunteers appear to be universal with similar findings in Australia, Norway and the UK (Auld and Cuskelly, 2001; Seippel, 2004; Nichols *et al.*, 1998a).

Pressures on the voluntary sector

There is a consistent view in the literature that volunteering in contemporary developed societies is under pressure from a number of factors that intersect and impact on volunteers at different levels (Lockstone *et al.*, 2002; Robinson and Godbey, 1997). These include broader socio-demographic patterns such as an ageing population, increasing social inequalities, disruption of marriage and family ties, reduction in religious attachment, suburbanization, and, the fragmentation of traditional community life and interaction patterns due to residential mobility. Factors related to time use and work also appear to influence volunteering including changes in workforce participation and composition (especially as more women have moved into the workforce), perceived time squeeze and increased television viewing, the pressures on dual income families, and the focus on consumerism and materialism with the concomitant need to increase paid employment time to afford a consumer lifestyle. Nichols *et al.* (1998b) developed an extensive list of potential reasons for declining volunteerism. These included:

- changed attitudes to volunteering (people are now less willing to devote as much time or commit themselves to a long term of office);
- an increase in family commitments;
- a perceived decrease in time left over after paid work;
- government policy that gives consumer rights precedence over the rights and responsibilities of citizens therefore creating a perceived need to work longer hours in order to claim those consumer rights;
- an increasing demand for 'professionalism' (e.g. accountability, technological skills, the ability to submit 'professional' grant applications and an increased need to be aware of legislative requirements).

Some authors have thus argued that due to these pressures and consistent with Putnam's views about a reduction in social capital, there has been a decline in volunteering (Lyons and Fabiansson, 1998; Nichols *et al.*, 1998a and 1998b; Gaskin, 1998; Davies, 1998; Daly, 1991). Others have suggested that the future of volunteering is 'grim' (Oppenheimer and Warburton, 2000: 7). Besides these trends, there are other emerging factors impinging on third sector organizations and volunteers. Such changes appear to be consistent internationally and are influencing the nature of volunteering. Nichols *et al.* (1998a and 1998b) argued that increasing professionalization, bureaucratization and commercialization have impacted on the nature of leisure service delivery organizations in the UK changing them from an informal and friendly culture to one more highly structured and professionalized. Thibault (2004) reported that volunteers felt 'tired' from working in such contexts and Hager and Brudney (2004) argued that these processes, and perhaps the bureaucratic style increasingly adopted by third sector organizations, were likely to impact on volunteer recruitment and retention. Hager and Brudney (2004: 9) suggested that

> some charities may supervise and communicate in a way that volunteer experiences feel too much like the grind of their daily jobs rather than an enjoyable avocation, thereby diminishing the experience for volunteers and reducing their desire to continue volunteering.

Furthermore, as professionals gradually assume more responsibility, volunteers may feel they are no longer required and because someone is now being paid to do the job wonder why they should continue to contribute for nothing (Auld and Godbey, 1998; Auld, 1997a; Abrams *et al.*, 1996). Furthermore, some potential volunteers may feel they do not have the skills required to be effective in this new professionalized and more accountable environment particularly when society is becoming more litigious (Auld and Cuskelly, 2001). These perceptions are likely to be felt more keenly by younger volunteers who may lack the necessary life experiences and confidence to cope with such pressures.

International trends

What do the data actually reveal about volunteer trends around the world? Despite definitional and methodological differences there are some data that can provide indications of broad patterns of national participation rates in volunteering. While it should be noted there needs to be caution in drawing firm conclusions about differences or similarities, at the very least, the data seem to indicate that volunteer participation rates are variable. Curtis *et al.* (2001) argued that there were four main factors that could be used to explain varying levels of voluntary association membership between different nations. These were: high levels of economic and industrial activity (positively associated with higher levels of voluntary association activity); higher levels of Protestant religion and/or mixed Christian type religions (associated with higher levels of voluntary association activity); the number of years of continuous democracy (a significant positive impact on volunteerism); and liberal and social democracies ranking highest in voluntary association activity.

Statistics Canada (2000b: no page) reporting on the National Survey of Giving, Volunteering and Participating (2000), identified a 13 per cent decrease in the number of Canadians who volunteered in 2000 compared to 1997 (from 7.7 million to just over 6.5 million). However, this was countered to some extent by an increase in the number of hours contributed per volunteer rising from 149 hours in 1997 to 162 hours in 2000. The survey also revealed a 5 per cent decline in the number of religiously active Canadians who volunteer from 46 per cent in 1997 to 41 per cent in 2000. In the UK the 1997 National Survey on Volunteering found that the level of volunteering had decreased slightly in the previous six years, down from 51 per cent of the adult population in 1991 to 48 per cent in 1997. However, similar to Canada, the survey also found that existing volunteers were contributing more time to volunteering, up from 2.7 hours a week in 1991 to 4 hours a week in 1997 (Institute of Volunteer Research, 2005). Conversely, according to the US Department of Labor, the number of Americans who volunteered increased by almost 5.4 per cent from 2002 to 2003 (from 59.8 to more than 63 million) followed by a 1.2 per cent increase from 2003 to 2004 (to 64.5 million). The volunteer participation rate increased from 27.4 per cent in 2002 to 28.8 per cent in 2004 and remained steady in 2004. The number of hours contributed by volunteers also remained steady at a median of 52 hours annually. Australia recorded a 24 per cent increase in volunteer numbers between 1995 and 2000. In 2000 volunteers contributed a total of 704.1 million hours of voluntary work, a 37.6 per cent increase from 1995 (ABS, 2002b). However, in the sport and recreation sector some evidence suggests that the hours contributed by individual volunteers decreased by 20 per cent during this period and volunteers also tended to stay with sport organizations for shorter periods (Cuskelly, 2001).

As indicated above there are potential problems when working with the macro level data usually collected by government agencies. For example, Oppenheimer and Warburton (2000) suggested that interpretation of data on volunteer trends is made difficult by variations in the way in which volunteering is defined. It should also be noted that because most of this type of data is on the formal volunteering context, the absolute levels of volunteering that occur in most communities are likely to be substantially under reported. Furthermore, most data collected in macro level surveys, while providing some broad indicators of reasons for engaging in volunteering, do little to illuminate the complexities of volunteer motives and behaviour.

Concluding comments

The material presented in this chapter has set the scene for the more specific coverage of sport volunteers in the remainder of the book. The sport context is an important arena for volunteering and in many countries sport volunteers typically represent the largest category of volunteers. Sport provides opportunities for a wide range of people to volunteer in a variety of ways usually in a positive, friendly and relaxed environment. The data outlined in Chapter 2 reveal the extent and significance of the contribution made by sport volunteers, the complex roles of sport volunteers and the nature of the setting in which this activity occurs. In addition to its direct contribution to sustaining communities, sport volunteering is also important because it has been suggested that the initial volunteer experience for many individuals, particularly young people, occurs in sport. Therefore sport may act as an important nursery for volunteers. Eley and Kirk (2002) found that sport volunteering can encourage prosocial behaviour and citizenship among young people. Houlihan (2001: 1) argued that 'as a source of empowerment for citizens and as institutions of civil society in their own right sport and recreation professions have a significant contribution to make'.

Chapter 2

Sport volunteers

Working with volunteers in sport necessitates an understanding of the nature of the voluntary sport sector context including the scope of the volunteer workforce, the characteristics of the volunteers and their involvement in the sport system. The previous chapter addressed definitional issues related to volunteering and outlined the nature, scope and impact of volunteers' contributions socially, culturally and economically. The purpose of this chapter is to provide a more focused overview of volunteer involvement in sport. It introduces definitions of sport, VSOs and sport volunteers as a context for exploring the importance and significance of volunteer involvement in sport. Building on the dimensions and categories of volunteering discussed in Chapter 1, the size and nature of volunteer involvement in sport is compared and contrasted across sport systems in several nations before exploring broad categorizations of volunteer participation. Subsequent chapters discuss the structural elements of voluntary sport systems and organizations and explore volunteer involvement in more detail.

Sport is such a widely known and utilized term that it may seem redundant to explore formal definitions. However, due to the ubiquity of sport, the nature and scope of VSOs, and the varied roles and characteristics of sport volunteers, the boundaries of the sport system need to be defined. Further, government policy requires sport organizations, at least at the national level, to be able to demonstrate that they meet a number of criteria to be eligible for access to funding and other support mechanisms. The Australian Sports Commission (ASC) (ASC, 2004a: 5) defined sport narrowly as 'a human activity capable of achieving a result requiring physical exertion and/or physical skill which, by its nature and organization, is competitive and is generally accepted as being a sport'. Sport England (2004a) adopted a more encompassing view that incorporated physical activity and informal activities. In its framework for sport, Sport England (2004a: 4) used the 1993 Council of Europe European Sports Charter description of sport as 'all forms of physical activity which, through casual or organized participation, aim at expressing or improving physical fitness and mental wellbeing, forming social relationships or obtaining results in competition at all levels'. These definitions of sport are embodied in a five segment model (see Figure 2.1) of connected yet distinct categories of sports practice (Stewart *et al.*, 2004). At the core of this model is the idea that 'competitive sport that begins with community, school and local sport and culminates in elite sport, which includes national sport leagues, national championships, and international sport events' (Stewart *et al.*, 2004: 19).

These definitions imply that VSOs and volunteers are the core of sport systems in most Western nations. Such organizations, and the volunteers that sustain them, provide opportunities for formally organized participation in a wide array of sports and physical activities. VSOs have also been labelled amateur sport organizations, community sport organizations or community amateur sport clubs. Sport England (2005a: no page) defined community amateur sport clubs as

> properly constituted as a not-for-profit organisation, with no provision for payment to members during the life of the club or upon dissolution. It can be either unincorporated (i.e. an association of members with unlimited liability) or incorporated as a company limited by guarantee (not shares). The club must operate an open membership policy that allows anyone, within reason, to join and use its facilities.

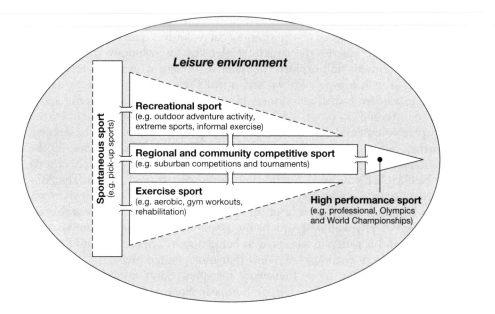

Figure 2.1 A typology of sport practice

Source: Stewart *et al.* (2004: 20). Reprinted by permission of Taylor & Francis Group.

For the purposes of this book, VSOs are defined as nonprofit organizations formally constituted to provide members with opportunities to participate in organized sport and physical activities within particular team or individual sports. VSOs are separate from the state, independently governed and operated by volunteer management committees or boards and do not return profits to their members. Most VSOs are formally affiliated with regional, state/provincial and ultimately sport national governing bodies (NGBs) and International Sport Federations (ISFs). In this book, the term VSOs incorporates sport organizations at the community (local) club, regional and state/provincial levels. Relationships between the various levels of VSOs are discussed in more detail in Chapter 6. Sport NGBs are known in some jurisdictions as national sport organizations (NSOs). However, for the purposes of this book the term NGB will be used and incorporates NSOs.

Volunteer participation is a central and defining feature of VSOs. The Leisure Industries Research Centre (LIRC) (LIRC, 2003) reported that of 2.01 million core and formal sport volunteers in England with named roles such as officers, committee members, coaches and officials, 75 per cent were club level volunteers. They accounted for 83 per cent of total hours volunteered. In contrast, sport volunteers in major events, educational settings, national governing boards and disability organizations accounted for a combined total of fewer than 10 per cent of volunteers and fewer than 5 per cent of volunteer hours. Statistics from the Australian Bureau of Statistics (ABS) (ABS, 2002d) based on research into 7,000 organizations with employees involved in the sports industries, revealed about half of those were employed by nonprofit organizations. In contrast, 98 per cent of volunteers worked for nonprofit organizations. This is not to deny that volunteers play an important role in the wider sport system at regional, provincial or state/national levels, particularly in the governance of sport, and in other sectors of the sport system such as schools, disabled sport and youth organizations such as the YMCA. However, volunteer involvement in sport is predominantly at the local level and within VSOs. The definition of VSOs used here does not preclude sport organizations that employ paid staff. Consistent with Sport England's definition of amateur community sport clubs, however, it excludes proprietary and private membership clubs. Such organizations rely on volunteer involvement to function effectively as do sport organizations based within institutions such as school sport, university sport and informal clubs within work organizations (e.g. social golf and tennis clubs). The structural elements of sport systems, the place of VSOs within these systems and internal and external operating environments of VSOs are explored in some depth in later chapters. In most instances, volunteer involvement in sport cannot be disaggregated accurately by type of organization. Perhaps such disaggregation is unimportant if it is acknowledged that VSOs are the dominant site of volunteer involvement in sport.

Because volunteers are integral to the functioning of the sport system it is important to be able to define the term sport volunteer. Chapter 1 explored generic definitions of the term volunteer and examined dimensions, categories and types of volunteering. There has been a tendency to define sport volunteers by roles, frequency of involvement and whether the activity of volunteering occurs within formal organizations such as clubs, projects, programmes and events. The ABS (2002c: 39) defined sport volunteers as those participating in 'roles undertaken to support, arrange and/or run organized sport and physical activity'. The ABS definition included coaches, instructors or teachers; referees or umpires; committee members or administrators; scorers or timekeepers; medical support people and other roles. Consistent with its definition of sport, Sport England (2005c: 9) defined sport volunteers in broader terms

> as individual volunteers helping others in sport and receiving either no remuneration or only expenses. This includes those volunteering for organisations (formal volunteers) and those helping others in sport, but not through organisations (informal volunteers). However, it does not include time spent travelling which may represent significant additional time inputs.

Sport England (2005b) further specified that 'to be included the individual must have undertaken voluntary activities at least once in the last year (once during the season for seasonal sports/activities and at least once for session based programmes)'. Such definitions of sport volunteering are not inconsistent with the generic dimensions and categories of volunteering of Cnaan *et al.* (1996), explored in Chapter 1. Sport volunteers vary widely in the extent to which their participation is on the basis of free choice (ranging from free will to obligation), they are remunerated (none to stipend/low pay), the structures within which volunteering occurs (informal or formal) and the intended beneficiaries (others/strangers to oneself) of their involvement. These dimensions of volunteering will be explored in more detail in later chapters as sport volunteering is examined across various roles and within differing organizational contexts in sport.

Sport volunteers work and interact at various levels within and across the spectrum of the sport system. Volunteers' contribution of time and effort within particular VSOs involves a complex array of interrelationships between those working at strategic and operational levels in managing and delivering services and programmes to members. Increasingly, these interrelationships are mediated by the involvement of paid staff, and impacted by government policies and accountability to governing bodies in sport. A current government policy environment aimed at increasing sport participation is a significant contextual factor in understanding VSOs and the greater strains being experienced by sport volunteers. Through the contribution of volunteers, VSOs are a substantial provider of services and opportunities for participation in organized sport and physical activity. Government policies in several nations including Australia, Canada and England are pushing the sport system and by implication, VSOs, to expand their capacity to cope with increasing levels of participation in organized sport. Sport policies such as Backing Australia's Sporting Ability (BASA) (Commonwealth of Australia, 2001), Active Communities (Sport England, 2000), and Enhanced Participation (Government of Canada, 2002) all include goals of increasing sport participation through VSOs. If it is assumed that the current number of VSOs and volunteers is sufficient to cope with existing levels of participation, then increasing sport participation will require an expansion of the capacity of VSOs. In reality this can be achieved only by increasing the number or size of VSOs, which, in turn, implies the need for more volunteer labour. Such an outcome is possible only through the recruitment of more volunteers, extending the careers of current volunteers through greater retention, increasing the number of hours contributed by each volunteer or a combination of these. Any such changes will have significant implications for sport volunteers and VSOs.

The size and nature of the voluntary sport system

Just as it is important to define and describe VSOs it is important to describe the size of the sport system within the wider third sector. To some extent the absolute number of VSOs varies in accordance with total population. Statistics from Canada indicate that more than 33,000 sport and recreation organizations comprise 21 per cent of all voluntary nonprofit organizations and that 71 per cent of sport and recreation organizations serve local communities (Doherty, 2005). In a report for Sport England, the LIRC (2003) conservatively estimated the number of volunteer run sport clubs in England as more than 106,000. Aside from Doherty who separated local organizations, these statistics do not describe the number of organizations across the various levels of the sport system from local clubs to NGBs. However, the typical pyramid structure of sport suggests that there are relatively few organizations at the national level, more at state/provincial, and regional level and many more at the local level. Using Canadian data as a guide, the proportion of sport organizations at the local level is in the vicinity of 70 per cent. Conservatively, there is a total of more than 150,000 local sport clubs in England, Canada and Australia alone. The distribution of sport organizations across various levels within the system provides further support for the view that volunteer involvement in sport is much more prominent at the local club level than at the regional level or above.

Using these data to describe the size of the voluntary sport system belies the complex nature of the organizations of which it is comprised. VSOs are sometimes categorized naively as a homogeneous sector of the sport system.

Even at a superficial level of analysis, this provides only a partial picture of an important and significant sector of the sport system. As discussed, while VSOs are the dominant feature of local level sport, they are also part of the sport system at regional, state/provincial, national and international levels. Even the International Olympic Committee (IOC) and many ISFs such as Fédération Internationale de Football Association (FIFA) are nonprofit entities. VSOs vary in terms of their size, structures, cultures and traditions and importantly their capacity to respond to changes in their external environments. In discussing the challenges to sport laid down by government policy which aim to increase sport participation in organized sport, Taylor (2004) identified and characterized two types of VSOs that lie at opposite ends of a spectrum (see Table 2.1). At one end of the

Table 2.1 A spectrum of VSOs

Traditional/informal VSOs	Contemporary/formal VSOs
Motivations compatible with mutual enthusiasm and social benefits: friendship and enjoyment, giving something back, and parents wanting to help their children.	Motivations include friendship, giving something back, parents wanting to help their children. More likely to want the club to do well in organizational performance and not just playing performance.
Proud culture of informality. More of a cooperative than a business. Active resistance to the relevance of terms such as management.	Formal and managerialist. More likely to use procedures such as mentoring, job descriptions and training. Some have volunteer coordinators.
Pragmatic solutions to resulting problems. Key volunteers staying longer and taking on more duties as other volunteers are not replaced.	More systematic in promoting an explicit contribution culture. Each member is expected to help in the organization of the club.
Reactive rather than proactive. A spirit of mucking in, reinforcing the cooperative culture, but often this spirit is only manifested in a loyal core of key volunteers.	Proactive in anticipating development and in planning to resolve problems and taking actions to deliver the plans.
Professionalization, in the sense of more formal management, is seen as a fundamental threat to the culture of the organization.	Professionalization is seen as a response to pressures. More likely to adopt paid work procedures and more receptive to paying for work e.g. coaches or officials.
Mistrust of assistance offered from an external source that is perceived as extra work. These organizations are too constrained in resources to acknowledge, investigate or seek assistance from outside.	Receptive to external assistance, welcoming it and seeking it for resolving problems and for development. Some planned exploitation of external assistance, others more opportunistic. Not mistrustful of, or hostile towards, external agencies.

Source: adapted from Taylor (2004).

spectrum are traditional/informal sport organizations described by Hoggett and Bishop (1985) as groups of mutual enthusiasts which have strong collective identities, operate as cooperatives and view professionalism and external assistance as threats. At the other end are contemporary/formal sport organizations that tend to be systematic, business-like and receptive to external assistance. Because the characteristics of VSOs vary widely, the characteristics and motives of the volunteers they attract and retain are likely to be representative of a wide cross-section of the population.

Volunteer participation in sport

The scale and nature of volunteer participation in sport depends very much on how volunteering is conceptualized, defined, measured and reported. As discussed, volunteers participate in a wide variety of formally and informally designated roles and positions, across a range of organizational settings, and at varying levels of frequency from as little as once per year to several times per week. Volunteer participation in sport can be reported numerically or expressed as either a proportion of the population or a proportion of all volunteers within the population. Hours contributed by volunteers in total or on average are important indicators of the scope of volunteer participation in sport as is the number of years contributed by volunteers. This section attempts to summarize sport volunteer participation data from several nations as well as noting important similarities and differences. Subsequently, volunteer participation is examined in terms of the characteristics of volunteers. Comparisons of volunteer statistics can provide an overview of participation but they should be treated with caution. Substantial differences in survey methods and sampling techniques can result in misleading conclusions.

By any measure, the scale of sport volunteering is extensive (see Table 2.2). In Australia between 1.1 and 1.4 million people volunteer for sport organizations. These numbers are comparable with Canada's more than 1.1 million sport volunteers. In England this figure is in excess of 5.8 million. Formal volunteering through a sport organization reduces the figure for England to 4.5 million volunteers. Counting only volunteers in formal roles (e.g. committee members and coaches) this number is reduced further to 2 million sport volunteers.

Because of significant population differences between these nations, sport volunteer participation rates provide a common basis for comparison. The sport volunteer participation rate expressed as a percentage of the population reveals that 5 per cent of Canadians are sport volunteers compared to between 8.2 per cent to 10 per cent of Australians and almost 15 per cent of the English population (5.1 per cent when only formal, core volunteers are included). Sport volunteers account for more than one-quarter of the total volunteers in Australia (26 per cent) and England (26.5 per cent) and

Table 2.2 Sport volunteer participation statistics for Australia, Canada and England

Volunteer participation	Australia (2000)[a]	Canada (2000)[b]	England (2002)[c]
Total volunteers ('000s)	4,395[a]	6,513	22,000
Volunteer participation rate (total volunteers/ population)	31.8%[a]	26.7%	48.0%
Volunteer participation (sport volunteers)	1,141,000[a] to 1,420,200[d]	1,170,000	5,821,000
Volunteer participation rate (sport volunteers/ population)	8.2[a] to 10%[b]	5.0%	14.8%
Volunteer participation rate (sport volunteers/ total volunteers)	26.0%[a]	18.0%	26.5%

Sources: [a] National Centre for Culture and Recreation Statistics (2003). [b] Doherty (2005). [c] LIRC (2003). [d] ABS (2002c).

Note: Volunteer and population statistics for persons aged 15 years or older (Canada), 16 years or older (England) and 18 years or older (Australia).

almost one-fifth of Canadian volunteers (18 per cent). Consistent with participation rates in Australia and England, the sport volunteer participation rate in New Zealand is 27 per cent of adults (SPARC, 2005a).

The extent of sport volunteer participation can also be examined in terms of hours contributed to sport organizations (see Table 2.3). The total volunteer hours contributed to sport per year is approximately 130 million and 167 million in Australia and Canada, respectively. Sport volunteers in England provide more than 1.2 billion hours. Across the three nations these hours account for between 77,000 and 720,000 full-time equivalent jobs. In England, volunteer hours exceed paid employment in sport (see Table 2.3). Using the average annual hours per volunteer serves as a useful basis for comparing the relative significance of the hours contributed by individual sport volunteers. Australian sport volunteers contribute a mean of 98 hours per volunteer per year. Clearly, the ABS used a method other than dividing the total volunteer hours by the total number of volunteers (see Table 2.3). In contrast, at 208 hours per volunteer per year, English sport volunteers put in more than twice as many hours annually as Australian volunteers. Closer examination of the Australian statistics reveals that hours per volunteer are positively skewed with a median of 40 hours compared to a mean of 98 hours (ABS, 2002d). In 2000, 25 per cent of sport volunteers contributed 20 hours or less per annum compared to 7.3 per cent who volunteered for 300 hours or more per annum (ABS, 2001b). In England a large proportion of sport volunteers (43 per cent) are involved for less than 50 hours annually whereas 13 per cent of volunteers each provide 500

Table 2.3 Hours volunteered and paid employment in sport

	Australia[a]	Canada[b]	England[c]
Total hours volunteered in survey year ('000s)	130,000	167,310	1,209,600
Average annual hours per volunteer	98	143	208
Volunteer hours full-time equivalent paid workers	77,000	87,140	720,000
Sport employment full-time equivalent paid workers	98,267[d]	262,325[e]	450,000

Sources: [a] National Centre for Culture and Recreation Statistics (2003). [b] Doherty (2005). [c] LIRC (2003). [d] ABS (2001a). [e] Statistics Canada (1998).

Note: Includes 59,122 sports manufacturing, wholesaling and retailing jobs.

or more hours annually (LIRC, 2003). In terms of years involvement, in Canada 57 per cent of volunteers had been with their sport organization for three or more years whereas 61 per cent of Australian volunteers had been with their sport organization for five years or less.

The substantial differences in hours provided by sport volunteers between nations are difficult to explain except for variations in the population sampling and data collection methods. The Australian statistics suggest that volunteer hours are distributed quite unevenly with a relatively small number of volunteers providing a disproportionately large number of hours to sport. There are no directly comparable data for years of volunteer involvement.

Characteristics of sport volunteers

In addition to exploring the scale of the volunteer contribution to sport, working with sport volunteers requires an understanding of their characteristics. Selected demographic characteristics for sport volunteers are displayed

Table 2.4 Characteristics of sport volunteers (%)

	Australia[a]	Canada[b]	England[c]
Gender			
Male	60.2	64.0	67.0
Female	39.8	36.0	33.0
Age group			
Less than 24 years	12.9	19.0	28.0
25–34 years	21.6	13.0	22.0
35–44 years	31.4	41.0	21.0
45 years and over	34.2	27.0	29.0
Employment status			
Employed (full-time or part-time)	84.0	84.0	70.0
Not employed (unemployed or not in labour force)	16.0	16.0	30.0

Sources: [a] National Centre for Culture and Recreation Statistics (2003). [b] Doherty (2005). [c] LIRC (2003).

in Table 2.4 and, except for age groups, there are some strong similarities between Australia, Canada and England. Sport volunteers are more likely to be male (60–67 per cent) and in paid employment (70–84 per cent). Sport volunteers tend to be drawn from the 35 years and over age group in Canada (68 per cent) and Australia (66 per cent) whereas sport volunteers are equally likely to be under or over 35 years of age in England.

Sport volunteer motivation and involvement

The motivation of sport volunteers is introduced in this section but reviewed in more depth in subsequent chapters that focus on event volunteers, coaches, officials and administrators. The motives examined in the Australian, Canadian and English research reviewed earlier are not so much based on motivation theory as they are lists of reasons for volunteering. Amongst Australian sport volunteers the most frequently cited reasons for volunteering are personal or family involvement, personal satisfaction and to help others or the community (ABS, 2001b). In order of frequency, Canadian sport volunteers list their motivations as to help a cause in which they believe, use skills to help an organization's cause or because someone they know such as a child or an adult partner is affected by the organization or its activities (Doherty, 2005). Using a focus group approach the LIRC (2003) identified social benefits, giving something back and parental involvement with their own children as the most frequently cited attractions for sport volunteering. Interestingly, sport volunteers in Australia are more likely than non-sport volunteers to list personal or family involvement (43 per cent of sport volunteers compared to 27 per cent of non-sport volunteers) and less likely than non-sport volunteers to list help others or the community (38 per cent compared to 50 per cent) as reasons for volunteering. Broadly, sport volunteering is motivated by a desire to help others as well as for social or personal rewards, termed altruism and self-interest respectively by Stebbins (1996).

It is beyond the scope of this chapter to introduce and review complex motivation theories in relation to sport volunteers. The purpose of this section is to introduce the concepts of altruism and self-interest as a heuristic for understanding what initiates and sustains volunteer participation in VSOs. Altruism and self-interest are examined within the context of a two dimensional space of degree of involvement (peripheral and core) and extent of involvement (short and long term) for sport volunteers. Where relevant, links are made to the traditional/informal and contemporary/formal ends of the spectrum of VSOs characterized by Taylor (2004).

Just as VSOs can be characterized across a wide spectrum, volunteers themselves exhibit various degrees of contemporaneous involvement. Pearce (1993) identified two groups of volunteers that she described as core and peripheral. Core volunteers usually hold a formal office often as board or committee members, are seen as the leaders and those who run things, and have higher levels of involvement and commitment (Pearce, 1993). Core volunteers can be identified by all volunteers in an organization and compared to peripheral volunteers, contribute 'significantly more time to the organization and felt that their work was more demanding' (Pearce, 1993: 49). In contrast, peripheral volunteers, though not necessarily apathetic, can be classified as steady contributors who do not want a higher degree of involvement, are occasional contributors, or those who have tried out an organization and decided to leave. Often it is a sense of altruism that attracts individuals to volunteer initially, most likely in a peripheral sense through a desire to help others without becoming overcommitted. In contrast, the motivation to continue volunteering and take on greater responsibility is often the intrinsic satisfaction of the activity itself. Sport volunteering is sustained by the social and personal rewards that are integral to the activity of volunteering.

In a VSO context, core volunteers tend to be the committee or board members who make policy and operational decisions. Because of their higher degree of involvement they may also hold more than one formal position such as being a coach or team manager as well as a committee member. Core volunteers are analogous to career volunteers described by Stebbins (1996). Career volunteers are motivated to continue 'in good part because volunteering requires certain skills, knowledge and training – and, at times, two or all three of these' (Stebbins, 1996: 216). While Pearce (1993) described the boundary between core and peripheral volunteers as fluid, peripheral volunteers are more likely to be found in operational, service delivery and informal roles in VSOs. In these roles they can contribute effectively without having to be fully involved or informed about an organization's activities.

VSOs across the full spectrum of traditional/informal and contemporary/ formal dimensions require both core and peripheral volunteers to function effectively. The culture of traditional/informal VSOs is such that they tend to be dominated by a loyal core of key volunteers who resist assistance from external sources. According to Taylor (2004) there is a tendency for such volunteers to muck in, stay with organizations longer and take on more duties as other volunteers leave. This is akin to Pearce's (1993) notion of martyred leaders who, during difficult periods for an organization, are willing to exploit themselves, work long hours and rally the support of others, through some degree of moral obligation. In contrast, contemporary/formal VSOs are more likely to develop a culture of contribution in which all members, core and peripheral, are expected to help. Taking a more systematically planned and proactive approach, leaders are more likely to exploit external sources of assistance, use mentoring and training to increase volunteer involvement and be receptive to paying for work such as officiating or coaching.

Sport volunteering varies not only on contemporaneous degrees of involvement but also on extent of involvement. As alluded to in the discussion on career volunteers, many sport volunteers undergo training and develop significant levels of knowledge and skills, often quite specific to a particular sport. Sometimes they become long-term volunteers, measured by years of involvement, and therefore important to the stability and continuity of VSOs as other volunteers and members come and go. Short-term sport volunteers are willing to help with one-off tasks on an as needed basis but are not willing or able, for whatever reason, to commit to longer-term roles or positions within VSOs. Stebbins (1996: 219) described such volunteering as casual in that 'it is momentary . . . [and] . . . requires little skill or knowledge'.

It is tempting to contemplate a direct association between the degree and extent of involvement of sport volunteers. It could be argued that volunteers with a high degree of involvement are more likely to be long-term volunteers. However, some peripheral volunteers 'were former core members, who wanted to reduce their involvement and no longer held any office' (Pearce, 1993: 48). Changes in volunteer involvement, at least in the Australian context, suggest that volunteering may be becoming more peripheral and short term. Statistics from consecutive ABS surveys (1996 and 2001b) revealed that the hours contributed per volunteer and the duration of volunteer careers have both decreased. Over a five-year period the median hours per volunteer displayed a marked decrease from 60 hours to 48 hours. These changes are evident in the proportion of volunteers contributing less than 40 hours per year, which has increased from 36 per cent to 45 per cent. In contrast, the proportion of volunteers contributing more than 140 hours per year has decreased from one in four (26 per cent) to less than one in five (18 per cent) volunteers. These trends suggest that sport volunteering is in decline.

Problems and pressures for sport volunteers

An important question in relation to the sustainability of the sport system is whether sport volunteering is declining and if so, what might have precipitated such a decline. This apparently simple question does not lend itself to a straightforward answer. The response depends upon how sport volunteering is conceptualized and measured. In this chapter, research on volunteer work has been analysed from several perspectives. These include total numbers of volunteers, rates of volunteer participation, hours contributed in total and per volunteer (mean and median values), years contributed by volunteers and the number of organizations and roles in which volunteers participate. Statistics from two volunteer work reports provided by the ABS (1996 and 2001b) may provide some insights to the complexity of this matter. Between 1995 and 2000 the total number of sport volunteers increased by as many as half a million and the total hours contributed increased by approximately 43 million whereas the median hours per volunteer per year decreased by 12 hours to 48 hours (Cuskelly, 2005). Doherty's (2005: 10) analysis of Canadian sport volunteer data concluded that 'there are fewer volunteers doing more work'. These findings are inconclusive in terms of whether sport volunteering is declining. What is clear is that VSOs and sport volunteers themselves are facing a number of problems and pressures. Reflecting on a 2003 Sport England report Taylor (2004) summarized these as:

- not enough people volunteering in sport clubs and falling volunteer numbers in the last five years;
- volunteer recruitment difficulties in more than a third of NGBs and clubs leading to multitasking and merging key positions;
- an ageing volunteer force with core administrative roles filled by older people;
- increased time inputs from volunteers and bureaucracy with pressures to implement and disseminate changes largely in response to sport NGBs and legislation;
- a pay and play attitude by members and a childminding attitude by parents of young members.

Some of the difficulties identified here may limit higher levels of involvement among current volunteers and probably act as barriers to individuals considering whether to volunteer in sport. For example, traditional/informal VSOs in which the core administrative roles are dominated by older volunteers tend to experience problems in replacing volunteers and have little appeal to potential volunteers from younger age groups.

Concluding comments

This chapter focused on the importance and significance of sport volunteers largely within the context of VSOs and against a backdrop of government policy intent on increasing sport participation. Sport volunteers and VSOs are at the core of the sport system and the contributions of volunteers to sustaining and developing the sport system clearly indicate that volunteers are of central importance to the sport systems in a number of nations. A prominent feature of VSOs and sport volunteering is diversity. The characteristics of volunteers, the organizations in which they participate, and the nature and degree of their involvement need to be understood and acknowledged in order to maximize the effectiveness and efficiency of working with sport volunteers in the planning, management and delivery of organized sport and physical activity to the population.

Chapter 3

Volunteers and sport development

This chapter outlines the significant role of volunteers in sport development in the areas of organizational governance, and in the development of administrators, players, coaches and officials. It reviews national policies regarding sport development and the roles of volunteers in facilitating the implementation of these policies. The increasing demands placed on volunteers and the organizations that rely on volunteers to facilitate sport development are also examined.

Sport development

Defining sport development and drawing a definitive boundary around the scope of its activities and stakeholders is recognized as a difficult task (Houlihan and White, 2002). The problem in defining sport development is exacerbated by the various forms it has taken over the last 40 years. Houlihan and White (2002) argued that sport development in the UK was conceptualized as facility development between the mid-1960s to mid-1970s, as a welfare instrument from then until the early 1990s, as a suite of differentiated programmes during the early to late 1990s, and presently as two discrete programmes, namely elite and community focused. Similar transitions are evident in how sport development has been conceptualized by governments in Australia, Canada and New Zealand over this period (Eady, 1993; Stewart *et al.*, 2004; Watt, 2003).

The first and perhaps most widely recognized model of sport development was based on the premise that sport participation comprised four hierarchical levels. Sometimes labelled the 'pyramid model' the four levels were: (1) Foundation – where individuals acquired the basic motor and perceptual skills to participate in physical activity; (2) Participation at a social or regular level through a local club system; (3) Performance – where the emphasis was on providing opportunities to improve performance through access to enhanced coaching and competition opportunities; and (4) Excellence – where the emphasis was on elite performance. The pyramid model emphasized the interdependence between the hierarchical levels, in particular the need for the lower levels to provide resources (i.e. athletic talent) to improve the outputs of successive levels (i.e. better performing elite athletes). One of the problems with this model is that it assumes every participant in organized sport wishes to move through the system until they reach their desired level or the limit of their capabilities. It fails to recognize that the vast majority of sport participants are unlikely to make such transitions, particularly beyond the participation level. The pyramid model was subsequently revised to incorporate the idea that individuals could 'shape their pattern of participation to meet changes in lifestyle, family and employment circumstances' (Houlihan and White, 2002: 42). The revised sport development model is presented in Figure 3.1.

The differences in how sport development is conceptualized leads to variations in perceptions of the roles to be played by government, sport governing bodies, the education system, health departments and local councils in the development of sport. Considering that sport development policy and funding priorities are often subject to the 'whim and caprice of governments or indeed individual ministers' (Houlihan and White, 2002: 206), it is difficult to define the extent of sport development activities and the full range of organizations and institutions that might be involved in or affected by the development of sport.

The environment in which sport development policy has been developed and enacted has undergone many changes in the last 15 years. Using the UK sport system as an example, Houlihan and White (2002) highlighted changes in administrative arrangements, patterns of interdependency between government and the nonprofit sport sector, growth in the power of sport consumers to influence sport development policy, a trend towards neo-liberalist philosophies such as privatization and contracting, and the

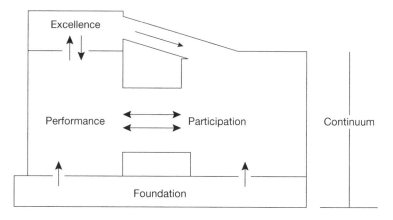

Figure 3.1 Model of the Sports Development Continuum

Source: Houlihan and White (2002: 42). Reprinted by permission of Taylor & Francis Group.

increasing professionalization of the sport industry as some of the drivers of change in delivering sport development. These changes have led to a 'decline in deference towards voluntarism and amateurism in sport clubs and governing bodies' (Houlihan and White, 2002: 212) which is manifested in central governments being much more inclined to influence the sport sector. Government influence is achieved through targeted funding schemes and the provision of other resources that are geared towards the fulfilment of particular policy goals.

Sport development in the early part of the twenty-first century now encapsulates strategic goals such as facilitating opportunities to participate and compete in sport, promoting sport to specific sectors of the community, direct service provision by way of managing sport events, and providing opportunities to achieve excellence. In other words, sport development is designed to increase the participation rate and performance levels of people involved in sport. Houlihan and White (2002) argued that sport development has been conceptualized as managing inputs (e.g. facilities, people and programmes) to create opportunities for participation at a variety of levels, as well as the outcomes of participation (e.g. health benefits, social capital development, national pride). Government policy concerned with sport has therefore been focused on two distinct goals: first, using sport as the vehicle for the development of society; and second, the development of sport systems and infrastructure for its own sake. Additionally, government sport policy occupies a space at the intersection of services as diverse as education, health, foreign policy, social services and sport itself (Houlihan and White, 2002). Direct government intervention in sport has changed dramatically in the last 15 years, as governments have sought to influence both the outcomes of sport and the way in which sport systems operate (Watt, 2003). Government intervention in sport is considered in detail in the next chapter, and for now attention is focused on the place of volunteers in sport development.

Volunteers are involved in all aspects of sport development, fulfilling roles in policy development, governance and committee work, facilitating opportunities through fundraising and facility development, and for the vast majority of volunteers, direct service delivery roles such as coaching, officiating and team management. These roles extend to specific functions of sport development including:

- facilitating involvement in community sport participation and competition opportunities;
- developing and promoting the delivery of sport to specific groups including disabled athletes, women, indigenous groups and older participants;
- identification of athletic talent and promoting individuals' progression through representative levels of sport, including elite and professional competitions;

- providing support to elite and professional competitions by developing the abilities of athletes or players, officials and coaches.

The nonprofit organizations that sport volunteers join are vehicles for citizen engagement, enabling individuals to contribute their talent, energy and time to be involved in group activities and causes that are not otherwise provided by the public or private sectors (Statistics Canada, 2004a). Nonprofit sport organizations are governed by volunteers and depend on the time and money contributed by volunteers to deliver sporting opportunities. The extent of this dependence on volunteers is highlighted by data indicating that Canadian sport organizations are largely self-sufficient with only 12 per cent of their income being provided from government sources. They rely more on membership dues and direct user fees to sustain their operations. Sport and recreation organizations also rely on volunteers more than other third sector organizations. They account for 28 per cent of all volunteers and 23 per cent of all volunteer hours in Canada. In contrast, religious organizations are the next largest sector and account for 11 per cent of volunteers and 12 per cent of volunteer hours (Statistics Canada, 2004a). Based on Canadian data 93 per cent of volunteers in nonprofit organizations are engaged in 'activities such as delivering, or helping to deliver, programs and services and engaging in fundraising and campaigning activities . . . with the remaining 7% engaged in governance' (Statistics Canada, 2004a: 31). Most nonprofit sport organizations in Canada also have no paid staff, further highlighting the reliance of these organizations on voluntary labour, time and resources to sustain their operations and develop sport.

Further evidence of the central role volunteers play in sport development is found in the research conducted by the LIRC, which argued that 'volunteers are hugely important to sport in England and they are not substitutable by commercial or public sector activity' (LIRC, 2003: 151). The LIRC report concluded that volunteering is crucial for the ongoing sustainability of the sport sector and 'remains the bedrock of opportunity in many sports' (LIRC, 2003: 33).

The Targeted Sports Participation Growth (TSPG) Program of the ASC also illustrates the central role volunteers play in sport development. The TSPG Program is a fundamental part of the ASC's junior and grass roots sport development agenda, designed to increase participation in formal organized sport (Stewart et al., 2004). The TSPG Program is designed to foster partnerships between business, government and the sport sector in 21 established sports such as netball, rugby league and Australian Rules Football that have sufficient 'infrastructure to be able to implement programmes that will have a meaningful impact on the policy objective of increasing organised sport participation' (Stewart et al., 2004: 112). The ASC provided funding to these NGBs to support a range of initiatives (e.g. the Australian

Football League's (AFL) Auskick Program). Auskick is comprised of junior clinics conducted over periods of 6 to 12 weeks to provide participants with promotional packs about Australian Rules Football, sponsor products, sporting equipment and engage them in modified forms of the game (Stewart *et al.*, 2004). The success of Auskick and similar programmes is largely dependent on volunteer efforts to deliver sporting experiences to participants. While the sport governing bodies facilitate the promotion of the scheme and provide the material resources to clubs and schools, it is volunteers who organize and deliver programmes at the local level.

Volunteer sport development roles

Sport development in countries such as Canada, New Zealand, Australia and the UK is dependent on local or community sport clubs, referred to as VSOs. As discussed in the previous chapter, the vast majority of sport volunteers operate at the community club level. The following section examines how volunteers and staff work in the club environment and their contribution to sport development.

The most striking feature of local or community sport clubs is their diversity. In a report for Sport Scotland, Allison (2002) provided a snapshot of sport clubs and highlighted the many functions, structures, resources, values and ideologies evident in sport clubs and the enormous range of opportunities they provide for sport participation and involvement. Not surprisingly, Allison found that most clubs provide single sport activities and focus on facilitating the enjoyment of sport, rather than competitive success. The average number of members in Scottish sport clubs was 133, with most catering for both junior and adult participants. The majority of clubs operate with simple structures, minimal staffing, relatively small amounts of income and expenditure, and often rely on a small group of paid or unpaid individuals to maintain their operations. Local sport clubs also tend to be fairly autonomous, relying almost exclusively on membership payments as their major source of income and little government funding. Allison (2002: 7) concluded that the management of local sport clubs in Scotland is an 'organic and intuitive process based on trust and experience rather than formal contracts and codes of practice', highlighting the informal and friendly nature of the volunteer experience at the local club level (see Nichols *et al.*, 2005).

The characteristics of local sport clubs (VSOs) in other countries are similar. Sport volunteers in England are multitaskers, fulfilling an average of 4.65 roles per year in these areas within the local sport club environment (LIRC, 2003). In a large sample of Norwegian sport clubs Seippel (2002) found that more than 90 per cent of the work for approximately 88 per cent of clubs was performed by volunteers. The findings of Doherty (2005), discussed briefly in the previous chapter, show that the majority of Canadian sport volunteers are also involved in more than one organization. Doherty

(2005) reported that most volunteers take on multiple roles within sport organizations. The roles undertaken by volunteers in the development of sport can be categorized broadly as either strategic or operational. Strategic volunteer roles include fulfilling administrative positions such as committee or board members of sport clubs, regional, state/provincial VSOs, NGBs or ISFs. Operational roles include acting as officials, coaches, event volunteers or general volunteers. The roles undertaken by volunteers and their impact on sport development are somewhat dependent on the level of involvement sought by individuals. These roles are briefly explained below.

Administrators

Committee or board members are charged with the responsibility for the overall guidance, direction and supervision of the organization, at all levels in the sport system from local clubs to ISFs. According to the ASC (2000a: 2) the responsibilities of the management committee of a sport club extend to:

- conducting long-term planning for the future of the club;
- developing policy and procedures for club activities;
- managing external relations with other sport organizations, local governments or sponsors;
- managing financial resources and legal issues on behalf of the club;
- carrying out recommendations put forward by members;
- communicating to members on current issues or developments;
- evaluating the performance of officials, employees (if any), and other service providers;
- ensuring adequate records are kept for future transfer of responsibilities to new committee members;
- acting as role models for other club members.

The ability of volunteers to carry out these tasks effectively will vary according to their individual experiences, qualifications, motivations, commitment, along with the culture and quality of the resources within a VSO. The important administrative roles within local sport clubs are the chairperson or president, secretary, treasurer and volunteer coordinator. Other committee roles might involve responsibility for organizing or coordinating coaching, officiating, representative teams, match day arrangements, fundraising and marketing.

The chair or president has overall responsibility for setting the agenda for how a committee operates, working to develop the strategic direction of the club, chairing committee meetings, and coordinating the work of other members of the committee and the organization overall. Club secretaries act as the link between club members, the committee or board and other organizations and have responsibility for managing correspondence, records and information about club activities. The treasurer's responsibilities include preparing the annual budget, monitoring expenditure and revenue, planning for future financial needs and managing operational issues such as cash receipts, payments and banking. Volunteer coordinators are responsible for developing systems and procedures to manage volunteers such as planning, recruitment, training and recognition and reward schemes. These roles are discussed in more detail in Chapter 8.

Officials

The majority of individual sports officials (referees, umpires, judges, scorers or timekeepers) are unpaid. Some sports such as football (soccer), Australian Rules Football, basketball, cricket and other football codes pay officials at all levels, enabling a small minority at the elite level to earn a living as full-time professional officials. Other sports such as netball, softball, swimming or tennis rarely pay officials other than those who officiate at or above state/provincial level tournaments and competitions. While sports officials are critical to facilitating sporting opportunities they often are the most difficult positions to fill at the voluntary level. Increasing abuse from players and spectators towards officials, excessive training and accreditation requirements and rising costs are some of the reasons why officiating is not an attractive volunteer role compared to other sport opportunities (Hoye and Cuskelly, 2004a).

All sports provide a structured training and accreditation scheme for officials to ensure high standards of officiating occur at local, state/provincial, national or international levels. In some cases governments seek to coordinate such efforts across sporting codes. In Australia the National Officiating Accreditation Scheme (NOAS) was established in 1994, and aims to develop and implement programmes that improve the quality, quantity, leadership and status of sports officiating in Australia (ASC, 2005a). The roles of sports officials are discussed in more detail in Chapter 9.

Coaches

The majority of coaches working in the local sport club system are also volunteers. However, depending on the nature of the sport and the resources of individual clubs, some coaches are paid. Coaches that rise up through the ranks and coach at elite levels are more likely to be remunerated, as are coaches in particular individual sports such as golf, swimming and tennis. The role of the coach is central to developing an athlete's skills and knowledge, in helping them learn and enjoy their sport. Coaches also act as important role models for players and athletes.

Standards of sport coaching have long been recognized as having an important impact on the development of sport. Similar to the NOAS programme, most NGBs provide structured training and accreditation schemes for coaches to develop their knowledge and skills. In Australia, for example, a National Coaching Accreditation Scheme (NCAS) was established in 1978. Through this scheme coaches can undertake a Level 0 basic course, Level 1 introductory course, Level 2 intermediate course and Level 3 advanced courses in coaching. NCAS training programmes comprise three elements: (1) coaching principles that cover fundamentals of coaching and athletic performance; (2) sport-specific coaching that covers the skills, techniques, strategies and scientific approaches to a particular sport; and (3) coaching practice where coaches engage in practical coaching and application of coaching principles (ASC, 2005a). The roles and impacts coaches are detailed in Chapter 10.

Event volunteers

Volunteers involved in sport events are somewhat different to volunteers who are regularly involved in sport organizations. The commitment of event volunteers tends to be short term, whereas volunteers regularly involved in sport organizations develop a relationship with the organization and other volunteers over a longer period of time (ASC, 2000a). Volunteers involved in events fulfil a variety of roles often requiring specialist skills or knowledge, and require a more intensive approach to managing them due to the timelines involved in recruiting, selecting and training event volunteers. The roles of event volunteers are discussed in Chapter 11.

General volunteers

Volunteers also perform various other roles that assist in facilitating the development of sport. These include fundraising, managing representative teams, player registration, helping with match day arrangements such as car parking or stewarding and helping to promote sport clubs. The majority of these general volunteers have an existing link to a sport club such as being a parent of a child involved in the club, through friends and work colleagues involved in the club, or as a past player. This form of volunteering is generally less formal than being a committee member, coach or official to the extent that training and accreditation schemes have not been established and the job requirements are often less onerous. Nevertheless, general volunteers are an integral part of supporting the operations of sport clubs and contributing to the development of sport.

The roles played by volunteers and the contribution they make to sport development do not go unrecognized by state/provincial sport organizations and NGBs. Volunteers are an important means by which significant parts of the strategic plans and management processes of sport governing bodies at national and state/provincial level are operationalized. Most sport NGBs and state/provincial governing bodies have developed a number of initiatives to ensure that volunteers in administrative, officiating, coaching and event roles are trained and well managed to deliver strategically important sport development outcomes. These initiatives and the roles of volunteers in these core areas are explored in more detail in subsequent chapters.

Pressures on volunteers and VSOs

It has been argued that volunteers are integral for the achievement of the primary goals of sport development in increasing participation in sport and improving the performance levels of people involved in sport. However, volunteers and the system in which they operate are subject to a number of demands that have implications for government policy, volunteers themselves and the manner in which volunteers are managed.

In the previous chapter, the variable nature of VSOs in terms of their size, structures, cultures, traditions and their capacity to respond to external pressures was introduced and briefly discussed. Taylor (2004) identified and characterized two types of VSOs that lie at opposite ends of a spectrum. At one end of the spectrum are traditional/informal sport organizations, which have strong collective identities, operate as cooperatives and view professionalism and external assistance as threats. At the other end of the spectrum of VSOs are contemporary/formal sport organizations, which tend to be systematic, business-like and receptive to external assistance. Taylor (2004) contended that it will be very difficult to effectively deliver sport development programmes aimed at increasing the number of sport participants or performance standards through the traditional/informal VSOs. More contemporary/formal organizations will be better able to provide the necessary infrastructure and systems to support sport development initiatives. As discussed in Chapter 2, Taylor (2004) identified a number of pressures confronting sport volunteers and VSOs in England. These pressures and the variable capacity of VSOs 'conspire to create considerable constraints to the development potential of voluntary sports organisations' (Taylor, 2004: 107). In other words, these pressures might force the more informal/ traditional VSOs to concentrate more on core operational tasks and less on strategic developments that enable growth and improvements in sporting experiences. Taylor (2004) argued that these pressures are not new to the sporting system, citing earlier research published in 1996 by the London Sport Council that had identified similar issues. However, there are indications that the situation has deteriorated. Based on the research conducted by the LIRC (2003), Taylor (2004: 107) listed several underlying societal and institutional reasons why the pressures on the sport system, and the volunteers that operate within it, are greater than they were a decade earlier:

- increased choice and competition for people's leisure time and expenditure;

- a 'time squeeze' caused not only by this greater choice of leisure options but also increasing time devoted to paid work and child care, particularly in the higher socio-economic groups that have the strongest representation in sports participation;
- a lack of time is the most important reason for people giving up volunteering in sport and the most important constraint preventing interested non-volunteers from volunteering;
- greater expectations of higher quality service delivery by VSOs;
- central government and Sport England requirements and initiatives (e.g. greater accountability for funds received, social inclusion, equal access and child protection);
- NGB standards and requirements (e.g. coach training, accreditation and registration, and member registration).

While these pressures may well limit the ability of the traditional/informal VSOs to contribute strategically to the development of sport, Taylor (2004: 108) asserted that more contemporary/formal VSOs 'have the managerial skills and techniques to promote development and respond to external initiatives'. In part, this view may be based on the fact that while some VSOs have falling volunteer numbers, an equal portion have increasing volunteer numbers and therefore have a reasonable pool of skilled volunteers. Taylor (2004) concluded that there is sufficient evidence to suggest that some VSOs at least are well placed to cope with the increasing workloads and complexity facing the sport sector. The lesson for policy makers and VSOs seeking assistance from their volunteer labour force in achieving sport development outcomes is that they must balance the risk of adversely affecting the motivations of volunteers against imposing higher levels of professionalism on VSO operations that are more akin to a service delivery organizations (LIRC, 2003).

A model of barriers to volunteering in sport developed by Doherty (2005) identified both personal and organizational barriers. Personal barriers include work commitments, lack of time, family pressures, past experience, lack of skills and an inability to make a year round commitment. Organizational barriers include the poor management, increasing demands placed on volunteers and organizations not inviting people to volunteer. Some of these barriers are beyond the control of VSOs, while others can be addressed, at least in part, by innovative organizational policies and strategies. The pressures confronting VSOs and the voluntary sport sector and the barriers that inhibit volunteering within VSOs have changed the ways in which volunteers participate in and contribute to sport development. They also create drivers for how VSOs might go about facilitating the engagement of volunteers in sport development activities.

In order for VSOs to contribute to sport development in the future they will need to compete for time, expenditure and enthusiasm from their members. VSOs face increased competition from local government and commercial providers as sport participants are faced with a wider variety of choice to occupy their leisure time and spend their disposable income on. This creates the need for VSOs to improve their service delivery systems for members which, in turn, may alter the relationship between members and their respective VSO from one of participation to purely consumption of services. This would have implications for how volunteerism might be viewed within the organization and the ongoing effects of possibly moving to a service provider approach rather than a member driven organization. The ongoing societal pressures placed on individuals' time and their capacity to volunteer may diminish the ability of VSOs to act as vehicles for citizen engagement and developers of social capital. VSOs may need to create attractive volunteer opportunities and benefits to enable member involvement to continue within sport.

Nichols *et al.* (2005) argued that pressures from NGBs are also changing the way VSOs operate. VSOs are continually asked to respond to increasing demands for the implementation of professionalized management systems. In Australia for example, the Australian Rugby Union (ARU) has implemented a centrally controlled database management system that requires club volunteers to register individual membership details via the ARU website for direct loading to a central database. Irrespective of their size, this necessitates clubs follow the same procedures for registration days to gather the same information from members each year. Such procedures can place considerable strain on smaller clubs and their volunteers to adopt more sophisticated and formalized procedures in their day to day operations.

The influence on sport volunteers of government policy enacted through government agencies such as Sport England, the ASC, Sport and Recreation New Zealand (SPARC) and Sport Canada is significant. Policies designed to increase accountability for funds received by NGBs, policies and funding schemes aimed at increasing levels of social inclusion and equal access to sporting opportunities, and regulatory requirements to increase child protection measures all place demands on national, state/provincial and local club level volunteers. Complying with the policies and allied funding agreement terms may add to the complexity and accountability of the work of volunteers at all levels within the sport system. Such compliance requirements may lead to a reduction in individual VSO autonomy (Houlihan, 1997) and constrain the operational flexibility of VSOs and their volunteers. Government policy requirements at the state/provincial and local level can also force change within sport organizations. These changes can be a source of tension as governments seek to support the voluntary sport sector but in so doing seek the assistance of VSOs in delivering government policy objectives related to sport. The relationship between government policy and volunteers and VSOs is considered in more detail in the next chapter.

Finally, VSOs must manage the opportunities and demands placed on them through technological change, a trend towards social risk aversion and increased legislation. VSOs are pressured to make use of the latest techno-logical improvements in sporting products and information technology, both of which may increase the costs of participation in a sport and the amount of volunteer time required to maintain websites and email addresses. VSOs are also subject to an increasing amount of legislation designed to regulate organizations and their activities in order to reduce risks to participants and volunteers involved in providing the activity. This often requires VSOs to deliver additional training to volunteers. It also highlights the risk of poten-tial exposure to legal proceedings faced by volunteers acting in their capacity as a coach, team manager, administrator or official. These changes have a direct impact on the ability of VSOs to attract and retain volunteers and thereby contribute to sport development.

Concluding comments

The sport systems of Australia, Canada, New Zealand, the UK and other countries with club-based sport systems depend on volunteers to deliver the majority of sporting opportunities for participants. Borrowing from Churchill, who said democracy 'is the worst possible system, except for all the others', it could be said that the reliance of sport systems on voluntary effort is problematic. Without huge investments by governments and a will-ingness on the part of consumers to pay far more for sport participation experiences, sports systems in Australia, Canada, New Zealand and the UK will continue to rely on the goodwill and efforts of volunteers. It has been argued that volunteers are integral to the achievement of sport develop-ment outcomes, that VSOs vary in their capacity to contribute to sport development, and that volunteers and VSOs are subject to a number of societal and institutional pressures. These pressures can create barriers to volunteering. Some VSOs are better placed than others to counteract these barriers and thereby build capacity for sport development. A key deter-minant of how VSOs are placed to tackle these pressures is the government policies designed to support and control the activities of the voluntary sport sector. The details and effects of government policies relevant to volunteers and VSOs are explored in the next chapter.

Chapter 4

Volunteers and government policy

This chapter explores the manner in which government policy impacts on volunteer activities in sport. It focuses on policies that have increased the compliance burden and complexity of volunteer tasks as well as policies that have been developed to foster volunteer involvement in sport. The chapter includes examples from Australia, New Zealand, the UK and Canada with the aim of summarizing the central tenets of government policy affecting volunteers in community-based sporting systems. The chapter comprises four parts: first, the foundations of sport policy and the mechanics of developing sport policy; second, the nature of the relationship between the government and the nonprofit sport sector; third, a summary of current sport policy; and fourth, examples of policies designed to foster volunteer involvement and those that have increased the compliance burden for sport volunteers.

Foundations of sport policy

Contemporary government involvement in sport is broad and extensive (Houlihan, 2005). Governments in Australia, Canada, New Zealand, the UK and most other Western countries have developed policies designed to foster community involvement in sport and physical activity, regulate the access and use of performance enhancing drugs in sport, improve the performance of elite athletes, deliver economic benefits through supporting infrastructure developments and major sporting events, and address issues of equity and access to sport by minority and disadvantaged groups in the community. Policies have also been developed to improve the management and operational performance of organizations involved in delivering sport, and to foster the development of social capital through programmes such as volunteer training and development programmes.

Government intervention in the voluntary sport sector is based on the principle that participation in sport is a merit good that is subject to two potential sources of market failure: efficiency and equity (Sandy *et al.*, 2004). Efficiency market failure occurs when sport delivery, although efficient for individual participants, may not necessarily be so for society at large if potential additional social benefits are not created due to the actions of individuals. Government therefore seeks to intervene through the provision of publicly funded programmes and facilities to increase sport participation which may have the effect of lowering expenditure on public health programmes. Government may also intervene in sport because of equity-related concerns where the market fails to distribute resources and programmes equitably to all sectors of the community.

The outcomes sought by government through various sport policies are to a large extent focused on delivering social benefits. Social benefits can arise from policies concerned with both elite sport and community or mass participation in sport. Stewart et al. (2004: 32) identified a number of social benefits that result from policies supporting the active participation of communities in sport and physical activity including improvements in community health and productivity, reduced medical costs, reduction in juvenile crime rates, development of character and sense of fair play, and the building of social capital, social cohesion and greater levels of civic engagement. Social benefits claimed to flow from policies that support elite sport include a sense of tribal identification and belonging, civic and national pride, international recognition and prestige along with economic development and tourism (Stewart et al., 2004: 32). Governments also seek to address inequities that may exist for individuals and groups accessing resources to participate or otherwise be involved in sport.

The extent of government involvement and attempts to intervene in the activities of VSOs is dependent on the ideology of the political party in power at any one time. Political ideologies provide a guide for how governments make decisions and seek to solve problems as well as the 'value positions, the ideals and prescriptions for action' (Bramham, 2001: 10). Political ideologies can be broadly categorized as conservatism, social reformism or liberalism. A conservative ideology seeks to maintain traditional values and customs, and preserve the status quo in which inequalities are perceived as natural and inevitable. Conservatism argues that individuals should be loyal subjects of the state and are therefore subject to a number of behavioural controls to maintain the order of society. Conservative governments tend to leave the market to decide the allocation of resources, with motivation for profits and market forces leading to optimal outcomes for society. Stewart et al. (2004: 22) argued that sport is 'not so much a blind spot as a vacant space' when it comes to conservative governments enacting sport policies. While on the one hand conservative governments recognize that sport delivers good outcomes for individuals and society, they believe sport is best left to its own devices with little if any government intervention. In contrast to the highly commercialized world of sport that exists today, conservative governments could be accused of retaining 'a romantic belief that sport fulfils its function best when it is done for its own sake, played by amateurs, managed by volunteers, and generally left to look after its own affairs' (Stewart et al., 2004: 22).

Social reformism is concerned with social justice and ensuring equity for individuals. Reformist governments also support the idea of a strong private sector but believe it needs to be tightly regulated and monitored to ensure fair and equitable outcomes. In terms of sport, reformist governments view it as a vehicle for social development, offering opportunities for the government to intervene in the market to ensure individuals have an equal chance to participate and enjoy the social benefits that sport can deliver. Stewart et al. (2004) noted that reformist governments tend to develop programmes for specific interest or minority groups such as aboriginals, women, the disabled and people of non-English-speaking backgrounds and that, in general, they focus on community sport rather than elite.

Liberalism is 'a political ideology that stresses both individualism and democracy: individuals should be free from governance, free to exercise rights to property, free speech and political suffrage' (Bramham, 2001: 12). Liberal governments view their main functions as to maintaining law and order, and avoiding interference in the affairs of the private and third sectors. Liberals view state-owned enterprises as inefficient and believe that most economic activity should be driven by the market, with little intervention by the state. Sport is viewed as 'an important social institution, but should not be strictly controlled' (Stewart et al., 2004: 23). Liberal governments do, however, recognize that sport has its value in nation building and economic development, leading to an emphasis on elite rather than community sport (Stewart et al., 2004).

These three ideologies provide different perspectives on the value and place of sport in society and therefore the extent and form that government involvement should take in influencing how sport develops and the activities of sport organizations. This creates several challenges for VSOs as 'each ideology will produce different sport policy outcomes, strategies and programmes, and the ideology often overrides the claims of interest groups and stakeholders' (Stewart et al., 2004: 23). In pursuing the wide range of outcomes that sport can deliver, governments enact policies that in a broad sense, either seek to regulate or directly support the activities of organizations involved in the delivery of sport. As discussed in previous chapters, the vast majority of sport organizations are dependent on volunteers, and thus sport volunteers are directly and indirectly affected by government policy initiatives and requirements. Governments employ a variety of policy instruments to achieve policy outcomes: direct funding support for organizations or programmes, enacting legislation or regulations to prohibit or restrict activities of individuals or organizations, acting as an advocate for a cause or idea, or pursuing direct action such as establishing an agency or department to deliver specific programmes directly or via contract (Bridgman and Davis, 2000).

Examples of direct funding provision by government to sport include the construction and operation of major stadia and community sporting facilities, providing operational grants to NGBs or state/provincial level VSOs, and financial support of bids for national and international sporting events. Government enacts legislation to control access to free-to-air broadcasting of sporting events in Australia, the distribution of lottery funds for sport in the UK, and the creation of national elite sport agencies in many Commonwealth countries. Legislation in areas such as taxation, food safety, privacy, human rights and incorporation also affect VSOs. Furthermore, government act as an advocate, directly promoting the benefits of sport participation to individuals through mass media campaigns and supporting the efforts of allied industries and groups that use sport as a vehicle to promote health benefits. Finally, governments are directly involved in delivering sport services and programmes in sport through agencies such as the ASC and Sport England and through elite sport institutes such as the Australian Institute of Sport (AIS) and UK Sport, respectively.

Policy developments are driven by the government of the day, the major opposition political parties that develop election policies that may subsequently become government policy, and/or the various stakeholder and interest groups involved in sport. Whatever form government policy takes or the policy instrument employed, the individuals and organizations involved are part of what is known as a policy community. The policy community for a particular sport policy may comprise organizations as diverse as ISFs and event organizations, NGBs, state/provincial VSOs, major sport leagues, health and physical education professionals, sponsors, major stadia, elite athletes, media organizations, universities, schools, sport clubs and volunteers. Policy communities provide governments the opportunity to consult with those who may be directly affected by policy, access to information about the likely impact of any new policy ideas and may help to reduce the potential for conflict over changes to policy.

Interest groups that form part of the policy community comprise four types of structural interest groups: demand groups (sport consumers such as club members or elite athletes), provider groups (service deliverers such as physical education teachers, coaches, club volunteers and VSOs), direct support groups (organizations that provide systemic support such as NGBs, sponsors, schools), and indirect support groups (local government authorities, non-sport funding agencies) (Houlihan, 2005). Volunteers play significant roles in the majority of these interest groups and thus are a core part of sport policy communities. The ability of volunteers and the organizations with which they operate within to influence sport policy depends largely on how governments perceive their legitimacy. Taylor and Warburton (2003) found that third sector organizations interpret their legitimacy as based on how well they represent the views of their constituents and promote values of social justice or equity, whereas governments consider legitimacy in terms of the ability of the organization to actually deliver policy outcomes. This discrepancy suggests that third sector organizations, including VSOs, need to demonstrate their capacity to contribute to delivering policy outcomes if they wish to be taken seriously by government and be actively engaged in the development of policy. However, this process should be carefully managed to ensure organizations maintain their independence and autonomy.

Stewart et al. (2004: 27) highlighted the increasingly complex nature of developing sport policy. Government interacts with numerous policy community members in a milieu of 'organizations, activities and facilities ... surrounded by a sport culture that has to balance the traditions and history of sport with its commercial imperatives'. Sport policy in countries with significant community club-based structures must strike a balance between economic reality of limited funding being available for sport and the need to deal with issues of gender, race, equity and the particular culture and traditions of different sporting activities. Houlihan (2005: 177) noted that there 'has been a steady growth in organizational complexity and specialization' for agencies that deal with sport policy. Subsequently, agencies have tended to 'develop relatively stable preferences for policy tools, perceptions of problems, and modes of working which constrain their response to new issues' (Houlihan, 2005: 177). The increasing complexity of the sport policy environment and the tendency for sport organizations to adopt a relatively narrow perspective for dealing with issues is a source of frustration for governments seeking to enact policy. In addition, Houlihan (2005: 177) cited the 'recurring complaint from sports ministers that making sport policy normally involves liaison and negotiation with a large number of other departments who have a secondary interest in the area' such as education, health and community development.

Developing sport policy is a messy business (Stewart et al., 2004). The multiplicity of outcomes that sport can deliver, the different ideologies that exist within governments, the utility of different policy instruments, the varied source of policy ideas, the wide range of structural interest groups that are involved in delivering policy outcomes, and the inherent complexity of sport issues that cut across different areas of government activity preclude the application of a routine, linear and rational policy process. Sport policy formulation can involve the application of rational planning, political opportunism, the development of sub-optimal solutions designed to appease the demands of disparate interest groups, incremental changes and a lot of muddling through (Stewart et al., 2004). There is no single way that governments can best be involved in sport, or fully understand 'what forms of assistance and regulation will produce the best outcomes' (Stewart et al., 2004). The following sections further explore the nature of the relationship between government and sport and the detail of policies that impact on the ways in which volunteer activities are undertaken in sport.

Government and sport relationship

The impacts of government policy were briefly discussed in Chapter 1 where it was argued that governments have generally scaled back their involvement in the direct delivery of welfare and social services and now rely more on nonprofit organizations and their volunteers to deliver services. The relationship between government and the nonprofit sector generally has shifted 'towards notions of social contract, mutual obligation and partnerships between individuals, communities and the state' (Warburton and Mutch, 2000). This trend presents a number of challenges for VSOs as their activities are increasingly tied to government policies and accompanying programme guidelines, directives, and funding and reporting requirements.

The extent and nature of the relationship between sport and government differs by type of organization involved (NGBs to local sport clubs) and the level of government involved (national to state/provincial to local) (Anheier, 2005). The relationship is also dependent on the funding arrangements between government and sport organizations, which may range from grants, fee-for-service contracts, or government loans, and other non-monetary support such as facilities, expertise or organizational support. Relationships also involve mandates where government is required by law to engage with nonprofit sport organizations to implement policy, as well as fulfilling the requirements of regulatory and accountability mechanisms.

Najam (2000) developed a model of government and nonprofit relations based on the extent to which their respective organizational goals and means overlap (see Figure 4.1). The model proposes that the relationship is cooperative, complementary, cooptive or confrontational. If the goals and means are similar then this leads to a cooperative relationship between government and the nonprofit sector. In sport this would describe the relationship between an elite sport agency or organization such as the AIS and NGBs striving to improve the performance of elite athletes and teams. A complementary relationship would evolve if the goals were similar but

		Organizational or policy goals	
		Similar	Dissimilar
Means of achieving policy outcomes or organizational goals	Similar	Cooperation	Cooptation
	Dissimilar	Complementarity	Confrontation

Figure 4.1 Government nonprofit relations

Source: Adapted from Najam (2000: 338).

the means were dissimilar, such as government promoting higher levels of participation in sport through a mass media campaign supported by NGBs and VSOs offering clinics in schools. If the goals are dissimilar but the means are similar, this leads to a cooptive relationship where, for example, government may support the funding of a new multipurpose sport stadium with matching funds from NGBs or VSOs that wish to use the facility for their own discrete purposes. Finally, if the goals and means are both dissimilar, this creates a confrontational relationship such as a sports organization lobbying government for more funding to the sport sector or criticizing current sport policies.

The value of Najam's model is that it emphasizes that all organizations, whether government or nonprofit, are 'driven not just by the grand schema of sectors and politics, but by the reality and rationality of their institutional interest and priorities' (Najam, 2000: 391). The relationship between government and VSOs is highly variable based on the policy and organizational goals sought by each and the strategies each seeks to employ for their achievement. As governments increasingly look to VSOs for assistance in achieving policy outcomes, VSOs must balance the need to maintain positive relations with government against the needs and interests of volunteers, who provide the dominant means through which VSOs deliver services to their members.

In the previous chapter sport was identified as being influenced by government policy, which has implications for how volunteers are managed, their roles and their workloads. One example of how the relationship between government and nonprofit organizations is becoming more formalized and interdependent is exemplified in the attempt by the British government in the later half of the 1990s to develop a 'compact' or agreement between government and the nonprofit sector. The agreement sought to foster a closer relationship between government and the nonprofit sector in policy development and reviewing the performance of organizations charged with carrying out government policy. Plowden (2003: 430) argued that a compact is indicative of 'an attempt to change the culture of government/voluntary sector relationships'.

Sam and Jackson (2004) highlighted a contradiction of sport policy in New Zealand in which the central government sought to coordinate the activities of the sport sector but at the same time empowered organizations within the sector to act more autonomously, seek independent funding and adopt more commercialized management practices. Such contradictions are also apparent in Australia and the UK where central government policy is increasingly focused on funding VSOs for specific policy outcomes but simultaneously requires them to be self-sufficient and independent. The following section explores recent government sport policies in Australia, Canada and the UK in an attempt to identify the elements of contemporary sport policy that directly affect volunteer involvement in sport.

Sport policies and volunteers

Contemporary sport policies developed in Australia, Canada and the UK follow a similar pattern as each government has attempted to balance supporting a community club-based sporting system while channelling significant funding towards elite sport. Green (2005: 161) argued that 'the interests of elite sport development have dominated the sport policy making process in Australia and Canada over the past two to three decades, with a similar scenario emerging in the UK over the past 10 years'. The dominance of elite sport has, however, not been the result of sustained lobbying from elite sport interests. Rather it is the result of government 'specifying, constructing, and maintaining through resource control and dependency the patterns of values and beliefs supportive of elite achievement' (Green, 2005: 161). Nor has community sport been ignored as governments have recognized the need to support other priorities such as 'club development, regional development or mass participation' (Green, 2005: 161).

The current Australian government sport policy, BASA, is focused on securing four outcomes: maintaining a national sport system that will deliver international success, increased participation in grass roots sport, improved management standards for Australian VSOs, and combating the use of performance enhancing drugs in sport. The majority of government funds are allocated to elite sport (Stewart et al., 2004) but there are a number of elements of the policy that directly impact volunteers at all levels of the sport system. For example, BASA requires 'national sporting organisations to achieve greater rates of active participation and increase registered membership as a condition of funding' (Commonwealth of Australia, 2001: 7). The policy also seeks to ensure 'the adoption of sound business and management practices by national sporting organisations . . . (and) . . . a higher level of commercial activity on the part of local and national sporting organisations' (Commonwealth of Australia, 2001: 8). These outcomes are to be delivered by setting specific performance targets for NGBs in areas of elite sport, participation, fairness, funding, governance, anti-doping and requiring NGBs and their member VSOs to adopt more sophisticated management systems and communication technologies.

These policy goals and mechanisms used to achieve them require significant input by volunteers in terms of improving their skills, devoting time in VSOs for achieving national outcomes such as increased participation levels and improving the veracity of member registration systems and procedures. At the same time as imposing these requirements on NGBs and their volunteers in return for funding, governments are encouraging these same organizations to become more commercialized and financially self-sufficient (see Nichols et al., 2005).

The Canadian Sport Policy (CSP) also has four major policy goals: enhanced participation, excellence, capacity and interaction. These goals seek to address 14 major issues in the Canadian sport system. The issues are common across other community-based sporting systems and include declining participation rates, significant access barriers for minority groups, fostering an effective elite athlete development system, clarifying the values that sport at all levels can deliver to communities and increasing the ability of the sport system to access non-government funding sources (Government of Canada, 2002). The CSP also relies extensively on the efforts of volunteers to deliver outcomes. Their goal of enhancing participation requires VSOs to 'increase participation, by recruiting new participants and reducing dropout rates in their sports' (Government of Canada, 2002: 16), an activity that must be managed by local club level volunteers. The CSP also seeks to enhance the capacity of the sport system by supporting the 'development of volunteer and salaried leadership and organizations at all levels to strengthen their contribution to a healthy and ethically based, athlete/participant-centred sport system' (Government of Canada, 2002: 18).

The CSP also emphasizes the need to enhance interaction between the organizations that make up the Canadian sport system. For example, it aims to foster stronger relations between VSOs and educational institutions in areas such as 'participation, athlete/participant development, coach education and employment, access to facilities, and the provision of other services' (Government of Canada, 2002: 19). The CSP also aims to strengthen the relationship between government and VSOs to 'increase the overall effectiveness and accountability of the sport system' (Government of Canada, 2002: 19). The effect of the policy is to formalize the procedures used by VSOs, increase the reporting requirements of VSOs funded by the government, and influence the way VSOs interact with their volunteers.

Sport England launched its most recent sport policy, 'The Framework for Sport in England', in 2004, which also has the twin objectives of increasing participation and supporting elite success. Sport England has identified six policy priorities: promotion and marketing, legislation and regulatory change, quality accreditation and improvement, structures and partnerships, innovation and delivery, and strategic planning and evidence. Together, these policy priorities require NGBs and VSOs to enter into partnerships with other organizations, engage in more formal planning and reporting, and deliver specific outcomes, all of which require volunteer efforts, in return for increased funding. The value of volunteers is recognized in the policy as are the 'increasing burdens on volunteers relating to bureaucracy, concerns around litigation, and time pressures from other areas of life' (Sport England, 2004a: 14).

Sport England has also produced a policy specifically for sport volunteers that recognizes volunteers as one of the key drivers for change in enabling the sport policy to be implemented and 'the growing number of pressures that compromise volunteer contribution to sport' (Sport England, 2005c: 4). The central tenet of the sports volunteer policy is a commitment by

Sport England to 'work with partners to develop a dynamic, coordinated and sustainable infrastructure for volunteering in sport at national, regional and local levels' (Sport England, 2005c: 5).

The success of contemporary sport policies of the major Commonwealth nations is largely dependent on volunteers continuing to provide the labour for basic service delivery, and increasingly, the targeted programme and policy support required at all levels of these sport systems. As governments devise more sophisticated policy responses to a wide range of issues within the sport system, and look to sport to assist in addressing allied issues such as childhood obesity and poor community physical activity levels, volunteers and VSOs are being asked to meet an ever growing number of demands. The impacts of these demands are addressed in the following section.

Impacts on VSOs

Changes in government sport policy and funding requirements and the subsequent change in the nature of the relationship between government and sport have resulted in a number of challenges for VSOs. Houlihan and White (2002: 213) identified that

> the steady erosion of the privileged position of sports organizations has enabled local authorities and the Sports Councils to raise their expectations of the contribution that clubs and NGBs might make to public sports development policy in return for access to public funds, National Lottery income and other public resources.

One of the most significant challenges confronting sport volunteers and VSOs is the erosion of their autonomy and the costs of compliance if they agree to receive government funding and other support initiatives so that they may access the resources needed to deliver or expand their services. Contemporary sport policies of Australia, Canada and the UK highlight the shift from government simply providing grants to sport, to contractual-based partnership arrangements between government and sport with government viewing sport funding as an investment with specified outcomes. Aside from the increased compliance burden of adopting new business practices and more stringent reporting requirements as a result of changes in government sport policy, VSOs and their volunteers have been confronted with many other changes in recent years.

In Australia, VSOs have had to deal with significant changes to the taxation system with the introduction of a Goods and Services Tax in 2000, which required a significant increase in volunteer time, increased skill requirements for club treasurers, changes to accounting practices and training costs. Australian VSOs have also been subjected to the introduction of child protection legislation requiring changes in operations dealing with adult supervision of children and police checks of volunteer backgrounds, more stringent food safety requirements for VSOs operating canteens and kiosks as fund raising activities, and legal requirements for incorporation, volunteer protection legislation and insurance for volunteer directors.

Nichols *et al.* (2005) cited similar increases in compliance burdens for VSOs in the UK as a result of government funding requirements and policy directions. While government policies emphasize the use of partnerships, these 'are a compromise of objectives, and are influenced by the power relations between partners' (Nichols *et al.*, 2005: 40). There is also evidence of resistance on the part of NGBs to implement government policy with the associated increases in paperwork and reporting requirements. The increased compliance burden has a direct impact on individual volunteers when 'pressures to comply with the conditions of partnerships between NGBs and government cascade down to the volunteers in the sports clubs' (Nichols *et al.*, 2005: 40). Further, the partnership arrangements between government and NGBs can be a source of tension if NGBs, and their member organizations, are viewed by government as service delivery organizations whose funding is tied directly to the achievement of specified outcomes. If government controls the funds, sports have little scope to counteract this control, so volunteers are inevitably asked to perform tasks focused on achieving government policy outcomes.

The response of VSOs to these policy requirements is to adopt more professionalized and formalized operating systems, something that may well be at odds with the motivations and expectations of many volunteers. There is evidence to suggest that the adoption of more formalized management practices by VSOs is determined by the motivations of a core set of volunteers, particularly at club level (Nichols *et al.*, 2005). If the core volunteers perceive that adopting such practices as part of the response to government policies and NGB requirements will benefit their club or organization then they are more likely to do so.

The success of these government policies is largely dependent on the voluntary sector of sport having the capacity and motivation to respond appropriately. At the 2001 National Summit on Sport held in Ottawa, as precursor to developing the CSP, building capacity in the Canadian sport system was deemed one of three priorities. The highest priority in building capacity was the development of human resources, in particular developing the skills, knowledge and abilities of volunteers (Government of Canada, 2001).

While there have been many additional compliance requirements imposed on VSOs, governments have also sought to support volunteering through a number of specific programmes. These include the Volunteer Management Program (VMP) in Australia and the Volunteer Investment Program (VIP), now packaged as Running Sport in the UK. Both programmes seek to improve the capacity of VSOs and sport volunteers in sustaining their

respective sport systems by increasing 'the recognition of the important roles of volunteers in sport, encourage good practice in recruitment and retention of volunteers, and to help volunteers develop their leadership and managerial skills' (Jackson and Nesti, 2001: 155). These programmes are discussed in more detail in Chapter 7.

Government policy has also attempted to influence VSOs to adopt member protection policies that enable players, administrators, coaches, officials and other volunteers to participate in sport free from inappropriate behaviours such as harassment, discrimination or abuse (Sport and Recreation Victoria, 2005). The rationale for the introduction of member protection policies is that

> as membership and volunteer numbers decline, organisations need to look at practices and procedures that create safe, welcoming and enjoyable environments. Organisations must comply with legislative requirements (such as anti-discrimination and racial and religious vilification laws), identify the potential for any incidents relating to harassment and abuse of its members and develop strategies to reduce the likelihood or severity of its occurrence.
>
> (Sport and Recreation Victoria, 2005: no page)

Developing member protection policies requires VSOs to adopt formal guidelines and procedures for the recruitment and selection of individuals, particularly those involved with children and adolescents, providing education to members about appropriate standards of behaviour, and appointing volunteers as member protection officers. These officers are the first point of call in a club or sporting organization for any enquiries, concerns or complaints about harassment and abuse by providing information and moral support to the person with the concern or who is alleging harassment. Volunteers must complete a two-day training course approved by the ASC before being appointed to such a position.

A host of other government policy initiatives have added to the complexity of running sport in areas such as anti-doping, conditions under which pregnant women may play sport, insurance, privacy requirements, human rights, incorporation and associated legal requirements, risk management, junior sport policies, and access and equity policies. These are in addition to policies concerning the core business of VSOs in athlete, coach and official development, hosting events, and delivering sport participation and competition opportunities.

Concluding comments

This chapter has explored how government policy impacts on the way in which volunteer activities are undertaken in sport, including policies that assist in fostering volunteer involvement in sport and others that have increased the compliance burden for sport volunteers. It has been argued that the multiplicity of outcomes that sport can deliver, the different ideologies that exist within governments, the utility of different policy instruments, the varied source of policy ideas, the wide range of structural interest groups that are involved in delivering policy outcomes, and the inherent complexity of sport issues that cut across areas of government activity preclude the application of a rational policy process. The relationship between government and VSOs has evolved towards contractual-based partnership arrangements between government and sport with government viewing sport funding as an investment. The success of these government sport policies is largely dependent on the voluntary sector of sport having the capacity and volunteers with motivation to implement such policies. Government sport policy is an important driver of how volunteering takes place in the sport sector and while it provides many opportunities for sport it also imposes a number of constraints on the operations of VSOs.

Chapter 5

Legal issues

In recent years the nature of sport volunteer involvement has changed due to the increasing complexity of the legal environment in which sport organizations operate. More so than ever VSOs need to manage risk and to protect the organization itself, their members and volunteers from legal action. Given the continuing trend towards increasing legal pressures on sport, it is vital that sport volunteers receive appropriate training and develop the skills and knowledge necessary to carry out their tasks safely and efficiently. This chapter examines the major legal issues associated with managing sport volunteers and VSOs. While it is beyond the scope of this book to address all relevant legal issues at an operational level of detail, key current and emerging concerns are discussed. Furthermore, given the international focus of the book, detailed analysis of specific legislation is not provided but rather, this chapter focuses on legal principles. It should be noted that while Chapter 5 contains legal information, it does not constitute legal advice and any individuals or organizations that require specific legal advice should consult a qualified legal practitioner.

The changing organizational and legal context in the sport sector

One of the main external pressures currently influencing third sector organizations is the changing legal environment in which these organizations function. Over the past decade voluntary organizations have come under more intense legal scrutiny as societies have tended to become increasingly litigious. Mahoney (1998) asserted that there had been an 'explosion' of litigation in the US in the previous decade. Citizens have developed a heightened awareness of their rights and, perhaps more importantly, are now more prepared to exercise those rights by seeking resolution through the courts when disputes occur (Healey, 2005). VSOs in particular have faced mounting legal pressures because of these factors coupled with the inherent risks associated with active participation in many sports and the incidence of escalating compensation payouts. Despite a traditional reluctance to intervene in the affairs of nonprofit sport organizations (Champion, 2000; Conn, 2003), the courts are also now more likely to take increasing interest in both the on and off field activities of VSOs as these organizations pursue activities that could be classified as increasingly commercial in nature (Healey, 2005). In addition, sport participants, volunteers and VSOs themselves have been more willing to seek satisfaction to a wider spectrum of disputes through the legal system (e.g. team selection, tribunal decisions, doping allegations and player contracts).

One of the key catalysts underpinning the altered legal landscape for VSOs is the enhanced level of professionalization witnessed in sport over the last 20 years. This trend has resulted in higher expectations of service and standards of behaviour by clients and members, the community and the legal system itself. According to the Centre for Sport and Law (2005), the public is now more litigation oriented and expects voluntary organizations to be more accountable and business-like. Thus, along with the myriad of benefits resulting from professionalization also come added responsibilities as sport club members and sport consumers come to demand more from 'professionalised' VSOs. However, it seems that 'in some cases, the outlook of administrators and others involved has not kept pace with changing circumstances' (Healey, 2005: 12).

Expanded levels of professionalization mean that sport organizations now operate in more complex ways. They are likely to be engaged in a wider variety of revenue raising and commercial activities, to enter into contracts (e.g. with suppliers, sponsors and lessees), and to have paid employees, including players. Furthermore, as the financial rewards from sport increase, there is more scrutiny of VSO actions in areas such as athlete selection and tribunal decisions, even at the community level. In response to these increased levels of external pressures and internal complexity, VSOs have developed correspondingly more sophisticated administrative structures and processes. Ironically, such processes are themselves more likely to be subject to legal intervention due to their complexity and subsequent potential for variations in the consistency with which rules and policies are interpreted and applied. It is now commonplace for lawyers and the courts to intervene in what have previously been internal sport club affairs. Concomitantly, this also places increased public pressure on VSOs and individual volunteers as their decisions and actions are more frequently featured in the media.

Sport volunteers thus find themselves working in an increasingly complex environment, contextualized within a more interventionist legal system. These changes have resulted in a number of implications for VSOs and sport volunteers. For example, there is evidence that the recruitment and retention of volunteers have been adversely affected due to 'a growing sense of apprehension' (Healey, 2005) and 'unease' (McGregor-Lowndes and Edwards, 2004) about possible exposure to personal legal liability and the subsequent potential for financial loss. Mahoney (1998: 36) previously argued that litigation was an 'obstacle to becoming more involved' and Martinez (2003) later reinforced the view that fear of litigation dissuaded people from volunteering in the US context. Oppenheimer (2001) suggested that the Volunteer Protection Act (VPA) (1997) was introduced in the US after it was perceived that people were less willing to volunteer due to concerns about the potential for liability actions and noted that a similar trend was evident in Australia. Some research, however, indicates that such perceptions do not reflect reality. The actual number of lawsuits is relatively low and has not changed substantially in recent years in Australia, the UK or the US (Martinez, 2003; McGregor-Lowndes and Nguyen, 2005).

Role of government

Governments at all levels have been partially responsible for the mounting legal pressures on VSOs, mainly as a consequence of more involvement with sport as an instrument of government policy. Houlihan (1997: 109) concluded that governments clearly perceived sport almost exclusively in instrumental terms and in the past three decades the trend 'has clearly been for central governments to become more closely involved in sport and to seek to exploit sports in pursuit of a broad range of domestic and international policy objectives'. This trend is also evident at the local government level (Nichols *et al.*, 1998a). As discussed in previous chapters, sport is often seen as a panacea for a number of local community problems (e.g. health, youth delinquency, social integration) and also as a vehicle for government to pursue broader systemic policy objectives (e.g. national pride, economic revitalization, international relations). Subsequently, as governments have invested more resources in sport, there has also been a similarly enhanced expectation of higher levels of performance and accountability on the part of the VSOs benefiting from such investment. This is especially so as the nature of government involvement has become more contractual rather than grant based with more onerous reporting and audit requirements. Subsequently, VSOs are involved in much more demanding compliance and accountability processes that often require a sophisticated legal and operational framework. The policy background to the increased compliance burden on VSOs was addressed in more detail in Chapter 4.

A recent initiative by government has been an attempt to reduce some aspects of the legal burden on individual volunteers. In a number of countries there has been growing recognition of the moral and ethical imperative to shield voluntary workers from potential legal action. Furthermore, concerns about decreasing volunteer numbers and the problem of rising insurance premiums, with increases of up to 350 per cent according to Pybus (2003), have also prompted government action. Responses to these concerns have been manifested in a number of countries by legislated measures to protect volunteers from incurring personal civil liability, especially for tort liability. For example, in the US the VPA was passed in 1997. According to Jacobs (1997) the aim of the VPA was to grant immunity from personal liability to those who volunteered for nonprofit organizations and, in so doing, encourage volunteerism. It also was introduced to provide a standardized national scheme for volunteer protection. The VPA effectively transfers the liability from the individual volunteer to the organization and, as suggested by McGregor-Lowndes and Edwards (2004: 54), this is 'analogous to the common law principle of vicarious liability and creates a statutory exception to the basic rule that vicarious liability only attaches to the relationship of employer and employee'. The VPA provides that volunteers would not be liable for harm if

> they were acting in the scope of the volunteer activity; they were properly licensed (if necessary); the harm was not caused by wilful or criminal misconduct, gross negligence, reckless misconduct, or a conscious, flagrant indifference to the rights or safety of the claimant; and, the harm was not caused by the volunteer operating a vehicle.
>
> (Jacobs, 1997: 40)

Australia introduced similar measures from 2001 to 2004 as each state and territory passed a range of civil liability acts introduced either as new legislation or as amendments to existing legislation. McGregor-Lowndes and Edwards (2004) argued that the purpose of such legislation was to arrive at a balance between the interests of injured people and the general community, ease the pressure on insurance premiums but still maintain appropriate levels of protection for consumers. Dietrich (2005: 39) suggested that the 'gist of the Acts is to limit liability of defendants by expanding defences, narrowing liability rules and capping damages awards'. According to McGregor-Lowndes and Nguyen (2005: 45–46), despite variations in different jurisdictions in Australia, the legislation encapsulates five common requirements:

> [T]he person must come within the definition of a volunteer; the volunteer must be performing community work; the community work must be organized by a community organization; the volunteer must not fall under an exception to protection; and, the liability incurred by the volunteer must not come within an excluded liability.

While New Zealand is yet to enact similar legislation, it has provided some measure of protection to volunteers via the Injury Prevention, Rehabilitation and Compensation Act (2001). The Act establishes an accident compensation system based on a no fault scheme to compensate people who suffer personal injury and prevents sport participants taking common law action against sporting event volunteers. According to SPARC

(2005b: 6), the Act has 'largely removed the right of individuals to sue and claim compensatory damages for personal injury' although 'affected persons can still seek exemplary damages'. However, for an exemplary damages claim to be successful, 'the defendant must have acted with outrageous, flagrant or high-handed disregard for the plaintiff's rights' (SPARC, 2005b: 8) or with gross, as opposed to ordinary, negligence according to Duley (2005). While insurance provides some protection from large payouts, high premiums may act as a deterrent to their widespread adoption.

Although the UK has also not enacted specific volunteer protection legislation, the recently drafted Charities Bill provides for the establishment of a Charity Commission that will be given powers to remove the liability of trustees where they have acted reasonably and in good faith. The Bill, although introduced in December 2004, was not passed by Parliament before the general election was called in April 2005. However, the newly re-elected Blair government re-introduced the Charities Bill which subsequently passed through the House of Lords in late 2005 and was due to be debated in the House of Commons during 2006. If the Bill is enacted, it may raise questions as to the extent to which NGB and VSO officers and general volunteers are categorized as 'trustees' and, if not, whether such organizations can or should alter their legal status in order to afford such protection to their volunteers.

While legislation restricting the civil liability of volunteers generally provides substantially enhanced levels of protection, loopholes are evident and volunteers should not assume they will always be protected. For example, the legislation may not apply in instances where the 'volunteer was involved in a motor vehicle accident, was affected by alcohol or certain other drugs or was acting outside the scope of the activities authorized by the community organization or contrary to its instructions' (Volunteering Australia, 2003a: 6). Therefore, sport volunteers must be vigilant in assessing the nature and degree of risk associated with their involvement and also the manner in which they go about their volunteer participation. Similarly, VSOs must carefully monitor the activities of their volunteers and retain adequate levels of insurance coverage for a range of different types of volunteer involvement (e.g. coaches, directors, committee members and event volunteers).

Despite widespread agreement that legislative protection measures have improved conditions for volunteers, they are not without their critics. Concerns tend to centre on issues such as:

- Variation between different jurisdictions (e.g. provinces or states) and the subsequent complexity and uncertainty this causes for national organizations.
- The problems arising for VSOs associated due to the transfer of liability from the individual to the organization for whom they are conducting the work.

- Moral issues regarding the rights of those that may be injured from the actions of volunteers.

While Eburn (2003) argued that the legislation has resulted in the law being more, rather than less complex, it is the latter two issues that seem to be most cause for concern, mainly due to the uncertainty of potential legal relief for plaintiffs. Dietrich (2005: 39) argued that the legislative reform agenda has identified 'deserving' defendants and 'undeserving' plaintiffs and established immunities from liability 'to protect such defendants or disentitle such plaintiffs' and further that such an approach 'suggests a very one-sided . . . view of personal responsibility' (Dietrich, 2005: 25). Orchard and Finch (2002) reported that plaintiff advocate groups in Australia have urged that there should be no restriction of common law actions because injured sport participants have no form of legal redress other than through the courts.

Rights and responsibilities of VSOs

Volunteering Australia (2003a: 3) asserted that 'liabilities do not just arise from physical risks – they also arise from not meeting regulatory requirements and from financial, moral or ethical issues'. VSOs should be aware of the duties and responsibilities imposed upon them both at common law and through legislation, as well as acknowledge the moral requirements to protect their volunteers. VSOs must ensure that they are not only willing to accept the benefits of the efforts of their volunteers but also meet or exceed the legal obligations and responsibilities associated with managing volunteers. Volunteers are central to the sustainability of VSOs and this should be reflected in actions taken by such organizations. VSOs need to regularly monitor the degree to which their actions may expose volunteers to possible legal action and provide appropriate legal protection.

VSOs also need to provide safe working environments for volunteers. In many jurisdictions this is governed by workplace health and safety legislative requirement although the extent to which such legislation applies to volunteers is variable. For example, SPARC (2005b) indicated that the New Zealand Health and Safety in Employment Act (1992) requires employers to provide safe environments and workplaces for all employees and volunteers engaged in work activities. However, volunteers who are, among other things, fundraising and/or assisting with sport or recreation are excluded. Although the Act provides that the person responsible for these volunteers should take all practical steps to ensure their health and safety, this duty is not enforceable. The scope of the exclusion has yet to be tested in the courts but, according to SPARC, a likely interpretation is that the exclusion will only apply to volunteers involved in amateur or local sport clubs and sport club fundraisers. Volunteers involved in competitive events, provincial or national sporting organizations and promoters may not be excluded. Given this lack of clarity, SPARC urges sport and recreation organizations to take all practical steps to ensure the health and safety of their volunteers.

Rights and responsibilities of sport volunteers

Just as VSOs have rights and responsibilities, so do sport volunteers. While the rights of volunteers are addressed implicitly in the preceding section, Volunteering Australia (2003b) has developed a comprehensive list of volunteer rights:

- to work in a healthy and safe environment;
- to be interviewed and engaged in accordance with equal opportunity and anti-discrimination legislation;
- to be adequately covered by insurance;
- to be given accurate information about the organization;
- to be reimbursed for incidental expenses;
- to be provided a copy of the organization's volunteer policy and other policies that affect their work;
- not to fill a position previously held by a paid worker;
- not to do the work of paid staff during industrial disputes;
- to have a job description and agreed working hours;
- to have access to a grievance procedure;
- to be provided with orientation to the organization;
- to have confidential and personal information dealt with in accordance with the principles of the Privacy Act 1988;
- to be provided with sufficient training to do the job.

Volunteers must also be prepared to honour the responsibilities that come with making a commitment to volunteering. These responsibilities entail not only fulfilling their scheduled duties but doing so in a manner that minimizes or avoids placing either themselves or the organization in a potentially liable situation. Therefore, volunteers must act within the scope of their job, follow directions from the VSO, familiarize themselves with VSO policies and procedures, and be mindful of potential dangers for participants and spectators. However, this is not always straightforward in the sport context. As pointed out by the Centre for Sport and Law (2005: no page) 'wearing several hats is not uncommon in the sport realm, and remembering which hat you're wearing can be confusing!'. This suggests that the nature of a volunteer's legal responsibilities may vary according to which role is being fulfilled in which particular context thus further confounding an already complicated situation for individual sport volunteers and those that manage them, whether in a paid or voluntary capacity.

VSOs should provide training and opportunities for volunteers to gain appropriate certification especially in the coaching and officiating areas. However, these requirements, though consistent with meeting the responsibilities associated with being a sport volunteer, are problematic. One of the main issues in the volunteer literature is that of 'professionalizing' volunteers through compulsory training needed to meet the increasingly bureaucratized and rationalized environment of modern sport (Nichols, 2005a). Government agendas, seeking to inject more accountability into the sport sector, have increasingly placed more pressures and higher expectations on volunteers and some have argued that these factors are contributing to the difficulties of recruiting and retaining volunteers (e.g. Nichols *et al.*, 1998a and 1998b). The potential consequences and philosophical inconsistencies of 'compulsory' involvement in training programmes and other 'professional' requirements in the largely volunteer-dependent sport system need to be acknowledged and addressed.

Specific legal issues for sport volunteers and VSOs

While other sections in this chapter have discussed the broader legal trends impacting on the sport sector, the key issue for VSOs and volunteers is how these trends eventually manifest themselves at the organizational and individual levels. What can VSOs and volunteers do to respond to and protect themselves while at the same time provide appropriate sport experiences for members, participants and the general public?

Risk management

An overriding legal consideration for VSOs is the need to protect the interests of their members, participants, spectators, staff and volunteers. One means of facilitating this is to assess the degree of risk associated with organizational activities and develop a risk management plan. Not to do so in the increasingly complex sport environment with the resultant level of legal scrutiny applied to VSOs would seem somewhat foolhardy. Risk management is important because many activities can have consequences for organizational effectiveness, as well as for the welfare of volunteers, staff and other stakeholders.

Volunteering Australia (2003a: 3) defined risk management as 'the process of managing your organization's exposure to potential liabilities . . . by identifying risks in order to prevent them or reduce them and by providing for funds to meet any liability if it occurs'. Martinez (2003) suggested that potential liability is determined by asking three interrelated questions. First, is the organization liable to third parties for acts performed by volunteers and if so how can it reduce its exposure? Second, is the organization liable if a volunteer is injured while carrying out their duties? Third, are volunteers

liable to third parties for their actions while volunteering for the organization and if so how can they reduce their exposure?

Volunteering Australia (2003a) argued that risk management is not only
about legal compliance or getting as much insurance coverage as possible
and should not prevent organizations taking calculated risks, or exclude
volunteers from participating in the activities of the organization. A risk
management plan should, among other things, identify, analyse, assess and
monitor risks in areas such as volunteer/customer dissatisfaction, misman-
agement, threats to the physical safety of volunteers/customers and breaches
of legal or contractual responsibility. 'Risk management of potential liabilities will include making sure that there are adequate systems to ensure
that volunteers are trained, supervised and effectively managed, and there
is insurance if it is available and cost effective' (McGregor-Lowndes and
Edwards, 2004: 55). The key to developing a workable risk management
plan is to identify and focus on 'appreciable' risks (Martinez, 2003) rather
than developing a list of all potential risks. According to Martinez (2003:
163) the organization must ensure it does not allow its time, attention and
resources to be 'devoted to addressing miniscule problems'. A risk management plan that is carefully developed and communicated to all stakeholders
should also assist with volunteer recruitment and retention. Volunteering
Australia (2003a) suggested that risk management plans reassure volunteers
that the organization has considered the needs of volunteers and has established an environment that will allow them to maximize their contribution.

Insurance

Insurance is a common risk management technique and involves transferring the potential liability to the insurance company. Insurance provides
VSOs with a means to minimize or remove the possibility of a substantial
financial loss. However, it appears that VSOs are 'poorly informed' about
many aspects of insurance (Healey, 2005). A further concern is the alarming
increases in the cost of premiums. This trend may be a major disincentive
or even preclude some VSOs from being able to fully benefit from insurance.
The Centre for Sport and Law (2005) argued that insurance requirements
are complex and advice should be sought from a lawyer or insurance broker.
Despite the complexity and potential costs of insurance, VSOs have a moral
obligation to ensure that they protect the interests of their volunteers
through appropriate types and levels of insurance. SPARC (2005b: 13–14)
suggested that essential insurance cover for VSOs should include:

* professional indemnity: for negligence in the conduct of professional
  duties, such as instructions and decisions;
* public liability: for accidents that occur on the premises or at venues
  involving third parties such as spectators and visitors;

- directors' and officers' liability: for officers of sporting clubs, especially if the club is not incorporated;
- participants' insurance: for injuries to athletes or officials. It may only provide cover for serious injuries or death, and should be carefully checked to ascertain its limits; such insurance may provide cover during organized training as well as competition;
- legal expense: for any legal costs incurred in defending certain criminal or civil court actions brought against sports organizations, administrators or participants.

VSOs should carefully consider the benefits of incorporation. While the nature of incorporation may vary among different jurisdictions, incorporation provides a number of protective measures for VSO and volunteers who work within them. As indicated by the ASC (2000b), the process of incorporation means that the VSO will exist as legal entity separate to that of its members, may enter into contracts, own property, accept gifts and bequests and be sued or sue. In the event of a lawsuit, incorporation means that the VSO tends to be the target rather than individual members.

Child protection

'The term child abuse is used to describe ways in which children are harmed, usually by adults and often by those they know and trust. It refers to damage that has been or may be done to a child's physical or mental health' (National Society for the Prevention of Cruelty to Children, 1998: 14). While sport has not been immune from sexual abuse incidents and must do its utmost to rid sport of this type of behaviour, it is incumbent upon VSOs to also guard against other less 'newsworthy' types of abuse. In sport these may take the form of physical and emotional abuse. A number of internationally publicized child abuse claims in a wide range of youth oriented organizations, including sport, has resulted in an increased awareness of the responsibilities of sport administrators to ensure the safety and wellbeing of children involved with their programmes. However, although Brackenridge (2002) argued that child abuse in sport has become a 'moral panic' in Britain, Brackenridge et al. (2004: 30) suggested that apart from a few countries, 'child protection is not yet widely recognized as an issue for sport and leisure managers'. There is also evidence of resistance by sport administrators to the issue and in some cases a culture of complacency (Brackenridge, 2002).

The responsibilities of VSOs and individual sport volunteers in terms of child protection are established through legislation in many, but not all jurisdictions. The ASC (2005b) developed a summary of the main provisions in relevant acts in Australia and indicated that the goal of most legislation is to provide environments where children are safe and protected. This goal is achieved by preventing unsuitable people from working with children and young adults. The main implication for VSOs and volunteers is the requirement that anyone working with children under the age of 18 years must undergo what is termed a 'working with children check'. This process entails the applicant completing a form and agreeing to a criminal history check prior to their appointment. If the applicant is found suitable, in most cases they are issued with a 'blue card' identifying them as having being appropriately screened to work with children. There are shortcomings with this process in that only convictions are recorded and interstate and international databases are not usually linked.

VSOs must develop appropriate policies to effectively deal with issues of child protection. Brackenridge *et al.* (2004) suggested there are four dimensions to child protection policies and procedures:

- protection through referral – recognizing and referring a participant who has been subjected to misconduct;
- protection through leadership – observing and encouraging good practice;
- protection against false accusations – taking precautions to avoid false accusations by athletes, their peers or families;
- protection of the sport – safeguarding the good name of the sport.

Screening volunteers

As suggested earlier, it is mandatory in many countries to screen volunteers prior to them beginning a voluntary role that potentially has direct contact with children. According to Volunteering England (2004) screening usually means checking if someone has a criminal record as a means of reducing the risk of selecting volunteers who may be unsuitable to work with children or other vulnerable groups. While screening is useful in identifying unsuitable volunteers, it is not infallible. Volunteering England reported that 90 per cent of child sex offenders have no relevant criminal record and even those with a criminal record may avoid detection by using an alias. The need to screen volunteers places an extra load on VSOs and the volunteers who manage them to balance the right to privacy of volunteers with the responsibility of the organization to provide a safe experience for participants, particularly children.

Although screening raises issues of privacy and data security, the process is often governed by relevant legislation designed to balance the needs of the organization, members, participants and the volunteers concerned. This is especially the case where children or vulnerable adults are involved. In the UK for example, the Protection of Children Act (1999), Registered Homes Act (1984) and Care Standards Act (2000) require that all potential employees and volunteers are checked against the Protection of Children Act list (Department of Health), and List 99 (Department for Education and Skills). Volunteering England suggested that organizations should not assume that screening volunteers alone is sufficient and recommends that screening should be augmented by good recruitment practices as well as training and supervision of staff, and a reporting system in case anyone has concerns about an individual working in the organization. In some jurisdictions, while it may not be a requirement to screen volunteers, it is normally good risk management practice to do so. Screening provides the organization with some protection against possible liability as the organization can argue that it has done everything 'reasonable' within its power to protect others from harm and thus exercised an appropriate standard of care.

Privacy and data security

A corollary to screening is the need to provide confidentiality to those screened and ensure that VSOs have an adequate privacy and data protection policy in place. The need for these measures extends to all aspects of employee, member, participant and volunteer management. It is not unusual for VSOs to collect a range of data about these groups through their usual club member registration procedures. The ubiquity of computer technology coupled with the expanded compliance requirements expected by government, NGBs and other stakeholders, such as sponsors, means that the personal information collected is often quite detailed. Such a situation warrants care and VSOs must ensure that the data they collect and store are managed in a manner that ensures privacy. In many jurisdictions, sharing personal information with a third party without the consent of those affected may constitute a criminal offence even if the purpose was innocent and did not involve remuneration (e.g. passing on member contact details for research or for a competition administered by a sponsor). Therefore, members and volunteers may in some circumstances sue an organization that breaches confidentiality. According to Volunteering England (2004), in the UK, Article 8 of the Human Rights Act specifies the right to respect for private and family life. Furthermore, the Data Protection Act (1998) outlines guidelines for how personal information should be managed. In Canada, privacy and data security are governed by the Personal Information Protection and Electronic Documents Act (2004). In Australia, individual data security has been a legal requirement since the enactment of the Privacy Act (1988). Therefore VSOs should have policies outlining how such information will be stored and with whom it will be shared. Access to personal information should be restricted to only those with the need to use it to administer the VSO. Those involved should be specifically informed of their responsibilities to maintain confidentiality. Furthermore, policies concerning the length of time for which data are held and processes for their destruction should be developed and communicated to relevant personnel.

Directors liability

Statistics Canada (2000b) revealed that over 40 per cent of Canadian volunteers hold positions on voluntary boards and committees. However the Centre for Sport and Law (2005) argued that many volunteer board members were not fully aware of the possible legal implications of their involvement. They may become exposed to litigation on a personal level due to a failure to carry out their responsibilities as directors of the organization. As suggested by Sievers (1992: 2) 'it is now clear that it is not enough for a member of the governing body to attend an occasional meeting or social event and leave matters of policy and management to the association's executives'. Sievers (1992: 15) also argued that courts were now moving 'in favour of a more stringent approach to the enforcement of director's duties'. A management committee normally runs most VSOs. Management committees should provide overall direction to the VSO and the role of committee members is to represent the interests of the club members in managing the affairs of the organization and to do so within the law (Centre for Sport and Law, 2005). A director is someone who is a member of such a management committee or board. In VSOs, directors are normally elected by the overall membership to manage the VSO on behalf of the members.

According to the Centre for Sport and Law (2005) directors have three basic duties: diligence – to act reasonably, prudently, in good faith and in the best interests of the organization and its members; loyalty – not to use the position as director to further private interests; and, obedience – to act within the remit of organizational policies and other laws, rules and regulations relevant to the organization. A director who fails to carry out these responsibilities may be liable. Liability generally occurs in four situations:

- statute – a law is broken;
- contract – a contract is breached or violated;
- tort – an act, or a failure to act, whether intentionally or unintentionally, causes injury or damage to another person or property;
- wrongful acts – errors, omissions, actions or decisions that harm others through interfering with their rights, opportunities or privileges.

Despite legislation in some jurisdictions that affords protection for volunteers it is prudent for VSOs to retain directors' liability insurance (Centre for Philanthropy and Nonprofit Studies, 2003).

Concluding comments

VSOs and individual volunteers are certain to face an increasingly complex and dynamic legal environment in the future. Societies are becoming more litigious and damaged parties are more likely to seek redress through the courts. This is especially the case with sport, as consumers perceive that

VSOs are now more professional and therefore are required to take more responsibility for their actions. While there have been attempts to ameliorate the potential for legal liability of individual volunteers, this process has resulted in more legal pressures being exerted on VSOs. The responsibilities of VSOs can largely be addressed by developing a comprehensive risk management plan that incorporates legal issues relevant to volunteers, provides adequate insurance coverage for all volunteers, develops and communicates appropriate policies and procedures, and provides legal training to volunteers.

There is little doubt that the increasing legal requirements imposed on volunteers and VSOs bring with them both costs and benefits. Increased expectations and compliance requirements place an extra load on volunteers, many of whom perceive they are relatively ill-equipped to cope. Even though recent civil liability protection legislation may ease some of these fears, there is some evidence that such perceptions and fears of litigation can act as barriers to either initially becoming involved or continuing as a volunteer. Conversely, the members of VSOs and those who participate in activities organized by VSOs are, to a large extent, the beneficiaries of the legal requirements imposed on VSOs and volunteers. They can now expect to participate in a safer environment as VSOs increasingly recognize and meet the enhanced levels of responsibility associated with their emerging professional status. One lingering concern for participants, however, is the extent to which new types of volunteer protection legislation may impact on their ability to seek legal redress if injured through the actions of VSOs or volunteers.

Chapter 6

Structural dimensions of VSOs

This chapter explores the structural dimensions of VSOs and their implications for volunteers working in sport. The chapter comprises four parts:
first, a description of the organizations that comprise the nonprofit sport
sector is provided including a number of examples; second, attempts to categorize VSOs through the development of taxonomies are analysed; third,
the structural issues facing VSOs are discussed; and finally, the implications
of these structural issues for volunteers and how volunteers contribute to
maintaining the structures of VSOs are examined.

VSOs

The diversity of VSOs, in particular the range of functions, structures,
resources, values and ideologies evident in sport clubs, has been highlighted
in earlier chapters. At the community level, VSOs tend to be run informally and are reflective of the social nature of the volunteer experience at
the local club level. An important attribute of many VSOs is that they are
member benefit organizations in the sense that they are created, developed
and maintained by the individuals (athletes, players or participants) and
those most closely connected to them (family and friends) who consume
the services the organization provides (Smith, 1993). Organizational
members are therefore involved in the governance of their organization
through being elected, appointed or invited to serve on their respective
management committee or board and to vote at elections. Smith (1999)
argued that the majority of nonprofit organizations are predominantly volunteer run, locally based grass roots associations that employ few staff, and are
governed by volunteers with usually no involvement of paid staff. The
majority of VSOs, particularly local clubs and regional associations, could
be considered grass roots associations. Hoye and Inglis (2003) argued that
the majority of research on VSO structures and allied volunteer issues had
not considered the implications for those operating within grass roots sport
associations. State/provincial level VSOs, as well as NGBs and ISFs, face a
variety of issues in managing their structures. They are subject to a range

of internal and external forces to adopt more sophisticated and professional management systems and processes. In order to understand these issues it is necessary to first identify the range of VSOs that exist within the sporting systems of countries such as Australia, Canada, New Zealand and the UK as well as those that operate at the international level.

The structure of VSOs can be conceptualized as comprising five elements: members, volunteers, salaried staff, a council, and a board or management committee. The members of the organization may include individual players, athletes, participants, coaches, officials, administrators, other individuals, or in some cases organizations. Affiliated organizations that are classified as members can include clubs that compete in a league administered by a regional sports association, or state/provincial VSOs aligned with a sport NGB. In a small number of sports, member organizations also provide facilities for sport participation such as indoor soccer, netball/basketball or tennis facilities. The members, or their representatives, normally meet as a group once per year at an annual general meeting in a forum most commonly known as a council. The council comprises those people or organizations that are registered members and have been afforded voting rights on the basis of their membership status. One of the main tasks of the council is to elect, appoint or invite individuals to a board charged with responsibility for making decisions throughout the year on behalf of the membership. The boards of VSOs normally comprise individuals who represent the interests of various membership categories, geographic regions or sporting disciplines in decision making. If the organization is of sufficient size and has the necessary resources, the board may employ an executive and other paid staff to manage the day to day affairs of the organization. The executive is employed by and reports directly to the board with other paid staff reporting to the executive. The nature of VSOs means that staff work closely with a variety of volunteers to deliver programmes and services in areas such as coaching, player and official development, marketing, sport development and event delivery. The majority of these volunteers usually come from within the membership of the VSO.

Hoye *et al.* (2006: 169) argued that this typical VSO structure 'has been criticised for being unwieldy and cumbersome, slow to react to changes in market conditions, subject to potentially damaging politics or power plays between delegates, and imposing significant constraints on organizations wishing to change'. However, most VSOs are structured this way as it enables members to be directly involved in decision making and ensures a certain degree of transparency in decision making. In addition it enables organizations that are members of federated VSOs to enjoy a degree of autonomy in how they operate at the local, regional, state/provincial and national levels (see Figure 6.1).

The work of Allison (2002) was used to describe the characteristics of local sport clubs in Chapter 3. Local sport clubs rely extensively on volunteers to govern, administer and manage their organizations and to provide coaching, officiating and general assistance with training, match day operations and fundraising. The majority of state/provincial VSOs, NGBs and ISFs that provide sport opportunities are governed by volunteer office bearers, who fill positions on either committees or boards. Most of these organizations operate under a federated delegate system with club representatives forming regional boards, regional representatives forming state/provincial boards and state/provincial representatives forming national boards (Hoye et al., 2006). NGBs may liaise to form an ISF that coordinates activities between nations (see Figure 6.1). Examples of sport organizations at each of these levels are provided to illustrate their variety and the differing roles volunteers may perform within them.

Hoye et al. (2006) used the structure of netball to explain the relationships between the various levels of VSOs involved in governing a sport. The members of the International Netball Federation Limited (IFNA) comprise 39 national associations from five regions: Africa, Asia, Americas, Europe and Oceania. Each region elects two members to direct the activities of IFNA, which is responsible for setting the rules for netball, conducting international competitions, promoting good regional management, seeking

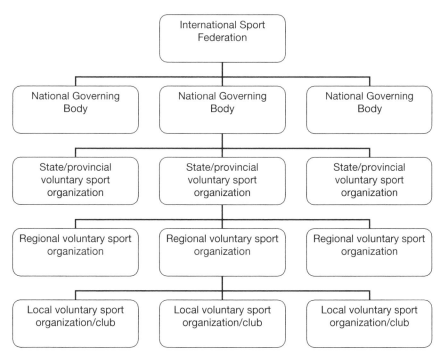

Figure 6.1 VSO federated structure

Source: Authors.

Olympic accreditation for netball, and increasing participation levels around the globe. Netball Australia is one of the 39 members of IFNA and has more than 350,000 registered players in 8 associations, one for each state or territory of Australia. Each of the state level VSOs has a delegate to the national board which, together with the staff of Netball Australia, is responsible for communicating rule changes from IFNA to their members, managing a national competition, promoting good management in the state/provincial organizations, increasing participation nationally, and bidding to host international events. One of the largest members of Netball Australia, Netball Victoria, has 250 affiliated associations organized into 21 regions and 6 zones across the state. Netball Victoria's role includes coach, official and player development, managing state competitions, promoting good management in the clubs, increasing participation in the state, and bidding to host national events. At the regional association level, local netball clubs field teams, recruit coaches and players, manage volunteers, conduct fundraising and may own and operate or lease a competition and training facility.

Typically, volunteers are involved in decision making at every level of these structures. The relationships between ISFs, NGBs and VSOs do not operate as top down power hierarchies. Organizations positioned at lower levels in the hierarchy do not always fully comply with the directives and policies developed at higher levels in the sport system. A spirit of cooperation and negotiation is necessary to ensure that such interrelationships operate effectively. This requires those volunteers who fill decision making roles within VSOs to act in the best interests of the organization they represent.

Watt (2003) contended that the key organizations involved in sport are NGBs and that regardless of their size or level of resources they have a number of distinct characteristics:

- They are grant aided, and the vast majority are dependent on national government funding to sustain their operations.
- They are autonomous in the sense that they are largely self-controlling and while dependent on government funding and subject to the views of a myriad of stakeholders, they ultimately decide their own strategies.
- They are voluntary, relying extensively on the time and efforts of volunteers.
- NGBs operate as a public voice for their sport, requesting support and interest in their respective sport and their participants.
- They rely on member contributions to fund a substantial portion of their activities.
- The volunteers involved in committees and other duties do so in the spare time away from their normal form of employment.
- VSOs at all levels rely on their links with public sector bodies such as elite sport institutes and local governments to assist with their activities.

- Most VSOs operate on an individual membership basis but many also have clubs or other organizations as members.
- Individual members are vital to garner support for initiatives and ideas that need to be instigated within the clubs and associations that comprise a sport NGB.
- VSOs are governed democratically with a general principle of one vote per member but are usually dominated by limited cliques of influential individuals.
- VSOs are also dominated by committees and committee structures, which causes slow and inefficient decision making but enables democratic processes to be enacted.

In addition to the VSOs that comprise the mainstream governing bodies for sporting participation and competition, there are a number of specialist voluntary organizations that focus on sport provision for specific community groups. For example, the International Paralympic Committee (IPC) is the international organization for elite sports for athletes with disabilities. The main roles of the IPC are to manage the Paralympic Games and other multi-disability elite level sports competitions. Volunteers are also central to the operation of two of the most influential sport event organizations in the world: the IOC and the Commonwealth Games Federation (CGF).

Volunteers are also involved in the operation of nonprofit professional service organizations in sport, some of which perform similar functions to accrediting organizations for medical practitioners, lawyers, accountants and other professions. These organizations assist in setting standards of practice in their respective industries, provide professional accreditation for qualified members and offer professional development opportunities through conferences, seminars or training programmes (Hoye et al., 2006). Examples of these organizations include the Australian Council for Health, Physical Education and Recreation, the Canadian Association for Health, Physical Education, Recreation and Dance, the British Institute of Sports Administration, and Physical Education New Zealand. Finally, most countries have a number of industry lobby groups, representing the interests of sport NGBs such as Confederation of Australian Sport and the Central Council of Physical Recreation in the UK. These volunteer driven organizations operate as independent peak industry organizations for state/provincial VSOs and NGBs to promote their interests to government and other stakeholders in the sport industry.

Categorizing VSOs

Given the wide variety of VSOs that exist at local through to state/provincial levels as well as NGBs and ISFs, there has been surprisingly little research that has attempted to categorize sport organizations. Kikulis et al.

(1989) were the first to develop a structural taxonomy for provincial (state) Canadian VSOs based on the organizational structure dimensions of specialization, standardization and centralization. They identified eight structural designs for VSOs. A central finding of their research was that 'important relationships among the variables composing structure indeed exist and importantly influence the feasibility of establishing consistent structural designs . . . [for VSOs]' (Kikulis *et al.*, 1989: 146). In other words, the structure adopted by individual VSOs is dependent on the level of professionalization (i.e. employment of paid staff) and the degree of bureaucratization (i.e. use of formalized and standardized processes). The impacts of professionalization and bureaucratization processes will be felt differently by VSOs that exhibit dissimilar structural designs.

Categorizing design types at the NGB level was the focus of a study by Kikulis *et al.* (1992) who identified three distinct designs – kitchen table, boardroom and executive office – based on a mix of organizational values and organizational structure variables. The organizational values included (1) orientation towards private or public interests; (2) the scope of activities conducted (ranging from broad participation based to a focus on high performance results); (3) the degree of professional involvement in decision making; and (4) the criteria used to evaluate effectiveness. The organizational structure variables were the same as used in the Kikulis *et al.* (1989) study – specialization, standardization and centralization. The design archetypes were considered representative with no individual sport organizations exactly matching the values and structure attributed to each archetype. Organizations of the kitchen table archetype focused on securing funds through traditional fundraising and membership contributions, delivered both mass and high performance sporting opportunities, had few if any staff in decision making roles, and judged its performance through meeting member expectations. NGBs in this category also used few rules and did little planning; decisions were dominated by a few volunteers and the roles adopted by volunteers were based on their personal interests. In contrast, the organizations categorized as the executive office archetype focused on securing funds through government grants and corporate sponsorship, emphasized high performance sport, were dominated by professional staff, and judged performance through international success. NGBs in this category also employed many specialized staff, used formal roles, rules and programmes, and decisions were decentralized to paid staff.

Theodoraki and Henry (1994) also developed a typology of structures for British NGBs. Adopting a similar approach to Kikulis *et al.* (1989), they utilized the structural elements of specialization, standardization and centralization to distinguish between various structural designs. Their study yielded six clusters of NGBs to which they designated titles based on Mintzberg's organizational structures, ranging from machine bureaucracy to simple structure. Significantly, their study highlighted the number of NGBs that were variations of Mintzberg's simple structure and that the type of sporting activity (i.e. high or low cost sport, newer versus more traditional sports) did not appear to influence the structure adopted by the NGB.

Structural issues for VSOs and NGBs

VSOs are faced with a number of structure related issues, namely: a heightened potential for conflict, the influence of size on structure, the introduction of professional staff, government policy impacts, and industry sector changes. Amis *et al.* (1995) argued that VSOs are more susceptible to conflict than other organizations. In a study of four separate Canadian sport NGBs, they found that structural issues were a major contributing factor to conflict. Sport organizations at most levels are subject to pressures for increased efficiency and specialization, which in turn leads to differentiation and interdependence of organizational sub-units. Coupled with the voluntary nature of VSOs and most NGBs, this 'adds considerably to the potential for conflict' (Amis *et al.*, 1995: 14). Furthermore, VSOs and NGBs have to contend with a combination of volunteer leadership and professional expertise, each with differing values and expectations, as well as a generally lower level of formalization and resource provision, all of which contribute to exacerbating the potential for conflict within the organization. Watt (2003) noted that the study by Amis *et al.* (1995) contributed to an understanding of the unique aspects of VSOs, in particular that while conflict often manifests as disputes between individuals, it occurs because of their membership in conflicting sub-units of the organization, suggesting therefore that the cause of conflict is often structural.

Organizational size also plays an important role in determining VSO structures. Organizational theory suggests that as organizations grow they become more formalized, with more specialist roles and departments and more levels of management compared with smaller organizations. Much of the research into the relationship between organizational size and degree of centralization suggests that as 'organizations become larger, decision making becomes more decentralized' (Amis and Slack, 1996: 83). In a study of Canadian sport NGBs, Amis and Slack (1996) found that as these organizations expanded, control over organizational decision making remained at the voluntary board level, albeit in an informal fashion. They concluded that a 'central role of decision making as a means of control and the desire for volunteers to retain this control' (Amis and Slack, 1996: 84) meant that the boards of many VSOs and NGBs were reluctant to relinquish control to professional staff. This reluctance was attributed in part to the 'levels of mistrust and antagonism that often exist between the professional workers and their volunteer superiors' (Amis and Slack, 1996: 84).

The impact of professionalization on sport organizations has been a recurring theme of sport management research since the early work of Slack

(1985). While this is discussed in more detail in Chapter 8, it is briefly addressed here in the context of its impact on VSO structures. The introduction of paid professional staff has been a deliberate strategy adopted by VSOs in response to increases in government funding for sport in most club-based sporting systems around the world. Thibault *et al.* (1991) explored the impact of professionalization on the structure of Canadian provincial VSOs and found that specialization and formalization increased after the introduction of professional staff. However, centralization, after initially increasing, actually decreased over time possibly because volunteer board members initially sought to retain control over decisions, and then allowed professionals to make some decisions as the relationship between board members and staff stabilized. This inherent resistance on the part of volunteers to structural change in VSOs was also noted by Kikulis *et al.* (1995b).

Government policy has also had substantial impacts on the structure of VSOs and was discussed in some detail in Chapter 4 (see also Green, 2005). These impacts include some erosion of autonomy and an increased compliance burden to which VSOs have responded by adopting more professionalized and formalized operating systems, which in turn has lead to changes in organizational structure. Oakley and Green (2001: 91) argued that the establishment and distribution policies of a National Lottery and the development of elite sport initiatives in the UK have created a 'more discrete and tightly focused policy community'. This policy community appears to be 'dominated by narrow performance principles above other interest groups' (Oakley and Green, 2001: 91), resulting in increases in targeted funding for Olympic and Paralympic sports and selective investment in those sports that are likely to deliver results at an international level. These changes in turn lead to an imbalance in resource allocation among VSOs allowing some to employ more paid staff, improve management systems and processes, and grow participation numbers on the back of better international results and subsequent market exposure. Similar shifts in government policy towards an emphasis on elite sport performance have been identified in Australia (Stewart *et al.*, 2004) and Canada (Thibault and Babiak, 2005). Taylor (2004) also suggested that while societal changes have caused many of the problems and constraints faced by VSOs, pressures from central governments should not be discounted. As discussed in Chapter 2 (see Taylor, 2004), VSOs tend towards being either more traditional/informal organizations or more contemporary/formalized entities with the latter more able to adapt to meet the demands of government policy requirements.

The final structural issue faced by VSOs is change itself, which has been examined extensively by Kikulis *et al.* (1995a, 1995b, 1995c). Kikulis *et al.* explored the patterns of organizational change influenced by federal government requirements within 36 Canadian NGBs between 1984 and 1988. Each of the NGBs was categorized as representative of either a kitchen table, boardroom or an executive office design archetype as outlined by Kikulis *et al.* (1992) and discussed earlier. The authors utilized the concept of centralization to explain: the structural changes that occurred within the organizations over this period (Kikulis *et al.*, 1995a); the role of values in defining the manner in which the organizations changed (Kikulis *et al.*, 1995b); and what impact human agents and choices had in determining the nature of structural change (Kikulis *et al.*, 1995c).

Kikulis *et al.* (1995a: 289) found that while there were no significant differences in the centralization of decision making between design archetypes, 'the data do show that decisions become more decentralized as we move away from the kitchen table to the executive office archetype'. They also found their data supported the notion that for a sport NGB to move into the executive office archetype, a shift 'in the level at which decisions are made' was required (i.e. decisions became more decentralized due to the inclusion of paid executives) and that volunteers were involved in fewer decisions and to a lesser extent in the decision making process within the executive office archetype. Importantly, Kikulis *et al.* concluded that while a change in the level of decision making is required for an organization to shift into the executive office archetype, the shift in values associated with moving decision making control into the hands of professional staff may not occur at the same time, reflecting the importance and impact of the informal structure on decision making in spite of formal structure realignments. The authors noted that 'it will take a long time before professionally led decision making displaces values for volunteer-led decision making so deeply embedded in the history of these organizations' (Kikulis *et al.*, 1995a: 297).

Kikulis *et al.* (1995b: 72) emphasized that the decision making structures in place for these organizations are high impact systems, in that they 'govern behaviour, determine whose interests matter, and establish how things should be done'. It was found that moving the organizations towards an executive office archetype will take a long time because 'these organizations support the tradition of volunteer control' (Kikulis *et al.*, 1995b: 96). The authors further argued that a 'qualitative change in the decision making structure will thus require a change in the core values of an organization . . . [and it] . . . is myopic, therefore, to treat decision making simply as a measure of structural design' (Kikulis *et al.*, 1995b: 96).

The third article, derived from the same study, considered the nature of the resistance to organizational change, specifically the role of human agents and choice in determining the nature of the change (Kikulis *et al.*, 1995c). The authors noted that in relation to centralization, 'while there were definite pressures for professional staff to assume much of the responsibility for decision making in NSOs, these pressures were resisted' (Kikulis *et al.*, 1995c: 147). While incremental changes in the centralization of these organizations were observed, the changes were 'characterized by the interest of organizational members in maintaining the tradition of volunteer-led decision making' (Kikulis *et al.*, 1995c: 148).

An underlying assumption in the attempts to categorize VSOs and NGBs is that the organizational forms adopted by these organizations would tend to coalesce as they are subjected to similar internal and external forces. This expected similarity is termed structural isomorphism which may result from coercive (coercion based on power differences), mimetic (imitation of successful organizations) or normative (influence of professionals or experts) influences (DiMaggio and Powell, 1983). Sport organizations can be expected to resemble one another because they are subject to such pressures. Those organizations that are dependent on government funding, especially at the state/provincial and NGB levels, are, consequently, subject to coercive forces. They are also increasingly networked and therefore aware of innovations and successes of other sport organizations and hence are subject to mimetic forces. NGBs and state/provincial VSOs are also becoming more professionalized, employing more paid staff in key positions of influence and thus are also subject to normative pressures. In contrast, Henry and Theodoraki (2000: 501) argued that the professionalization of sport organizations 'has not led to adoption of a single set of organizational structures or strategies, even within a given national context'.

The lack of structural isomorphism evident in VSOs and NGBs is mirrored in the wider nonprofit field. Leiter (2005: 27) found a higher than expected degree of heterogeneity in the structures of Australian nonprofit organizations, concluding that best practice had not become widespread and that 'ultimately efficient and productive organizational methods have not yet been discovered, disseminated, and institutionalized'. However, such variety fosters the ability to be innovative and 'means a broad organizational repertoire with which to face uncertainty and change in the future' (Leiter, 2005: 28). Volunteers within VSOs and NGBs are less likely to have similar attitudes and values to professionals, therefore, there are less normative pressures in volunteer 'only' sport organizations.

Implications for volunteers

The nature of VSOs and the associated structural issues have a number of implications for volunteers and the way in which volunteer activities are undertaken in sport. From what is known of VSOs, the majority of them are member benefit organizations where volunteers are involved in decision making at every level from local clubs and regional associations to ISFs. VSOs have a number of common structural elements relating to their resource base, membership structures, foci of activities and reliance on volunteers to govern, manage and administer their operations. However, there are differences in the degree of formality that exist within the structures of sport organizations from local VSOs to ISFs which are also evident even within VSOs operating at the same level.

In order for sporting systems based on VSOs to operate effectively, volunteers need to work cooperatively with the members of their own organizations and with other volunteers and paid staff from affiliated organizations. While VSOs have been subject to varying degrees of professionalization, particularly at the state/provincial level and above, there is little evidence to suggest that this has resulted in an optimal set of organizational structures or strategies for how to manage the introduction of paid staff into volunteer dominated organizations. In addition, VSOs and the volunteers who work within them are faced with a number of structural issues including a potential for conflict, managing the changes in formalization and centralization as a result of increases in size, government policy impacts, and industry-wide changes as the sport industry has become more commercialized.

These issues suggest that the voluntary and paid leaders of VSOs are best placed to manage the impacts of organizational structure on behalf of the volunteers who sustain these organizations. Papadimitriou (1999: 98) found that the constituents of NGBs 'agree on the need for motivated, competent and influential individuals on boards as contributing particularly to the effective operation of the organizations'. Papadimitriou (1999: 99) also found that the boards are led by 'volunteers who control the policy formulation mechanisms and the management of organizational resources, as well as fundamental elements of the daily routine activities and decisions'. However, these NGBs are run according to 'inflexible decision-making authority structures' (Papadimitriou, 1999: 98). In a later study of local sport clubs, Papadimitriou (2002: 212) found that the majority 'carry out their sports-related activities with the help of four to ten active voluntary board members'. Papadimitriou argued that this relatively low volunteer participation rate raised 'critical questions regarding the viability of values such as altruism and voluntarism in the management of the local sports delivery system' (2002: 212). The study also found that the structures of club level VSOs are

> dominated by the amateur practices of the boards of directors, which avoid separating formally the authority for overall management and policy, from the responsibility for policy implementation (and as a result clubs) operate on direct and casual interactions between individuals and groups who follow trial and error procedures.
>
> (Papadimitriou, 2002: 217)

This inflexibility and self-perceived ineffectiveness of the way NGBs are structured is likely to be a cause of some frustration for volunteers seeking to offer their time and effort to sustain the operations of these organizations. Watt (2003: 56) argued that within the context of VSOs one individual can 'dominate the sports setting: where this person is the club coach or the national governing body president, they can be the dominant figure leading the organization forward or holding it back'. He also suggested that the social cub ethos evident in most VSOs, where a small group dominates decision making, can pose a problem for individual volunteers 'penetrating the inner sanctum and having real effect on the operation of the organization' (Watt, 2003: 57). Volunteers seeking to make meaningful contributions to the leadership of VSOs may therefore be stifled in such attempts, further highlighting the need for VSOs to implement effective structures that facilitate volunteer experiences and particularly the inclusion of new volunteers. This may well suit the type of volunteer experience sought by volunteers at the local club level and goes some way to explaining the tensions that may develop in VSOs as they become more professionalized and adopt more formalized procedures and management practices.

Watt (2003: 86) also highlighted that volunteers serving on boards and committees are 'under tremendous pressure, with work coming from a wide variety of sources, while being subject to the pressures of any democratic organization which has political (with a small 'p') moves and issues to resolve on an ongoing basis'. Further, VSOs operate in a complex environment, and the volunteers in leadership positions should have a formalized approach to managing their organizations. Smith and Shen (1996) suggest that VSOs and other nonprofit voluntary organizations should adopt more formalized structures in order to be more effective.

Finally, the role that volunteers play in shaping the structure of their respective VSO should not be discounted. McDonald and Warburton (2003: 396) underscored the role of volunteers as 'institutional agents' in the sense that through their individual decisions and approach to their roles they help shape and define the organization in which they volunteer. Volunteers are confronted with the challenges of increasing professionalization within VSOs, a dual leadership environment, having to manage their working relationship with paid staff, and seeking to balance volunteer and paid staff influence within VSOs. These issues are explored in more detail in Chapter 8.

Concluding comments

This chapter has explored the structural dimensions of sport organizations and implications for working with volunteers in sport. VSOs tend to have a common resource base, membership structures, foci of activities, and reliance on volunteers to govern, manage and administer their operations. However, there are differences in the degree of formalization, specialization and centralization that exist within the structures of sport organizations at various hierarchical levels and within VSOs operating at a similar level. Attempts to categorize VSOs and NGBs through the development of taxonomies have illustrated the varied nature of organizations at all levels of the sport system. VSOs and the volunteers who work within them face structural issues such as a heightened potential for conflict, the need to manage changes in formalization and centralization, the impacts of government policy, and industry-wide changes as the sport industry has become more commercialized. In order to manage the impacts of these issues, VSOs often resort to more formalized structures and management practices. These processes may not fit well with the sport volunteer experience, particularly in local VSOs characterized as traditional/informal organizations.

Chapter 7

Managing sport volunteers

Volunteers are integral to the successful management and operation of VSOs and the services they deliver to players, members and spectators as well as to the wider community. As discussed in previous chapters, VSOs are under increasing demands through government policies, legislative demands and sport NGBs to increase levels of participation in organized sport and to do so in a more professional manner. At the same time, VSOs are reporting shortages of volunteers. Whether volunteer shortages are related to problems of recruitment, retention or both, sport volunteers are increasingly being looked upon and managed as human resources. It is no longer a question of whether volunteers ought to be managed but how should they be managed in a way that does not impinge upon a fundamental condition of volunteering – to freely choose when, where and how to volunteer in sport. The focus of this chapter is the challenging issue of volunteer management. It examines the application of traditional HRM principles and practices to the management of sport volunteers as recommended by government sport agencies in several nations. Before outlining the key processes of HRM, two approaches to volunteer management are compared and contrasted. Later sections consider the impact of volunteer management practices on the performance, commitment, satisfaction and retention of sport volunteers.

Government agencies responsible for sport policy have long recognized the pivotal importance of volunteers to the foundation of the sport system. Over the past decade, sport and club development programmes, such as those developed by Sport England and SPARC, and promoted as Running Sport and the ASC's Volunteer and Club/Association Management Program, devote significant space to the subject of volunteer management. Volunteering Australia (2001), a volunteer advocacy body, has formally documented and adopted a set of national standards for involving volunteers in nonprofit organizations. Among these standards are guidelines for establishing volunteer management systems as well as clearly defined procedures for the recruitment, selection, orientation, training and development, documentation and continuous improvement of volunteer management systems. Described collectively in this chapter as VMPs, these approaches use a traditional HRM paradigm (Frisby and Kikulis, 1996) either explicitly or implicitly.

Most VMPs recommend the appointment of a volunteer manager or coordinator whose job description includes recruiting, training and supervising volunteers and developing volunteer retention strategies. However, there has been little systematic research into factors that support and retain sport volunteers. For the most part, studies of sport volunteers have been narrowly focused on exploring volunteers' experiences or characteristics (Coleman, 2002), with little regard to how these experiences are influenced by volunteer management practices (Dorsch et al., 2002). While there has been some volunteer management research on major sport event volunteers (Farrell et al., 1998; Lynch, 2002; Strigas and Jackson, 2003, Cuskelly et al., 2004), the transferability of these research findings is problematic. As Grube and Piliavin (2000: 1118) noted, volunteer behaviour is rife with complexity and 'all behavior takes place within a situational context and the characteristics of the context must be considered in models of volunteer behavior'. Wood (1999) argued that it may be too simplistic to presume that a single optimal set of HRM practices is ideal for all situations. Criticisms of applying traditional HRM practices to managing sport volunteers are addressed throughout this chapter.

Applying HRM to sport volunteers

VMPs advocated by government agencies and subsequently adapted by many sport NGBs to their particular requirements, cultures and traditions are based on the principles and practices of personnel management. HRM represents a transition from personnel management in that HRM represents a stronger commitment to the development of human capital. In a more strategic view of VSOs, volunteers represent the human capital necessary for the achievement of longer-term organizational goals. However, there is an underlying tension in applying HRM practices to the management of sport volunteers. This tension is captured in the LIRC (2003: 80) report for Sport England when commenting on the merits of formal and informal management cultures relative to volunteer motives:

> In particular the importance of shared enthusiasm and social benefits from volunteering militates against a managerialist approach to volunteers, whilst motivations concerned with helping a club improve and succeed, and 'giving something back' are more compatible with formal approaches to volunteer management.

Frisby and Kikulis (1996) argued that traditional HRM has the advantage of a planned approach that links the abilities of individuals to organizational needs, but is limited by an emphasis on controlling behaviour and ignoring many of the dynamics that are more evident in interpretive and critical HRM paradigms. The traditional paradigm views HRM processes 'as objective realities that can be observed, measured and controlled by management' (Frisby and Kikulis, 1996: 109). Traditional HRM ignores matters such as the formation and impacts of groups and coalitions within organizations, organizational cultures and subcultures, as well as the broader social and political environments and the influences exerted on individual volunteer behaviour.

Because it is a planned approach, traditional HRM assumes that the relationship between volunteers and VSOs commences with the recruitment process. However, many volunteers have a long association with sport before making the decision to volunteer. A decision to volunteer often represents a changed involvement rather than the development of a new relationship with a VSO. Based on Atchley's (1989, 1999) continuity theory, Cuskelly (2004) advocated a transition-extension hypothesis to explain volunteer participation and retention in sport. Continuity theory argues that individuals are 'both predisposed and motivated toward inner psychological continuity as well as outward continuity of social behavior and circumstances' (Atchley, 1989: 183). Therefore volunteer recruitment practices need to be varied to take into account whether volunteers are being recruited from within or outside VSOs. Those being recruited from within the organization are likely to be extending their participation, perhaps making the transition from another role less difficult than it might be for volunteers recruited from outside the organization. Those recruited from outside a VSO experience a different and perhaps more difficult transition process as they are introduced to key volunteers, as well as organizational systems and processes, for the first time.

Contrasting management approaches

The dominant HRM approach and the one advocated by most VMPs closely resembles what Meijs and Karr (2004) described as programme management, which they differentiate from membership management. The programme management approach identifies specific operational tasks to be undertaken prior to recruiting volunteers to do these tasks. In contrast, membership management focuses on the volunteers themselves, taking into account the expectations of existing members and ensuring that the tasks fit these expectations (Meijs and Karr, 2004). A comparison between programme management and membership management is provided in Table 7.1. Meijs and Karr discussed a number of characteristics, advantages and disadvantages in contrasting programme and membership management approaches to volunteer management.

Membership management organizations may develop high levels of satisfaction with the volunteer experience because participation tends to be

Table 7.1 Comparison between programme management and membership management

Criteria	Programme management	Membership management
Structure		
Flexibility of approach	From task to volunteer	From volunteer to task/assignment
Integration	Free-standing programmes	Integrated approach
Direction of integration in national organization	Vertical	Horizontal (i.e. per branch)
Management	One single manager	Group of 'managers'
Executive committee	Arm's length	Close by
Culture		
Organizational culture	Weak	Strong
Volunteer involvement	Low	High
Volunteer involvement in more than one organization	Often	Sometimes
Level of homogeneity among volunteers	Low	High
Relationships between volunteers	People do not know each other	People know each other well or very well
Volunteers' motivation 1	Goal-orientated	Socially orientated
Volunteers' motivation 2	Increase in external status	Strengthening internal status
Process		
Cost of admission	Low social costs	High social costs
Cost of transfer	Low	High
Expectations	Explicit	Implicit
Recognition	On basis of performance	On basis of number of years as member
Hours spent/invested	Low	High
Environment		
Necessity of conforming to environment	Major	Minor
Possibility of conforming	Good	Poor

Source: Meijs and Hoogstad (2001). Reproduced by permission of Institute for Volunteering Research.

broad and multifaceted and the organization 'shapes itself to the needs and desires of its membership' (Meijs and Karr, 2004: 178). Loyalty to and identity with the organization tends to be high because of the risk of losing long-time friendships when leaving a VSO. However, membership management organizations tend to have problems coping with diversity and risk either stagnation or extinction because they are unable to adapt in a timely manner to changes in either their internal or external environments. In contrast, programme management organizations are focused on clearly specified tasks (e.g. delivering a particular service at a scheduled time) in which the priority of volunteer involvement is to carry out such tasks without fear of committing unlimited amounts of time. Volunteers' needs and interests tend to be secondary and volunteers themselves do not identify strongly with these organizations. Because involvement is limited, volunteer entry and exit is easily facilitated. Programme management organizations are more adaptable to their environments but are less personable, risk high rates of volunteer turnover and rely on recruiting new volunteers to ensure continuity of client services.

The programme management and membership management approaches vary both in terms of degree of formalization in volunteer management practices and their suitability for organizations across the spectrum of VSOs from traditional/informal to contemporary/formal as discussed in Chapter 2. Many membership management characteristics are evident in the traditional/formal VSOs, which suggests there is active resistance to formalized management and external sources of assistance. Volunteers' motives are compatible with shared enthusiasm and social benefits and there is a tendency for a loyal core of volunteers to take on more tasks as other volunteers leave. In contrast, the characteristics of programme management organizations are closely aligned with those of contemporary/formal VSOs except, perhaps, for volunteer motivation. The needs and interests of volunteers are important to contemporary/formal VSOs whereas in programme management, volunteer motives are subordinate to organizational tasks. Overemphasizing managerialist approaches to managing sport volunteers runs the risk of subordinating the needs, motives and interests of volunteers to increasing levels of formalization and standardardization. The dominance of organizational concerns has the potential to disempower sport volunteers.

The traditional HRM paradigm

Notwithstanding contrasting volunteer management approaches, their degree of formalization and suitability to various types of organizations, it has been argued that volunteer management is essential to the success of VSOs. The traditional HRM paradigm is considered here because it is dominant among VMPs developed and advocated by government agencies, sport NGBs and volunteer advocacy bodies. Because VMPs have logical and clearly defined processes such an approach is most likely to be adopted by VSOs seeking ways to improve volunteer management practices. Therefore, it is important to understand the processes and impacts of this approach on VSOs and their volunteers. Traditional HRM is prescriptive rather than adaptive and is based on the assumption that the motives, needs and interests of volunteers can be matched with the strategic and operational requirements of VSOs. Further, the performance, commitment, satisfaction and ultimately the retention of volunteers are logical outcomes of appropriately deployed HRM practices. This approach is closely aligned with programme management, discussed earlier. It focuses on the recruitment, selection, orientation, training, development, performance management, recognition and reward of volunteers. Traditional HRM is a cyclical process in which human resources are acquired, developed and either retained or replaced by VSOs. Significant components of these processes are outlined and discussed critically within the context of VSOs in the following sections.

Acquiring human resources

In most VMPs, the process of acquiring volunteers begins with an examination of organizational strategies and long-term goals along with estimates of current and future needs for volunteers to service existing and planned programmes and events. The planning task is seen as a key role for the volunteer coordinator who has responsibility for developing volunteer job descriptions and planning a recruitment campaign. However, the appointment of a volunteer coordinator is not widely practised in VSOs. The LIRC (2003) revealed that 10 per cent of NGBs have a volunteer coordinator at the national level and at the club level and 3 per cent of clubs have a volunteer coordinator. These statistics suggest that the processes involved in acquiring volunteers are either handled informally or are the responsibility of other volunteer committee or board members. The responsibility for recruiting a replacement, whether through normative pressures or organizational policies, often rests with the incumbent volunteer who has announced their intention to leave.

Volunteer recruitment and selection is the second major step in the HRM approach and is becoming increasingly complex in many jurisdictions as VSOs are required to incorporate child protection, member protection, privacy and other legislative requirements into their day to day operations. In theory, recruitment is designed to attract a pool of appropriately qualified and motivated applicants to a position. In practice, many VSOs operate under duress and almost three-quarters (74 per cent) of sport clubs reported 'there are not enough other people willing to volunteer in the club' and two-thirds (65 per cent) reported that 'increasingly the work is left to fewer people' (Nichols, 2005b: 3). Furthermore, VSOs have little control over recruitment and selection processes for some key positions. If more than one nomination is received for significant leadership and decision-making positions, such as president or chair, secretary or treasurer, most VSOs are constitutionally required to run an election usually on an annual basis. An assumption of managerial control that underpins the HRM approach is secondary to the democratic principles upon which most VSOs are founded.

Developing human resources

Orientation, training and performance management are important processes in the development of sport volunteers and are common to most VMPs. A significant event in the HRM process is the transition that occurs as an individual takes up a volunteer position for the first time. Whether a current or former player, parent or partner of a player, general member or previously playing no part in a VSO, volunteering, particularly for the first time, deepens or extends and sometimes enriches an individual's level of involvement. However, it cannot be assumed that even a long-term member has a thorough understanding of an organization, its strategic direction, its policies and procedures and the roles of key office bearers even if they know some or all of the these office bearers. A well-designed orientation session reduces stress on new volunteers, makes them feel welcome and may reduce the likelihood of turnover (Cuskelly, 1995).

Orientation is the first stage in formalizing the relationship between new volunteers and a VSO. Volunteers new to an organization and those continuing, either in the same or a different position, usually need specific and up to date knowledge and skills training to perform their tasks effectively. The choice of training method will usually depend upon factors such as cost, timing, specificity, flexibility, delivery mode, prerequisite knowledge and the availability of volunteers. With the increasing sophistication and ease of access to the internet, volunteer training and development programmes can be self-paced, customized and delivered at times to suit the schedules of volunteers irrespective of their physical location. Government sport agencies, sport NGBs, major sport event organizers and professional associations have long recognized the benefits of well-trained volunteers. They have become adept at developing and promoting volunteer training and development programmes for coaches, officials, administrators and sports trainers.

Having volunteers recruited, orientated and trained for the job they are expected to do does not necessarily guarantee job performance. Pearce (1993: 178) noted that 'it is widely assumed that volunteers are less productive than employees . . . [but] . . . we do not really know in what ways'. Volunteer job performance is likely to be affected by the personal attributes of volunteers and by organizational issues. Factors such as volunteers' abilities, motivation, commitment and competing demands (e.g. work and family) coupled with organizational factors such as management style and working conditions affect volunteer job performance and satisfaction.

Performance management is a process whereby organizations 'try to achieve strategic goals consistently through better formal and informal motivation, monitoring, evaluating and rewarding performance' (Pinnington and Lafferty, 2003: 158). Managing volunteer performance is problematic not least because 'volunteers are not as dependent on their organizations as are employees, and their independence . . . leads to less volunteer subordination to the system of organizational behavior' (Pearce, 1993: 128). Like many voluntary organizations, VSOs tend to operate on the basis of informal, interpersonal and value-based control mechanisms rather than bureaucratic control, particularly when the culture of the organization is strong and positive. Organizations can manage volunteer performance through informal social or normative controls or more explicit bureaucratic controls or use both approaches but 'no organization can be effective with neither one' (Pearce, 1993: 179).

There is a tendency for performance management to be tied to reward systems among employees. However, the benefits of volunteer work are not clear and 'rewards that seem to be most important . . . [to volunteers] . . . are not under the control of the organization' (Pearce, 1993: 181). Therefore, performance management is unlikely to be effective if it is simply adapted to VSOs from employment-based performance management systems. This is not to suggest that performance management is unimportant to volunteers or VSOs. Plainly, volunteers who feel as though their performance is supported and recognized by others are more likely to continue to contribute time and effort than those who feel unappreciated. Cnaan and Cascio (1999) found evidence that variation in volunteer performance could be explained in part by volunteer management practices. They concluded that screening practices and the use of symbolic rewards influenced commitment and tenure. Aside from a study of volunteers in tourism organizations, which found no significant differences in the quality of service provided by volunteers and paid staff (Jago and Dreery, 2002), it seems that research on volunteers has not ventured into measuring the quality or the management of volunteer performance.

Retaining human resources and motivation to volunteer

VMPs advocate the need to retain volunteers through appropriate management practices. Clearly, there is a direct relationship between volunteer retention and recruitment. Higher volunteer retention rates mean that VSOs can operate with lower levels of volunteer recruitment. Management practices include recognizing and rewarding volunteers for the time and effort they put into organizing, managing and delivering the programmes and services offered by VSOs. There is some evidence that the adoption of volunteer management practices influences volunteer retention. Hager and Brudney (2004) found that volunteer management practices, centred on making the volunteer experience worthwhile, positively influence volunteer retention in what have been described in this chapter as programme management organizations. Specifically, offering training and development opportunities to volunteers, screening to identify suitable volunteers and matching volunteers to appropriate tasks are associated with higher volunteer retention rates (Hager and Brudney, 2004). These findings are not inconsistent with those of a Canadian study that identified ongoing appreciation and respect, meaningful volunteer experiences, and communicating and being responsive to volunteers as important factors in volunteer retention (Phillips et al., 2002).

The recognize-reward-retain approach of VMPs assumes a direct cause and effect relationship between retention, rewards and recognition but raises the question of motivation to volunteer. There is a tendency for VMPs to ignore fundamental motivational issues such as the value of rewards, effort-reward probability, equity theory or the differences between intrinsic and extrinsic rewards, from the perspective of volunteers. Relationships between retention, rewards and recognition are influenced by complex interactions between motivation, performance, commitment and satisfaction, as well as management practices, much of which have only emerged recently as a topic of research on the retention of volunteers. It is beyond the scope of this book to introduce the extensive and highly complex topic of motivation theory even if it were limited to content and process theories in sport organization settings. Other authors, such as Chelladurai (1999), provide thorough reviews of motivation theory in the context of sport organizations.

Motivation to volunteer was introduced in Chapter 1 and described as a desire to help others, as well as for personal and social rewards. Labelled altruism and self-interest, respectively, by Stebbins (1996), these rewards coexist in motivating volunteers in formal organizations. Knoke and Prensky (1984) have been influential in the field of volunteer motivation. They identified and described three motives, labelled incentives, which are discussed later – utilitarian, affective and normative incentives. Other researchers have developed motivation to volunteer models that are unidimensional (e.g. Cnaan and Goldberg-Glen, 1991), based on two factors (e.g. Smith, 1981; Stebbins, 1996), or more complex models with as many as six unique factors (e.g. Clary et al., 1992; Clary and Snyder, 1999) as discussed in Chapter 1.

Utilitarian incentives, sometimes described as material incentives, align with self-interest and are personal benefits gained from the experience of volunteering. Unlike employees, volunteers by definition are not financially recompensed, beyond reimbursement for expenses, for their efforts. However, sport volunteers are often motivated by personal benefits such as gaining work experience, tapping into community networks or assisting their child to participate in sport. Policies in some sports that prevent parents from coaching their own children are likely to be a disincentive for volunteering and may result in failing to attract or retain volunteers motivated by such utilitarian incentives. Recognition in the form of symbolic rewards (e.g. club uniforms for volunteer coaches and team managers) may positively influence the performance and the likelihood of retaining volunteers motivated by such materialistic incentives.

Affective incentives, sometimes described as solidary incentives, are derived from social benefits, which also align with self-interest. Interpersonal relationships that develop into friendships, group identification and group status serve to motivate many sport volunteers. VSOs whose purpose and operational environments encourage social interaction among volunteers are likely to retain volunteers motivated by affective incentives. VSOs that find the operation of food and drink services burdensome might consider the extent to which sociability is an important incentive to volunteers before deciding to discontinue or contract out such services.

Normative incentives, sometimes described as purposive incentives, appeal to concerns of a suprapersonal nature in which volunteers share a genuine and unselfish concern for others. This incentive aligns with altruism as a motive for volunteering and is linked to the intended beneficiaries component of Cnaan *et al.* (1996) categories and dimensions of volunteering introduced in Chapter 1. VSOs would do well to ensure that opportunities to help beneficiaries other than oneself or family and friends are part of the experience for volunteers motivated by normative or purposive incentives.

The HRM management approach advocated by VMPs is cyclical in nature and the loop is closed at the point where volunteers make a decision about whether to continue volunteering. A volunteer may decide to either continue in their present position or, if a there is a vacancy, continue but take up a new or additional position within the same organization. Continuing volunteers in new positions may require additional training, support and mentoring as they make the transition and extend their involvement by moving to other roles. However, continuing volunteers might normally be expected to have a good understanding of the organization, its purpose, reporting relationships, culture and traditions. When a volunteer decides to discontinue their involvement, the organization initiates what is described in VMPs as a succession plan, whereby it begins a recruitment process to fill the vacant position with a new volunteer. As discussed earlier, membership management organizations have high levels of volunteer loyalty and lengthy involvement. As a consequence they tend to have low rates of turnover but can find it difficult to fill some core volunteer positions. In contrast, programme management organizations are adept at dealing with volunteer turnover. Both organizational types may benefit from having a succession plan but for different reasons. Membership management organizations might use a succession plan to encourage turnover in key positions, avoiding the problems associated with martyred leadership (Pearce, 1993) such as burdening core volunteers with additional responsibilities. Programme management organizations might be in a better position to maintain high standards of service quality and continuity if they can minimize significant fluctuations by using past experience to predict volunteer turnover rates. A succession plan does not necessarily reduce turnover, but it can put a VSO in a stronger position to cope with the impact of turnover.

Volunteer commitment and satisfaction

The commitment of sport volunteers and the extent to which they are satisfied with the volunteer experiences are two important outcomes both from the perspective of individual volunteers and the VSOs that rely upon them. Commitment, conceptualized here as organizational commitment, is of particular importance because without at least a core of committed volunteers it would be difficult for VSOs to function effectively and with a reasonable degree of stability. This is particularly the case in membership management organizations. Organizational commitment provides a basis for understanding the linkages that develop between volunteers and VSOs and it is both a factor in the retention of volunteers and, to some extent, their performance. For example, Cuskelly and Boag (2001) found that organizational commitment was a significant discriminator between sport volunteers who stayed with or left the management committee of their organization. Mowday *et al.* (1982: 27) defined organizational commitment as

> the relative strength of an individual's identification with and involvement in a particular organization. Conceptually, it can be categorized by at least three factors: (a) a strong belief in and acceptance of the organization's goals and values; (b) a willingness to exert considerable effort on behalf of the organization; and, (c) a strong desire to maintain membership in the organization.

In contrast to the Mowday *et al.* conceptualization, commitment has also been described as the costs associated with leaving an organization. Becker's (1960) side bet theory argued that consistent lines of activity that persist over time lead to the rejection of alternative activities. In an organizational context, side bets were defined by Cohen and Lowenberg (1990: 1016) as 'the accumulation of investments valued by the individual which would be lost if he or she were to leave the organization'. Meyer and Allen (1991) further advanced the conceptualization of organizational commitment in developing a more comprehensive three-component model. Affective commitment embodies the notion that individuals want to become committed to an organization. This conceptualization is consistent with the definition of Mowday *et al.* (1982). Continuance commitment develops as a result of having to be committed due to a lack of alternatives or the sacrifice of a high level of sunk costs (i.e. side bets) if one was to leave an organization. The third component of their model, labelled normative commitment, develops as a result of feeling one ought to be committed. Normative commitment is based on socialization, organizational investment and the strength of the reciprocity norm.

The implication for VSOs and the management of volunteers is that commitment is important in developing attitudes and behaviours that are consistent with acceptance of organizational goals, working on behalf of an organization and maintaining membership. Furthermore, different components of commitment are related to different reasons for becoming committed to an organization. However, there is a degree of alignment between volunteer motivations and the three-component model of organizational commitment. The affective, utilitarian and normative incentives for volunteering are conceptually related to affective, continuance and normative commitment, respectively, and may explain, despite similar experiences, why some volunteers decide to stay with a VSO while others leave. Volunteers motivated by utilitarian incentives are likely to develop a stronger sense of continuance commitment than volunteers motivated by normative or affective incentives. VSOs, and by implication individuals in leadership positions, that understand the particular utilitarian incentives that motivate some sport volunteers may be able to better match volunteer management practices and rewards to volunteer experiences, particularly those incentives that are controlled by the organization. Though perhaps more enduring, affective and normative commitment are more difficult to influence directly because the incentives are more individualized and less likely to be influenced by volunteer management practices. As discussed earlier, the rewards that are most important to volunteers are mostly outside the control of the organization.

Satisfaction is a complex multidimensional construct that has been conceptualized and researched most extensively in management and organizational behaviour literature as job satisfaction. Chelladurai (1999) provides a review of a number of theories, dimensions and facets of job satisfaction within the context of managing human resources in sport organization settings. Chelladurai (1999: 232) argued that the extent of 'discrepancy arising out of psychological comparison between what one receives and a standard of comparison' permeates most theories of job satisfaction. However, many of the theories and much of the research on job satisfaction has been developed within the context of paid work. Some aspects of job satisfaction have application to volunteer work and satisfaction with the volunteer experience (e.g. the work itself and supervision) whereas other aspects have little relevance (e.g. pay and promotion). Understanding volunteer satisfaction is important for VSOs because 'satisfaction plays a role in not only the volunteer experience, but also in influencing the likelihood that volunteers will volunteer again' (Johnston et al., 2000: 165). Cnaan and Goldberg-Glen (1991: 28) argued that 'people will continue to volunteer as long as the experience as a whole is rewarding and satisfying to their unique needs'. From another perspective Pearce (1993: 90) stated that volunteers 'have no direct financial dependence on their work . . . [and] . . . dissatisfied volunteers can be expected to leave their organizations virtually the moment they become unhappy'.

Volunteer satisfaction, motivation and performance are complex and are interrelated concepts. From a traditional HRM or programme management perspective it is important to be able to differentiate the components of volunteer satisfaction that are controlled by an organization. Those aspects of volunteer satisfaction that are beyond the control of an organization are important for a more comprehensive understanding but cannot be used to directly influence the motivation, performance or retention of sport volunteers. Much of the research into sport volunteer satisfaction has been in the context of major events as well as in agencies with paid staff in which the programme management approach is the dominant volunteer management paradigm. Using a functionalist approach, Silverberg et al. (2001) found that volunteer satisfaction in a local government sport and recreation setting is a function of job setting and psychological functions met by volunteering. Their findings imply that if there is a match between the job assigned to volunteers and the psychological functions they are seeking through volunteer work then volunteers will be more satisfied. In particular Silverberg et al. found that volunteer coaches were more satisfied when their children were receiving the benefits of participation. In a major event setting, Johnston et al. (2000) found that relationships between volunteer motivation and satisfaction were influenced by volunteer management practices including communication with and recognition of volunteers. Understanding volunteer satisfaction among longer-term volunteers and those in VSOs which take a more membership management approach appear to be under researched. Speculatively, because volunteer satisfaction is multifaceted and shaped by the needs of members, compared with programme management organizations, satisfaction is less likely to be influenced either directly or predictably by management attributes in membership management organizations. Membership managed VSOs tend to have volunteers who are socially orientated with high levels of homogeneity (see Table 7.1 on p. 83). Doherty and Carron (2003) examined the influence of task and social cohesion on sport volunteer executive committee satisfaction, effort and intention to leave. They reported that task and social cohesion were significantly associated with sport volunteer satisfaction. Doherty and Carron also found weak but significant relationships between task cohesion, intention to stay and volunteer effort, but found no evidence of such relationships between social cohesion, intention to stay and volunteer effort. The cognitive and social processes that underpin these relationships are yet to be identified. Sport volunteer satisfaction seems to be largely beyond the control of VSOs and more likely to be derived from task enjoyment and interrelationships between volunteers than it is from formal recognition systems or formalized HRM practices.

Concluding comments

This chapter sought to examine the challenging issue of managing sport volunteers. It critically discussed the application of traditional HRM processes advocated by VMPs to VSOs. Volunteer management was considered within the context of the contrasting approaches of programme management and membership management advanced by Meijs and Hoogstad (2001). The application of traditional HRM practices to volunteer management has several significant limitations that include the underlying of assumptions of HRM, the lack of volunteer coordinators within VSOs, the complexity of volunteer roles and volunteers' perceived experiences in VSOs. This is not to deny the many benefits of a more planned approach to volunteer management to VSOs, their members, the volunteers themselves and sport development generally. However, Pinnington and Lafferty (2003) argued that all HRM models are based on the assumption that the interests of management are the most legitimate. This assumption does not sit well with VSOs because 'volunteers experience significant uncertainty stemming from the fact that they frequently find themselves holding contradictory formal positions in relation to the organization' (Pearce, 1993: 151). Not infrequently, sport volunteers are simultaneously owners of VSOs (e.g. as club members), workers expected to follow directives from other volunteers, and clients who are service recipients of the VSOs of which they are members. Each of these 'distinct formal organizational roles comes with its own set of behavioral expectations' (Pearce, 1993: 151). Even the appointment of a volunteer coordinator, as advocated by VMPs but not widely adopted, is unlikely to disentangle the complexity of volunteers' roles in VSOs or lead to significant improvement in volunteer management practices in the short term.

Chapter 8

Volunteer sport administrators

While many types of sport volunteers are a clearly visible component of the sport experience, this is not always the case with volunteer administrators. Despite the high public profile of a small number of volunteer administrators involved with elite international sport, it is more likely that at the club, state/provincial and NGB level most sport participants probably are not aware who is involved in planning and organizing the sport in which they participate. This is despite administrators typically being one of the largest categories of sport volunteers (see Chapter 2). Because volunteer sport administrators are involved in the day to day management of VSOs, they are the most likely volunteer group to feel the expectations arising from the more complex operating environment in sport. As a consequence of their large numbers and because they are instrumental to the viability of the sport system, volunteer sport administrators have attracted a great deal of interest from researchers, government and the sport industry. The purpose of this chapter is to review the roles and nature of the contribution made by volunteer sport administrators and to examine the critical issues in developing, managing and working with volunteer sport administrators. Furthermore, the chapter focuses on the process and impacts of professionalization and the dynamics of volunteer staff relationships introduced in Chapter 6.

Nature and scope of volunteer sport administration

Volunteer sport administrators are essential to the effective delivery of sport. As indicated by the ASC (2000b: 1), behind the scenes 'there is a structured system of administration and management' as sport programmes and events require careful planning, budgeting and organization. This is true even more so in the current climate, given the increasing levels of professionalization and commercialization evident in VSOs with resulting higher expectations by sport participants and their members. Some categories of sport volunteers (e.g. officials and coaches) are often more obvious to sport participants and the public than are volunteer administrators. Nevertheless, volunteer administrators are crucial to planning, organizing and delivering quality sport opportunities. For the most part, VSO administrators work in a variety of roles that include among other things, planning, budgeting and managing finances, managing human resources including paid staff and other volunteers, evaluating programmes and events, and liaising with external stakeholders (e.g. government, sponsors and affiliated VSOs). Volunteer sport administrators facilitate the planning and development of opportunities for sport participation that are usually delivered by other types of sport volunteers, although it should be reiterated that many sport volunteers fulfil multiple roles.

Volunteer administrators comprise a large proportion of third sector sport and non-sport volunteers. The ABS (2001b) reported that of the 4.4 million people who volunteered in Australia in 2000, 45 per cent indicated that they were involved in 'management/committee work/coordination' and a further 41 per cent that they were involved in 'administration/clerical/recruitment' though respondents could indicate more than one role. These two categories were among the four most frequently reported types of volunteer work. A later ABS (2005a) survey on participation in organized sport and physical activity indicated that volunteer sport administrators are a significant category of sport volunteers and make substantial contributions of their time to VSOs. The ABS (2005a) reported that almost 575,000 persons aged over 15 years in Australia (3.7 per cent of the population) were involved as a committee member or administrator in a sport organization during 2004 and this accounted for 25.5 per cent of all non-playing participation in sport. Approximately 53,000 of these volunteer administrators contributed more than ten hours per week to sport administration in 2004. The data also suggested that administrative roles require a greater commitment compared to other categories of sport volunteers. The demands of sport administration extend beyond the typical seasonal nature of sport and necessitate volunteer administrators to be involved almost all year round. The ABS data indicated that 42 per cent of volunteer sport administrators contribute to their VSO for 40 to 52 weeks per year whereas most sport volunteers tend to participate on a seasonal basis. The next highest proportion was for coaches, instructors or teachers, 27 per cent of whom worked beyond 40 weeks.

Data from other countries also suggest that management and administration are prominent roles for sport volunteers. Statistics Canada (2004b) reported that 1.7 million persons aged over 15 years (7 per cent of the population) were involved in sport as an 'administrator or helper'. Doherty (2005) found that 46 per cent of sport volunteers at the community level in Canada were members of a committee or board, 47 per cent were involved in fundraising activities and a further 32 per cent in administrative work. As reported in Chapter 2, the LIRC (2003) found that 85 per cent of sports volunteers in England had been involved in some form of administrative role in 2002. Seippel (2002) reported that volunteers in Norwegian sport clubs contributed an average of 8.3 hours per person per week to administration (second only to average hours devoted to coaching).

Management committees

Much of the work of volunteer sport administrators occurs in the context of VSO management committees or boards. The work of these committees is central to organizational effectiveness. Cuskelly and Boag (2001: 65) suggested that 'in many parts of the world, volunteer committees . . . are the backbone of community-based sport organizations'. Hence the roles and processes of volunteer committees have received considerable research attention in the sport management as well as the third sector literature. As indicated in Chapter 5, VSO committee members are normally elected and have legally enforceable roles and responsibilities. Management committees are charged with the responsibility to manage VSOs on behalf of its members. According to the ASC (2000b) the committee normally should:

- develop strategic and operational plans and budgets to ensure the aims of the VSO are fulfilled;
- coordinate the planning of programmes and activities;
- carry out the recommendations of members as expressed at the annual general meeting;
- provide members with detailed information regarding the management of the VSO;
- monitor the performance of VSO officials, subcommittees and paid employees;
- determine volunteer training needs and organize training opportunities;
- provide written and oral records and job descriptions to a newly elected committee.

Committee effectiveness has received much more attention in recent years particularly in the context of VSO governance (discussed in detail later). One of the key issues related to the effectiveness of volunteer committees is the turnover of members. The very nature of committee work means that inefficiencies can arise when there is a continual loss of organizational memory. Cuskelly (1995) found that perceptions of committee functioning were an important consideration in understanding the commitment of volunteers to VSOs. It seems that poor procedures and inefficiencies in committee operations impact on the willingness of members to maintain their involvement and like other areas of sport volunteering, the administration function is under threat from recruitment and retention problems. At the macro level, the ABS (2005a) reported that in Australia the number of volunteer sport administrators as a proportion of the population had declined from 5.1 per cent in 1997 to the 2004 level of 3.7 per cent. Cuskelly and Boag (2001) found an annual committee member turnover rate of almost 30 per cent in a study of Australian community sport clubs.

Volunteer sport administrator roles

Given the nature of the roles of sport administrators, much of the responsibility for dealing with the compliance, accountability and legal requirements discussed in previous chapters tends to fall on their shoulders. The work required to cope with these increased expectations occurs mainly in the committee context. While all committee positions are important to the successful management of VSOs, it is generally acknowledged that a smaller number of positions have higher levels of responsibility and play key roles in effectively managing sport organizations. In many VSOs these key positions often form a smaller executive committee although the extent to which this occurs and the composition of such executive committees may vary. Specific roles that normally comprise the executive committee include the chairperson and/or president, secretary and treasurer.

The chairperson/president

While some nonprofit organizations utilize both positions it is usually the case that a sport organization's president also has the role of chairing management committee meetings. The chairperson is the principal organizational leader, has overall responsibility for VSO administration and controls management committee meetings. According to the ASC (2000b: 9) the chairperson should:

- be aware of the future directions and plans of VSO members;
- have a good working knowledge of the constitution, rules and the duties of all office holders and subcommittees;
- manage committee and/or executive meetings;
- manage the VSO annual general meeting;
- liaise on behalf of the VSO at local, regional and national levels;
- be the supportive leader for all VSO members;
- act as a facilitator for VSO activities;
- ensure that planning and budgeting is carried out in accordance with the wishes of the VSO members.

Secretary

Many of the day to day administration tasks are carried out by the secretary who is essentially chief administration officer of a VSO. According to the ASC (2000b) the secretary is the coordinating link between VSO members, the executive committee and external stakeholders. As the secretary handles the majority of the correspondence and usually has responsibility for setting the agenda for meetings, they are in a position to significantly influence the operation of VSOs as they largely control the rate, amount and manner in which information is communicated to different internal stakeholders.

Treasurer

This position has responsibility for managing the financial affairs of VSOs and, given the more complex environment in which VSOs operate, it is an increasingly difficult role. Treasurers prepare the budget, help plan the VSOs financial future and may assist other committee members with financial issues. The volume and nature of the treasurer's work will vary in relation to the size of the organization, the degree of complexity of its activities and whether the VSO owns facilities or employs staff. Larger VSOs often have a finance subcommittee to assist the treasurer (ASC, 2000b).

While these are the central administration positions within most VSO structures, many VSOs also have a number of other operational areas or roles represented on management committees. These may include:

- volunteer coordinator;
- coaching coordinator;
- membership;
- publicity/promotions and media liaison;
- social events coordinator;
- fundraising coordinator;
- club captain;
- team managers.

There are well established career pathways available for volunteer sport administrators throughout the sport system. Despite the professionalization process, a large number of high level administrative roles are voluntary in nature and many volunteer sport administrators are sufficiently motivated to be involved at the higher levels of their particular sport. This includes, for example, volunteers representing their local club as elected or appointed delegates on either the regional or state/provincial management committee or representing state/provincial organizations at the NGB level. The delegate system is also evident at the ISF level with many positions comprising elected or appointed representatives from sport NGBs. The nature of involvement at higher levels in the sport system may vary according to the role to which one is elected or appointed. In some sports, volunteer administrators may be elected as delegates whose role it is to represent the organization or stakeholder group that elected them (e.g. state/provincial representative on a NGB). Such involvement requires the delegate to adopt a position in decision making that best protects the interests of the organization from which they derive their mandate. Alternatively, some volunteer administrators may be elected or appointed to a specific administrative position (e.g. treasurer, media liaison, national team selector) necessary to manage the next level of the sport system. In this case their responsibility lies with the higher level in which they perform this role.

However, the boundaries between these different roles and their responsibilities are sometimes blurred, resulting in problems and inefficiencies at the next level of decision making. For example, NGB committee or board members may bring a parochial state/provincial agenda to the meeting table rather than adopting a perspective that is in the best interests of the sport as a whole. Stewart-Weekes (1989, 1991) argued that the delegate system was an anachronistic feature of traditional/informal VSOs that has inhibited the ability of VSOs to keep pace with the changing sport environment and adopt modern management approaches better aligned with contemporary issues in sport. There have been calls to replace the representation/delegate system with skill-based appointments to management committees or boards particularly at the NGB and state/provincial levels of many sports but the traditional system is still common. The adoption of more corporatized approaches to sport governance and less representative structures are not without costs and may jeopardize the traditional democratic nature of decision making in VSOs.

Volunteer sport administrator and VSO support programmes

The development and management of volunteer administrators is important for sustaining sporting systems dependent on volunteers to govern and manage VSOs from the local, state/provincial to national and international levels. Within a context of growing interest in the standards of sport governance and administration, the critical role of these volunteers has been recognized by governments in a number of countries. Subsequently, education and training programmes aimed at supporting and improving the performance of volunteer sport administrators have been developed. Such programmes recognize that despite increasing professionalization, the key to optimizing the outcomes from government investment in sport rests largely with volunteer administrators. In Australia, there are two ASC programmes operating at different levels. The Governance and Management Improvement Program provides assistance and support to NGBs in relation to their structure, governance, management and strategic direction. The aim of the programme is to increase the capacity of NGBs to achieve their strategic objectives. Subsequently the programme adopts a sport-wide perspective, tends to concentrate on national issues, and services mainly chief executive officers and national boards (ASC, 2005c). The Active Australia Club/Association Management and Volunteer Management Program is focused more on the community club level. This programme incorporates a series of educational booklets on a wide range of topics that include planning, club development, legal issues, volunteer management and financial management.

The equivalent Sport England club development programme entitled Running Sport is designed to assist sport volunteers to effectively manage clubs. Running Sport addresses a number of key issues similar to those in the ASC programmes outlined above. Also in the UK, Sport England has introduced the 'Quest' quality assurance scheme for sport and leisure. Quest encourages the application and development of defined industry standards and good practice 'in a customer-focused management framework' (Sport England, 2005e: no page). Quest focuses on both facility management and sport development issues appropriate to a wide cross-section of VSOs. Similarly in New Zealand, the efforts of volunteer sport administrators are supported by SPARC (2005c) through the Business Improvement Program. This programme consists of a series of information resources including guides and templates on governance, board assessment and risk management. Further resources are planned for business planning, HRM, and sponsorship and fundraising.

The implications of professionalization for VSOs and volunteer administrators

As indicated earlier, the majority of the work of volunteer sport administrators tends to occur in a specific context – the VSO management committee. It is also within management committees that many of the consequences of professionalization are manifested. As sport has become more professionalized and commercialized, enhanced levels of specialized knowledge and different types of skills are required to manage in this more complex environment. From around the mid-1970s volunteer sport administrators began to work in an increasingly turbulent and dynamic operating environment with more bureaucratic performance, conformance and compliance requirements together with an expanding range of more demanding stakeholders, including government. As suggested by Deane (1992: 24) the sport environment became characterized by complex social, legal and economic issues, commercial interests and a 'more sophisticated ... bureaucracy'. Kikulis (2000: 293) argued that the changes in VSOs have been characterized by the 'adoption of more professional and business-like management practices due to the growth of these organizations and the complexity of demands placed upon them'. The developments in sport also occurred at the same time as broader social and demographic trends made it increasingly difficult for volunteers to find the necessary time to effectively manage

VSOs as their operations became more sophisticated and demanding. Given these developments many VSOs sought the assistance and involvement of paid staff.

The introduction of paid staff into VSOs was initially facilitated by governments through the provision of financial assistance for VSOs to improve their management performance and included direct grants to employ paid staff. However, government initiatives in this area were not entirely altruistic and frequently seemed to be driven more by concerns about protecting its escalating investments in the sport system. Macintosh and Whitson (1990: 27) reported that Canadian volunteer sport administrators learned that the pursuit of excellence in international sport 'requires both technical and bureaucratic rationalization'. Consequently, VSOs at many levels in the sport system developed from volunteer only managed organizations to a combination of paid and volunteer management (Auld and Godbey, 1998). However, professionalization is more than just the employment of paid staff by VSOs. 'Generally it involves the adoption of management practices to increase effectiveness; both at NGB level and through the support given to volunteers' (Nichols, 2003: no page). This trend was quite common in a number of countries throughout the 1980s and 1990s. Professionalization has perhaps been the single most important factor impacting on VSOs with far reaching implications as the process has continued to evolve. The evidence has generally suggested that VSOs have come to rely extensively on the knowledge and skills of paid staff to help run and strategically manage sport organizations (Auld and Godbey, 1998). This major change to VSOs has been the catalyst for a significant level of research that has focused on a number of themes relevant to this chapter. These themes include the potential conflict between paid and volunteer staff, power and influence in decision making, the effectiveness of management committees and VSO governance.

The volunteer-professional relationship

One of the key concerns emerging from professionalization is the relationship between paid staff and volunteers and nowhere is this experienced more acutely than in management committees. The increasing focus on professionalization has generated more attention and put increased pressure on both paid and volunteer administrators in VSOs. While much of the day to day work is facilitated through paid staff, the bulk of the governance responsibility still falls to volunteers. They must cope with the associated increase in accountability and compliance requirements but to do so requires effective working relationships between volunteers and paid staff. This setting is complex not only because of the external environment but also because of internal factors such as high committee member turnover rates that are exacerbated by the election and appointment processes in VSOs.

These normally result in committee membership changes on an annual basis meaning that 'the relationship between the executive and board members tends to be in a continual cycle of negotiation and re-negotiation' (Hoye and Cuskelly, 2003b: 71). In many nonprofit organizations, paid staff are employed and supervised by volunteer management committees and also frequently have a role on the committee, although not always voting rights. As the role of the committee is to manage the affairs of the organization and make decisions on behalf of members, the relationship between volunteer administrators and paid staff is critical. As indicated by Auld and Godbey (1998), because of the potentially problematic nature of these relationships, the issue of board/staff relations has been extensively researched in the third sector both in sport and non-sport organizations.

Much of the third sector literature reflects the normative view that suggests that the board sets policy and the executive implements policy. However, research in sport organizations suggests that the normative view is somewhat simplistic (Auld, 1997a) and does not capture the complexity of either the operating environment or the relationship between paid staff and volunteers. It is commonly acknowledged, however, that the differing values and motives of volunteers and paid staff are problematic. Pearce (1993) argued that together with other reasons, tensions result because paid employees develop high status due to both organizational knowledge derived from more continuous work in the organization and the values often ascribed to professionalism in the workplace. Concerns about the impact of occupational professionalization have permeated the literature for some time. Salaman (1980) argued that professional knowledge is used to legitimate interests and therefore decisions made by professionals, using such knowledge, are presented as inevitable or necessary. Furthermore, the authority granted to professional knowledge helps ensure the self-fulfilling nature of the process. These views were reinforced by Henry and Spink (1990) who argued that professionals legitimize their authority by reference to professional skills and qualifications. Sessoms (1991) argued that professional status and power has developed through creating dependency in others. Donovan and Jackson (1991) suggested that this approach characterized the dominance of professional managers as gatekeepers to limited resources.

In the sport context, Amis et al. (1995: 1) argued that the characteristics of VSOs 'render them significantly more susceptible to conflict than organizations in other institutional spheres'. They suggested that one of the key factors acting as antecedent to conflict in these organizations was the presence of volunteer and professional leadership and stated:

> While the combination of volunteer leadership and professional expertise is an appealing notion, it is also highly problematic. The differing values and expectations of each group, which results from their differing

backgrounds and motives, make the volunteer-professional relationship inherently conflictual.

(Amis *et al.*, 1995: 14)

This issue is not new to sport and was the subject of a report for the Canadian Olympic Association in 1986 entitled 'The state of the volunteer-professional relationship in amateur sport in Canada'. Gibson (1991) asserted that working with boards was the number one reported problem for Canada's paid sport directors. However, the issue has not been resolved and is still the subject of much ongoing interest with a special focus on the nature of the distribution of power and influence between professional and volunteers. According to Auld and Godbey (1998), although much of the research has indicated that increasing the level of management professionalization frequently results in declining levels of power and influence for volunteer board members, the situation is complex. Relative levels of influence may vary between different organizations and, given the turnover rates in committee membership, may also vary considerably within a VSO from year to year. Influence may also be specific to the type of decision area.

Power and influence in decision making

VSOs appear to go through a number of stages of development as they grapple with professionalization, rationalization and bureaucratization. As discussed in Chapter 6, Kikulis *et al.* (1992) found three main design types (kitchen table, boardroom or executive office) and one of the key distinguishing features between the different structures was the respective levels of influence and control by either volunteers or paid staff in decision making. Much of the early research on this issue in sport was conducted on provincial VSOs and NGBs in Canada. The results were mixed and, while there was some evidence to suggest professional staff were taking over decision making (Slack and Thibault, 1988; Kikulis *et al.*, 1989; Thibault *et al.*, 1991), later studies indicated that volunteers were retaining their power often due to the strong voluntary values inherent in VSOs. As indicated in Chapter 6, Kikulis *et al.* (1995a) argued that although volunteers were involved in fewer decisions and to a lesser extent in the decision making process within the executive office archetype, volunteer led decision making is deeply embedded in VSOs and is unlikely to be displaced by a professional dominated process in the near future. Kikulis *et al.* (1995b: 96) found that moving the organizations towards an executive office archetype will take a long time because 'these organizations support the tradition of volunteer control'. Kikulis *et al.* (1995c) reported that pressures for professional staff to assume the responsibility for decision making in NSOs were resisted and, further, that organizational members had an interest 'in maintaining the tradition of volunteer-led decision making' (Kikulis *et al.*, 1995c:

148). This group of findings was reinforced by Amis and Slack (1996) who concluded that control remained with the volunteer board, mainly because decision making was perceived as a means of control and was used by volunteers to retain this control.

Somewhat contrary to the volunteer led findings of Kikulis et al. (1995c), Chelladurai and Haggerty (1991) reported that the CEO had the most amount of influence over six of the seven decision making areas they researched and Inglis (1997) found that the amount of influence exerted by various board members varied according to the type of decisions being made. Auld (1997a) explored this phenomenon more directly by investigating the perceptions of influence in decision making of volunteer and professional administrators in Australian NGBs. Auld found that both volunteers and professionals perceived that professionals had the most influence and that specific roles and areas of decision making were perceived to be the responsibility of either paid staff or volunteers. Auld (1997a) also noted that although in 84 per cent of the organizations in the study the role of the professionals on the committee was reported as being advisory only, professionals were still perceived to have the most influence in decision making. A similar study of 61 Canadian NSOs by Auld and Godbey (1998) found that influence in decision making was not perceived as reciprocal between volunteers and professionals, and that some areas of decision making were perceived to be the domain of either the professionals or volunteers. An important implication from this research was the 'recognition that the policy development/implementation split between volunteers and professionals may be too simplistic' (Auld and Godbey, 1998: 20). In a later study, Amis et al. (2004: 158) found that VSOs in which volunteers were willing to share power with staff were able to complete the change process better than those VSOs characterized by 'a structure in which power was retained centrally by volunteer board members, and . . . by ongoing struggles among subunits to protect their own interests'. Taken together, these findings reinforce the point that VSOs have become dependent on professional staff who can exert tremendous power and influence, irrespective of their position in the formal structural hierarchy. Auld (1997a) cautioned that unless volunteer committee members were sufficiently engaged they may feel they have become marginalized in decision making and lose interest in their roles. In summarizing this area of research Kikulis (2000: 294) suggested that

> voluntary sport organizations have adapted the roles and responsibilities of volunteer board and paid executives to accommodate increased influence of paid executives while striving to maintain volunteer influence. From this perspective, then, adopting more professional and business-like management practices has meant a change in the governance and decision-making structures.

Management committee effectiveness and VSO governance

While the majority of sport management research examined relationships and power and influence in the VSO committee context, more recently researchers have begun to investigate the relationship of these phenomena to committee effectiveness and governance quality. Hoye and Cuskelly (2003a) argued that it is somewhat simplistic to view the board as either volunteer or executive led. Their research indicated that five patterns of board power distribution were evident in VSOs: executive dominated; chair dominated; fragmented power; power sharing; and powerless. They found that members of those boards perceived to be ineffective 'were more likely to describe their board as either fragmented, powerless or led by the chair . . . than were the members of effective boards' (2003a: 103). However, their results also revealed that 'if the board is perceived to be executive led there was no relationship to board performance' suggesting that despite the gradual influence of paid staff on committee processes this 'may not have had any effect on the ability of the board to perform' (Hoye and Cuskelly, 2003a: 115).

Using reanalysed data from a previous study, Auld (1997b) reported that the views and values related to influence in decision making expressed by executives and chairs were more similar than that of chairs and board members. Auld (1997b) suggested that the majority of decision making power was therefore likely to be vested within these two key leadership positions rather than disbursed throughout the board. Inglis (1997) argued that these core groups were common in VSOs and these findings were later reinforced by Hoye and Cuskelly (2003b) who found the dominant coalitions that existed within VSO boards were positively related to board performance. Hoye (2004) later extended this approach by using leader-member exchange theory to examine the quality of the leader-member exchanges and its relationship to board performance in state/provincial VSOs. He found that higher quality exchanges among all three pairings of stakeholders (chairs, members and executive) were positively associated with higher levels of board performance but that the board chair and executive seemed to enjoy 'a relatively higher quality working relationship than that which exists between executive and board members or between board chairs and board members' (Hoye, 2004: 67). Hoye and Cuskelly (2003b) found that board performance was related to a number of factors including the centrality of the executive due to their control over information flow to board members, the existence of trust between stakeholders and the sharing of leadership between a coalition comprised of the executive, the chair and a small number of senior board members. Doherty and Carron (2003) concluded that both task and social cohesion predicted volunteer satisfaction and perceived committee effectiveness but task aspects were more important in keeping the group together. Group integration around the task was particularly important for perceived committee effectiveness. They argued that volunteer sport administrators are more likely to be satisfied with their committee experience when they are attracted to the social aspects of the group and when the group is focused on its tasks.

In attempts to improve board performance a number of board processes has been recommended often through government agencies including the ASC and Sport England, with an interest in supporting the effectiveness of VSOs. Recommended processes include such items as written job descriptions and selection criteria for board members, new board member orientation programmes and board self-evaluation. Hoye and Cuskelly (2004b) investigated the relationship between the extent to which these processes have been adopted and perceived board effectiveness. They found boards perceived to be more effective used more of the processes than did boards perceived to be ineffective although a causal link was not established. Hoye and Cuskelly (2004b) qualified their results by adding that the relationship was dependent on the nature of the member representation system. They concluded that 'the application of models and theoretical frameworks concerning governance of the nonprofit sector, while generally applicable for the investigation of the governance of sport organizations, needs to be applied in light of member representation in the governance of VSOs' (2004b: 97).

The broader impacts of professionalization on sport

Little work has focused on the more subtle political impacts of professionalization or at least the broader implications for sport and those who utilize the services of VSOs. As suggested by Auld (1997a) professionals tend to seek control and exert professional 'expert' ideologies on the organizations for which they work. Whitson (1986: 59) argued that aspirant professions are 'characterized by strategies which seek to associate expertise with credentials and to privilege their own particular form of knowledge, in particular by systematically distinguishing it from the lay person's understanding. Such tendencies are likely to create barriers . . .'. This issue goes to the heart of the tensions described by Nichols et al. (1998b) as VSOs move along a continuum from less formal type of management to the more professional and formalized service delivery model. Based on Handy's (1988 cited in Nichols et al., 1998b) typology, Nichols et al. (1998b) argued that prior to professionalization most VSOs would be classified as 'mutual support organizations' that have informal unstructured management systems characterized by minimum organization and maximum enthusiasm. This category is similar to that of Smith (1993) who argued that 'member benefit groups' are more concerned about relationships than output and what Taylor (2004) characterized as traditional/informal VSOs. As VSOs become more professionalized they take on the attributes of what Handy termed 'service delivery organizations' in which management is formal, structured and focused on professional standards and efficiency. Paid and voluntary staff may work together and each has a delineated job description and is held accountable for the performance of their duties. As discussed, tensions arise in service delivery organizations with shared volunteer and paid staff leadership as it appears the presence of both is an antecedent to conflict (Amis *et al.*, 1995).

Furthermore, tensions may also develop between those that do and do not volunteer in VSOs. Nichols *et al.* (1998b) argued that volunteers are more likely to consider the VSO as a mutual support type organization in which they simultaneously produce and consume the sport experience. On the other hand, it was suggested that those who do not volunteer may regard the VSO more in service delivery terms in which they pay a fee in exchange for a service as a consumer. Nichols *et al.* (1998b) argued that as the volunteers and non-volunteers do not share the same objectives for the club, they are unlikely to share the same definitions of effectiveness thus exacerbating tension between these two groups.

Continuing this theme Nichols (2003) later indicated that tensions also arise because of different perceptions about the values and importance of the ends and means of VSOs. He suggested that due to the nature of voluntary associations, not only is the end product (i.e. sporting opportunity) important, but also the means by which it is produced. He argued that

> volunteers must get satisfactory rewards from the process of volunteering. The pressures towards professionalism will strain the motivation of volunteers such that those who remain are willing to accept an effort/reward package in which they contribute more time and skills, and accept greater accountability. These volunteers will either be motivated by the desire to maintain an effective service delivery organization, opposed to one characterized by mutual aid (Handy, 1988), or, more likely will be motivated by enthusiasm for the sport and identification with the club, but will realize, or have been sold the idea, that professionalization is required for it to survive.
>
> (Nichols, 2003: no page)

These arguments suggest that the impacts of professionalization extend beyond the relatively narrow consequences for volunteer sport administrators to also include VSO members and sport participants. Frey (1978: 367 in Slack, 1985: 146) argued that the bureaucratization of sport 'reduces the organization's legitimacy in the eyes of its constituents'. Wilson (1988: 33) argued that the goal of leisure professionals was the 'rational supervision of leisure' later echoed by McKay (1990: 144–146) who indicated that participation levels may be adversely affected by commercialization, state intervention and professional experts who 'frame the problem of leisure'. Hibbins (1996) argued that leisure is socially controlled by professionals. Coalter (1990) also suggested that meaningful participation is more than just consumption and should include opportunities to participate in decisions about what is provided. He argued that

> the liberative potential of leisure services is undermined by bureaucratic structures, 'managerialist' ideologies based on income maximising, . . . and the growing dominance of paternalistic professional groups in the determination of 'need' and 'relevant' provision. These all serve to produce restrictive definitions of 'appropriate' forms of behaviour . . .
>
> (Coalter, 1990: 168–169)

Concluding comments

Although there have been significant changes to VSO practices and procedures brought about by professionalization, the responsibility for effective service delivery still rests largely with volunteer administrators. Volunteer sport administrators make substantial contributions, often behind the scenes, to the provision of services to members and the public and ensure the continuing viability of VSOs. However their roles, probably more so than other types of volunteers, have been altered by the professionalization of sport systems internationally over the past two decades. Professionalization is a double-edged sword. VSOs must ensure that while they enjoy the many benefits of professionalization, they should also be acutely aware that professionalization may impact on committee functioning and board effectiveness, contribute to declining volunteer levels as well as alter the very nature of the sport experience. VSOs need to establish an appropriate balance between what may be frequently competing values and motivations that drive the involvement of professional and volunteer sport administrators in order to maintain sport as a buoyant, viable and satisfying community activity.

Chapter 9

Sports officials

From local parks, pools and sports facilities to high profile international events, sports officials are prominent in almost every sporting contest. Often maligned by players, coaches, spectators and the media, sports officials are an essential part of organized competitive sport. The knowledge, skills and performance quality of those who officiate at sport contests and events has an impact on the quality of the sport experience for all involved. Standards of officiating also affect the safety of participants in many sporting contests. Consistent with the five-segment model of sports practice (see Chapter 2), the bulk of the officiating workload is shared among volunteer or low paid officials, occurs at the foundation of the sports system, and, most often, within VSOs. Governments and sport organizations are becoming increasingly interested in the recruitment, retention of officials and the standard of officiating as they work towards the implementation of policies aimed at increasing participation in organized sport, the vast majority of which require the services of sports officials. The purpose of this chapter is to explore the importance and significance of sports officiating, the roles of sports officials, problems and issues in sports officiating, and the development and management of sports officials.

Nature and scope of sports officiating

The ASC (2005d: no page) defines sports officials as 'any person who controls the actual play of a competition by applying the rules and laws of the sport to make judgments on rule infringement, performance, time and score'. This definition is consistent with that of SPARC (2003a: 3) which defines sports officials as 'any person who controls or directs the actual play of a competition by applying the rules of the sport to make judgements on rule infringements, performance, time or score'. The ASC added that officials have a key role to ensure that games and events are 'played within the spirit of the rules'. Both the SPARC and ASC definitions are inclusive and encompass many officiating roles across a range of different sports. Depending upon the particular sport, sports officials undertake a variety of roles which may include umpire, referee, judge, scorer, timekeeper and, in some cases, adjudicator, marshal and scrutineer.

Sports officials apply the laws and rules of sport in many competitive contexts. Within the Stewart *et al.* (2004) five-segment model of sports practice, volunteer and paid sports officials are found in community, school and local sport through to elite sport such as national sport leagues, national championships and international sport events. They officiate at team and individual sports whether played on courts, fields or tracks, in pools or a variety of natural settings (e.g. rivers, lakes, oceans, mountains). Officials are sometimes situated within the contest itself (e.g. rugby) or adjacent to it (e.g. volleyball). At times they are required to make instantaneous decisions (e.g. netball) or delayed judgements (e.g. gymnastics) about the rules of the game or the performance of players or athletes. Unlike professional sport, most sports officials in VSOs carry out their tasks with minimal use of technology (e.g. video replay).

Based on the nature of officials' roles across sports, SPARC (2003b) categorized sports officiating as active, sedentary/low activity, time/distance measurement, or judging roles. These categories are not necessarily mutually exclusive because all categories of sports officiating require judgements to be made. For example, time/distance measurement officials often have to determine whether the performance of an athlete or a team is compliant with the rules. However, the SPARC categories are useful for understanding the diversity of contexts and settings in which sports officiating occurs. Examples of sports officiating in the active category are soccer (association football), rugby codes, netball, basketball and hockey. In the sedentary/low activity category are sports such as softball, volleyball, tennis, cricket and squash. The time/distance measurement sports officiating category includes rowing, cycling, swimming, shooting and archery. Sports officiating in the judging category includes gymnastics, diving, weightlifting, ice skating, equestrian and martial arts.

Sports officiating is among the most practised volunteer roles in sport. Reporting data from a national population survey volunteers in England, the LIRC (2003) found that in the previous year, 82 per cent of sport volunteers had undertaken activities as a referee, umpire or official for a match or competition. Only coaching (88 per cent) or administrative roles (85 per cent) for a sport organization exceeded sports officiating. In Australia, sports officiating accounted for 38 per cent of non-playing sport participation, which was higher than coaching, instructing and teaching (26.4 per cent) and committee work or administration (25.5 per cent) (ABS, 2005a).

On the basis of an estimated 5.8 million sport volunteers in England, approximately 4.7 million volunteers had, at some point in the year prior to survey, participated in some form of officiating (LIRC, 2003). The figures for England are much higher than those in Canada and Australia. In Canada, 937,000 people aged 15 years and over (4 per cent of the population) were involved in amateur sport as referees, officials or umpires (Statistics Canada, 2000c). The ABS (2005a) reported participation numbers separately for referees/umpires (335,000) and scorers/timekeepers (513,000) for a total number of sports officials of 848,000 people aged 15 years or over. As a proportion of the population aged 15 years and over, the participation rates for sports officials in Canada (4 per cent) and Australia (5.1 per cent) are similar.

The higher participation rate in Australia might be explained by the inclusion of both paid and unpaid involvement. Payment for officiating is not inconsistent with the Cnaan *et al.* (1996) remuneration dimension that categorizes volunteering from 'none' to 'stipend/low pay'. Of the 78,600 Australian sports officials who reported some level of paid involvement, 71,800 (91 per cent) were paid in goods or services only or earned less than AUD$5,000 from officiating in the year prior to survey. Nominal payments such as stipends or low pay have become increasingly important as sport organizations face the challenge of recruiting officials in sufficient numbers. Because of the public perception that receiving abuse is part of the job of officiating (SPARC, 2003a), it is becoming increasingly necessary to use match payments and other utilitarian incentives (see Knoke and Prensky, 1984) to attract new officials. Further, sports officials, irrespective of their age or the level of competition at which they officiate, are expected to perform at a high standard. Spectators, coaches and players make few concessions to young or inexperienced officials, which places their decisions under great scrutiny. These factors, in addition to requiring officials to be trained to high standards at all levels of competition, add weight to the argument for paying individuals to officiate.

The average number of officials per sport varies widely. In New Zealand, SPARC (2003a: no page number) estimated an average of 'around 578 officials per sport at all levels of competition' but added that the range was from less than 20 officials for sports such as archery and synchronized swimming to more than 2,000 officials for sports such as rugby (2,300), netball (2,750) and swimming (3,000). The proportion of officials to participant numbers varies within and across sports. For example, the ARU has 3,250 accredited officials including referees and touch judges which is equivalent to 2.2 per cent of its 150,000 registered players (ARU, 2004). The Rugby Football Union in England (2005) has a players to referee ratio target of 30:1 or 3.3 per cent in its 2005/2006–2012/2013 Strategic Plan.

Characteristics of officials

Statistics Canada (2000c) provided a breakdown of sports officials by demographic characteristics (see Table 9.1). The importance of young people filling officiating roles is underlined by the 12 per cent of Canada's population aged 15 to 18 years who are sports officials. Further evidence of the importance of young officials is revealed by the one out of ten students who

Table 9.1 Characteristics of Canadians who participate in amateur sport as a referee, official or umpire, 1998[a]

	Population '000s	Sports officials '000s	% of population	% of sports officials
Total	24,260	937		
Gender				
Male	N/A	537	4.5	57.3
Female	N/A	399	3.2	42.6
Age group				
15–18	1,644	194	11.8	20.7
19–24	2,415	142	5.9	15.2
25–34	4,615	143	3.1	15.3
35–54	9,353	412	4.4	44.0
55 and over	6,233	45	0.7	4.8
Labour force participation				
Full-time	11,388	524	4.6	55.9
Part-time	1,615	82	5.1	8.8
Student with or without employment	2,368	217	9.2	23.2
Not in labour force	6,742	102	1.5	10.9
Level of education				
Some secondary or less	6,286	187	3.0	20.0
Some college/trade/high school	6,057	285	4.7	30.4
Diploma/some university	6,201	302	4.9	32.2
University degree	4,094	150	3.7	16.0

Source: [a] adapted from Statistics Canada (2000c).

are officials. Fifteen to 18 year olds accounted for 20 per cent of the total number of Canadian sports officials. Among sports officials, 44 per cent are aged 35 to 54 years but as a proportion of the population, less than 5 per cent of this age-cohort are involved in sports officiating. With only 45,000 sports officials aged 55 years and over these statistics indicate that retirement from officiating probably occurs rapidly, in many sports, when officials reach 50 years of age. Participation increases with higher levels of education but decreases when people complete university degrees. Comparative statistics are available by gender for sports officiating in Canada and Australia. Excluding scorers and timekeepers from the Australian statistics, sports officials in Canada and Australian are more likely to be male. In Canada (Statistics Canada, 2000c) and Australia (ABS, 2005a), 57 per cent and 58 per cent of sports officials, respectively, are male.

Trends in sports officiating

Recent participation trends in sports officiating are displayed in Figure 9.1. In Canada, the number of sports officials increased at an average of 65,000

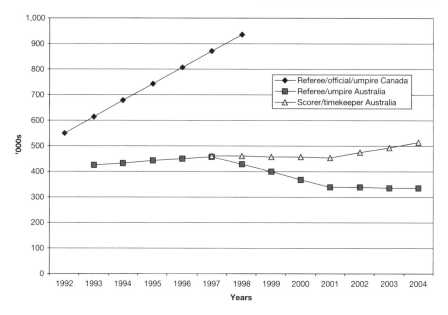

Figure 9.1 Trends in the number of sports officials in Canada[a] and Australia[b]

Sources: [a] Adapted from Statistics Canada (2000c). [b] Adapted from ABS (2005a).

Notes: Canadian statistics interpolated for years 1993 to 1997. Australian statistics interpolated for 1994 to 1996, 1998 to 2000, and 2002 to 2003.

per year from 550,000 in 1992 to 937,000 in 1998 (Statistics Canada, 2000c). In Australia, there has tended to be a declining trend in the total number of sports officials in recent years. From 1997 to 2004 when data were collected for all types of sports officials (referees, umpires, scorers and timekeepers) total numbers decreased from 918,000 in 1997 to 848,000 in 2004 (ABS, 2005a). The number of referees and umpires decreased, on average 29,000 per year from 1997 to 2001, but levelled from 2001 to 2004. The number of scorers and timekeepers was relatively stable from 1997 to 2001 and increased, on average, 20,000 per year until 2004. The Australian sports officiating trends have occurred despite the introduction of the NOAS in 1994.

Stress and burnout

Over the past two decades, a growing body of research has focused on stress, burnout and intention to quit among sports officials. The germination for most of this research was a study by Taylor and Daniel (1987) that investigated sources of stress among Canadian soccer (football) officials. Subsequent studies have demonstrated that stress is a predictor of burnout and intention to terminate among officials in a number of sports (Taylor et al., 1990; Schmidt and Stein, 1991; Rainey, 1995; Anshell and Weinberg, 1996; Rainey and Duggan, 1998; Rainey and Hardy, 1999).

Four sources of stress have been identified consistently among sports officials across a number of sports: performance concerns (or fear of failure); fear of physical harm; interpersonal conflict; and time pressure (Rainey and Hardy, 1999). Performance concerns include having a 'bad' game, making a bad decision and maintaining concentration. Fear of physical harm is associated with assault by a coach or player, whether actual or threatened. Interpersonal conflict includes dealing with abusive players, personality clashes with players or coaches and dealing with hostile or over-excited coaches. Time pressure is concerned more with extraneous factors not directly associated with the job of officiating. Time pressure includes conflicts between officiating, work and family or the social demands of others who would prefer that the official spent more time with them. Several studies have found evidence that burnout among officials is predicted by several sources of stress, particularly performance concerns (Taylor et al., 1990; Rainey, 1995), interpersonal conflict and time pressure (Taylor et al., 1990; Rainey and Hardy, 1999) and that burnout, in turn, is a mediator between stress and intention to quit (Rainey and Hardy, 1999). Notwithstanding the cognitive and emotional processes that cause individual sports officials to make a decision to quit, retention of sports officials is a significant concern for many stakeholders across the sport system.

The retention problem

Statistics from the ABS (2005a) revealed that the total number of sports officials (referees and umpires) in Australia declined 26 per cent over a five-year period from 1997 to 2001 from 456,800 to 340,000 but had stabilized by 2004 (see Figure 9.1). SPARC (2003a: 4) reported 'a small but significant decline in the proportion of volunteers involved as officials between 1997 and 2001' and that 'recruitment and/or retention are identified as significant problems for many sports, with few documented policies and strategies in place to address the issue'. Government agencies and many sport NGBs are acutely aware of the high levels of turnover evident among the ranks of sports officials, particularly early-career officials. The declining number of sports officials encouraged the ASC (2004b) to commission a research report to examine 'Problems and issues in the recruitment and retention of sports officials'. The ASC (2004b) found attrition rates of up to 60 per cent among first-year sports officials in some associations. Among the reasons for high rates of attrition among first-year officials were a lack of suitability for the role of being an official, facing up to the realities of abuse from players, coaches and spectators, the pressure to perform with proficiency despite low levels of experience, and unrealistic expectations of advancing quickly to higher standard competitions (ASC, 2004b). The findings of the ASC are consistent with the sources of stress identified and researched by Rainey and Hardy (1999).

The retention of sports officials is becoming problematic in the achievement of government policy objectives aimed at increasing participation in organized sport. Almost invariably, increases in the number of sports participants put pressure on the ranks of sports officials to increase their capacity to officiate at more competitions and events. Increased capacity can only be achieved through some combination of three possible alternatives: recruiting more sports officials; increasing the workloads of current officials through allocating more games or contests per official per season; or increasing the average career length of sports officials through increased retention rates. Sport Canada (2000) identified six key issues for officiating many of which are associated with the retention of officials:

- The lack of roles and responsibilities of provincial/territorial VSOs and sport NGBs for the training and development of officials and the need to make officials part of governing bodies.

Table 9.2 Conclusions of an ASC report into problems and issues in the recruitment and retention of sports officials

Retention of sports officials is a significant problem, particularly among inexperienced officials at the grass roots level of sport.

Incomplete data make it difficult to document the exact nature and extent of the retention problem.

NGBs and state/provincial sporting organizations have little influence in the recruitment and retention of sports officials at grass roots level.

Resources allocated by NGBs and state/provincial sporting organizations to sports officiating are disproportionately low in comparison to coach and player development.

Compared to metropolitan officials rural/regional officials incur significantly higher time and money costs in officiating.

Facilities and resources available to sports officials at the grass roots level are inadequate.

Poor integration of sports officials within the operation of sport governing organizations.

Significant shortcomings in the training provided for sports officials to deal with abuse and conflict situations.

Feedback provided to practising officials at the grass roots level is generally inadequate.

Education and training is based on the assumption that all sports officials are seeking career advancement.

Skills and abilities of sports officials' coordinators is a key determinant in the recruitment, development and retention of sports officials.

Source: adapted from ASC (2004b).

- The lack of recognition and understanding by sport organizations at all levels of officials as an integral part of the Canadian sport system.
- The need for strategies for the recruitment and retention of officials.
- The need to provide more officiating opportunities at the national and international level (currently hindered by a lack of financial support for official's expenses and international competitions occurring in Canada).
- The need to improve communication and relationships between officials and the Canadian sport community.
- Improve training materials for officials.

The ASC (2004b) has also focused its attention on recruitment and retention problems and issues and listed a number of structural, systemic and individual factors in relation to sports official retention problems. These are summarized in Table 9.2.

Independent or integrated governance structures?

A common theme in the Australian, Canadian and New Zealand contexts is the degree of integration of officials within the structures and strategies of sport NGBs. Structurally, there are two officiating models, termed the independent model and the integrated model, which are situated at the opposite ends of a spectrum. The independent model has the following features:

- a governance structure that ensures complete separation between the body responsible for sports officiating at local, state/provincial and NGB levels;
- an officiating governing body that assumes responsibility for all aspects of officiating including recruitment, training and accreditation, appointment to competitions, assessment, talent identification and development;
- a service provider approach whereby the officiating body enters into a contractual type of arrangement to officiate at competitions is officially sanctioned by VSOs or NGBs.

In contrast the integrated model has the following features:

- a governance structure in which sports officials are members of the sport NGB or VSO with similar rights and responsibilities as other members such as players, coaches and administrators;
- the NGB or VSO that assumes responsibility for all aspects of officiating;
- officials who work with and under the direction of the NGB or VSO.

The integrated model enables sports officiating to be more closely aligned with the strategies, policies and operations of NGBs and VSOs for the mutual benefit of both parties. Communication problems, which tend to exist between separate bodies, can be minimized. Matters such as the management of recruitment and retention, training, accreditation, development, support and recognition of officials are dealt with more effectively when they are part of the regular deliberations of committee and board members within a NGB or a VSO rather than the subject of ongoing negotiations between two separate entities. The integrated sports officiating model may also alleviate other officiating problems and issues that include support for officials, particularly when they are verbally or physically abused, over-rostering of officials to compensate for under-recruitment, lack of performance feedback and access to career pathways. Some of these issues were raised earlier in relation to stress and burnout among officials.

The ASC (2004b) reported that most officials expected conflict with and abuse from players, coaches and spectators would occur and accepted it as part of the job of officiating. However, officials were less likely to consider quitting if they felt they were supported by their organization, codes of conduct were applied when abuse occurred, and that tribunals displayed minimal tolerance of abuse in imposing sanctions on players and others. The issues of rostering officials, performance feedback and career pathways are interrelated. Officials with a desire to advance their career beyond junior and lower grade contests reported that they felt pressured to accept too many appointments, performance feedback was often insufficient, and career paths were both obscure and difficult to access, particularly for officials not based in major metropolitan areas.

Part of the solution to the retention problem is to come to terms with the inevitability of turnover irrespective of how much attention is focused on retaining officials. Whether through retirement, changing work or family demands, prioritization of other leisure interests, stress or burnout, a certain number of sports officials will quit officiating every year. The problem is compounded when a sport has increasing participant numbers. Notwithstanding retention rates and increasing participant numbers, recruitment of officials continues to be an important function for VSOs. As discussed in Chapter 7, many volunteers have a prior association with sport, often as a player, and the decision to adopt a different role, such as officiating, is essentially a transition process. Sport NGBs and VSOs need to gather information about transitions into officiating and progression through different levels of officiating. Examples of the transition into officiating are those that occur when a former athlete, player, coach or administrator or parent of a junior player becomes a volunteer official for the first time. Examples of progression through officiating are the transitions that occur as officials move from volunteer to paid status and the career transitions that occur as officials are promoted from local to state/provincial to national and ultimately to international level competition. Opportunities for career advancement are important for officials motivated by utilitarian incentives. As officials move up the ranks of officiating they create vacancies that need to be filled. Most often this occurs through recruiting and promoting others from within the ranks of currently active officials. It is therefore incumbent upon sport organizations to take a balanced approach to the recruitment and retention of officials at all levels of sport.

Government initiatives and the role of sport NGBs

Over the past decade government and sport NGBs have increasingly recognized the importance and value of sports officials. Officials are important in realizing policy initiatives aimed at increasing levels of participation in organized sport. Increasing participation levels and quality standards in organized sport also have consequences for sports officials through demands for more sports officials and standards at which they are expected to perform their duties. Many sport NGB strategic plans include objectives and targets for officiating in terms of recruitment, retention and development. Within their particular organizational structures and with partner organizations, NGBs work towards two broad goals of increasing the number of officials and increasing officiating standards. Specifically, sport NGBs or national associations of officials develop and govern matters including:

* the rules or laws of the sport and their interpretation;
* accreditation programmes, competency standards, performance monitoring, assessment and grading;
* roles of officials and officiating practices;
* codes of practice and participant safety;
* talent identification, career pathways and development of officials.

In its National Officiating Strategy, SPARC (2003a: 7) lists three strategic goals: to provide quality training and development opportunities for officials; to provide quality support and resources for officials and officiating; and to improve the public perception of officials and officiating. The New Zealand National Officiating Strategy outlines roles and responsibilities for stakeholder groups including SPARC, sport NGBs and provincial VSOs known as regional sports trusts. Longer term, the outcomes of this strategy are an increase in the number of active officials and the quality of officiating as well as improved support and recognition for officials. In contrast, sports officiating was not addressed in Sport England's (2004b) publication entitled *Driving Up Participation: The Challenge for Sport*. Furthermore, the only reference to sports officiating in the *National Framework for Sport in England* (Sport England, 2004a) is in relation to the issue of insurance for volunteers.

NOAS

For the past decade, the ASC has invested significantly in the development of the NOAS, which is modelled, to some extent, on the NCAS. While the training, accreditation and development of officials is the jurisdiction of sport NGBs or associations of officials, the NOAS programme was established to improve overall sports officiating numbers and standards.

Established in 1994 the NOAS aims to assist sport NGBs to develop and implement programmes that improve the quality, quantity, leadership and status of sports officiating in Australia (ASC, 2005d). NOAS training programmes include general principles (e.g. fundamentals of officiating), sport-specific (e.g. technical rules, interpretations and sport-specific roles for officials), and officiating practice. The NOAS provides accreditation for defined periods of time set by each sport (e.g. two years). Participants may apply to sport NGBs for recognition of prior learning or current competence. To retain accreditation NOAS officials are required to attend appropriate education activities designed to ensure that sports officials stay informed about rule changes in their sport, are aware of current officiating techniques and methods, and are reminded about participant safety. The process also ensures that sport NGBs and the ASC have a current register of active officials.

A national officiating scholarship programme was developed in 2003 and provides potential high performance officials with an intense learning programme. The structure for this programme is flexible to meet the specialized needs of different sports and can be up to 52 weeks duration. Officials are required to participate in hands-on officiating as well as undertake professional development courses and update or upgrade their level of NOAS accreditation. The programme is built on the desire to provide a career pathway for officials upon completion of the scholarship programme.

Ethics in officiating

The ASC apportions responsibility for the ethical conduct of sport equally with officials, players, administrators, coaches, spectators, media, educators, parents, governments, sponsors and team owners. The duty of sports officials is to impartially judge sporting competitions with accuracy, consistency, objectivity and high integrity. The ASC recognizes that to preserve and encourage confidence in the professionalism and integrity of officiating, officials must first foster ethical behaviour. The ASC (2005d) sports officials' code of ethics is to:

- place the safety and welfare of participants above all else;
- accept responsibility for all actions taken;
- be impartial and avoid any situation that may lead to a conflict of interest;

- be courteous, respectful and open to discussion and interaction;
- value the individual in sport;
- seek continual self-improvement through study, performance appraisal and regular updating of competencies;
- encourage inclusivity and access to all areas of officiating;
- be a positive role model in behaviour and personal appearance;
- refrain from any form of personal abuse or sexual harassment towards athletes;
- show concern and caution towards sick and injured athletes.

Breaches of the code of ethics for sports officials are handled by sport NGBs and their member associations, which may take disciplinary action against officials in accordance with the principles of natural justice. The code provides for a number of disciplinary measures that range from verbal or written apologies to deregistration or the withdrawal of the official's accreditation from a set time period, including life bans.

Match officials in the Football Association

The NOAS in Australia and the National Officiating Strategy in New Zealand each provide a focal point for addressing the number and quality of sports officials as well as improving the overall status of sports officiating in their respective countries. However, sport NGBs still have a considerable role to play in the recruitment, development and retention of sports officials. Government initiatives provide a framework designed to assist, rather than subsume, the role of NGBs. In a 2003 review of its Referees Department, the Football Association (FA) addressed a range of matters including referee recruitment, retention, training and education, incentives, referees academies, assessors, mentors and instructors.

The FA operates an integrated model of officiating with the FA Match Officials Association incorporated in the vision and mission of the FA. Typical of most officiating programmes, the FA referees development programme has a number of levels, specifically eight in this case, from level eight (local amateur football) to one (labelled the national list). The most talented officials move on to an international list. With an estimated 20 per cent of games in some parts of the country played without a qualified official, the FA aims to recruit 10,000 referees annually and ensure that every official receives training and support from its mentor programme and helpline. Recruitment is focused on young people and includes a mixture of training options. Females have also been targeted as officials because of the increasing number of girls and women playing football. In the two-tier training programme the laws of football are learnt at the first tier with no requirement to become an active official. The second tier is designed for those who want to become active officials and emphasizes practical training.

Consistent with the findings of the ASC (2004b) report, part of the retention problem for the FA was obtaining accurate data on the number of registered referees. The FA has put in place a number of initiatives to address the retention problem. These include in-service training, particularly for recently qualified referees, as well as incentive and mentor schemes. The incentive scheme is based on a system of reward points, which referees earn by officiating, attending training and meetings. Reward points can be traded for official merchandize and referee's kit. The incentive scheme is an interesting initiative and is likely to facilitate the retention of officials who are motivated by utilitarian incentives and symbolic rewards. However, such schemes are based on the recognize-reward-retain approach, a common feature in VMPs discussed in Chapter 7. Incentive schemes frequently ignore the complexity of individual motives for commencing and continuing to officiate. They also tend to increase the administrative load on VSOs and, if not administered with attention to detail, can raise concerns about the equity of rewards and effort among practicing officials.

Education and training are important components of development programmes for officials. The FA uses several training methods designed to suit different styles of learning. These include classroom-based basic training, skill development delivered in a practical manner and match officiating. These programmes are supplemented and supported by a number of assessor, mentor and instructor training programmes. Using in-service training, particularly targeting officials nearing the end of their careers, assessors and mentors are trained to use their experience to support and develop other officials. To ensure that their knowledge and interpretation of the laws of the game remain current, assessors and mentors are required to attend an additional training module and re-register every five years. Instructors are initially trained and accredited to offer basic training to those wanting to become officials. More advanced training is available to accredited instructors to become registered and licensed instructors. All instructors are subject to re-appraisal and re-accreditation on a regular basis to ensure that they are actively instructing officials at an appropriate standard. Referees academies and centres for excellence have been established to further develop talented officials in a structured, controlled and supportive environment with close links to county FAs and professional football clubs. The FA initiatives and programmes designed to recruit, develop and retain officials are consistent with the policies and strategies developed by the Australian and New Zealand governments that aim to increase the number of officials, improve standards of officiating and, longer term, create a more positive public perception of officials and officiating. Due to resource constraints many sport NGBs are not in the position to develop comprehensive recruitment, development and retention programmes for their officials to the extent that it has occurred in the FA. However, the problems faced by sports officials are unlikely to improve unless sport NGBs respond to the need for more and better trained and supported officials, particularly at the VSO level.

Concluding comments

This chapter focused on problems and issues in relation to the recruitment, development and retention of sports officials as well as the standards of sports officiating. The application and interpretation of the rules or laws of the game is a necessary but often thankless task in many sports. The standard of sports officiating has a direct impact on the quality, enjoyment and safety of the sport experience for competitors, coaches, other officials and spectators. Increasingly, government and sport NGBs are taking a strong interest in the recruitment and retention of officials, the overall standards of officiating and the public perception of sports officials. Stress and burnout are among a number of reasons for high rates of attrition among officials, particularly those who are new to the role. Pay and other rewards are being used as incentives to recruit and retain officials. It is also apparent that significant structural reform is necessary in some sports to ensure a more integrated governance structure in which sport NGBs and VSOs assume greater responsibility for officiating. It is important that officials enjoy the rights and responsibilities enjoyed by other members of NGBs and VSOs, such as coaches and players. Government policies, strategies and programmes in Australia and New Zealand seem to be well advanced in addressing the problems and issues associated with sports officiating compared with other countries.

Chapter 10

Volunteer coaches

Coaches are often the most tangible manifestation of organizational quality and effectiveness in the sport context and are a crucial component of the sport experience for most participants. They are highly visible due to their very direct involvement with many sport participants and there is a clear link between sport performance and coaching quality at all levels of sport. Moreover, coaches can facilitate rewarding experiences in sport, especially for younger participants that have direct and significant implications for individual wellbeing and levels of participation in physical activity. However, given the nature of the coaching role some of the strains felt by VSOs, especially in areas such as participant safety and child protection, may fall disproportionately on coaches more so than other categories of sport volunteers. The purpose of this chapter is to review the roles and nature of the contribution made by volunteer sport coaches and to examine the important issues and core principles required to effectively develop and manage this important cohort of volunteers. Furthermore, the chapter focuses on the critical issues of coach education and coaching in junior sport.

The role and scope of volunteer sport coaching

Coaching is one of the key roles in sport at all levels but given the size of the community sport sector its overall contribution is more significant at this level. As discussed in other chapters, a number of national sport policies has targeted increased participation rates in sport as significant and prominent goals. For example, the Commonwealth of Australia's (2001) BASA policy has placed increased focus on the community sport system and the management of its volunteers as the 'centrepiece of [the] policy is a new strategy to increase community participation in sport' (Commonwealth of Australia, 2001: no page). If the goal of increased participation in community sport is to be realized then one of the key success variables will be volunteer involvement, particularly coaches. Sports Coach UK (2005: no page) argued that any strategies to increase sports participation 'will be contributed to significantly by the quality and quantity of coaching opportunities available'. Wiersma and Sherman (2005: 325) suggested that 'the existence of community-based sport programs depends primarily on the leadership of volunteer coaches'. The role of sport coaches in helping to provide quality sport experiences and sustain community life cannot be under estimated. Although many sport organizations have instituted mechanisms and processes to facilitate growth, without a sufficient number of willing and skilled volunteers, including coaches, this potential capacity may never be realized.

The fundamental role of coaching is consistently acknowledged across a number of countries. SPARC (2004: 2) indicated that 'coaches have a huge impact on their communities . . . and have a positive influence on the life and values of those they come into contact with'. Wiersma and Sherman (2005: 324) argued that 'the vast majority of youth sport programs in the United States relies primarily on parent volunteers to serve as coaches'. A UK survey found that the adult population 'clearly views coaching as an important aspect of sport both at the elite level as well as the enjoyment it can help bring to participants at all levels' (Sports Coach UK, 2004: 8). Furthermore, two-thirds of respondents to the Sports Coach UK survey indicated that coaching was crucial for elite sport success while just over half suggested that coaching improves the enjoyment of sport participants no matter what their standard. A third believed that investment in coaching should be a government priority and 40 per cent of those who had not participated in sport in the previous 12 months felt that good coaching helped increase sport participation levels.

Data from a range of countries, despite methodological differences, support these views and indicate that coaches are a significant category of sport volunteers who make substantial contributions of their time to VSOs. Statistics Canada (2004b) reported that over 1.7 million people aged over 15 years (7.1 per cent of the population) were involved in sport coaching. A report commissioned by Sports Coach UK (2004) indicated there was a total of 1.2 million people providing sports coaching in the UK and of these, almost 1 million (81 per cent) were volunteers. Men were more likely than women to engage in coaching and the figures indicated that 4 per cent of the UK adult male population was involved in some kind of coaching in the preceding 12 months compared to 1.2 per cent of the adult female population. An analysis of the five sports in the UK with the highest numbers of current coaches revealed that even in sports regarded as relatively highly professionalized (e.g. football and rugby), volunteer coaches comprised over 80 per cent of all coaches in those sports. Some of the lower percentages for volunteer coaching levels were in those sports frequently perceived as being less professionalized. The lowest figure contained in the report was for gymnastics where 41 per cent of coaches were volunteers followed by swimming at 60 per cent. Furthermore, the report also suggested that approximately 6.25 million people who participated in sport in the previous

12 months had received some form of coaching. However, the extent to which this occurs may vary considerably between sports. Some activities, for example those needing high levels of technical expertise, are likely to require more coaching than those sports that are often more informal and casual in nature with lower skill level requirements.

The ABS (2005a) reported that almost 595,000 people aged over 15 years in Australia (3.8 per cent of the population) were involved as a coach, instructor or teacher in sport during 2004 and this accounted for 26.4 per cent of all non-playing participation in sport. Approximately 77,000 of these coaches contributed more than 10 hours per week to their VSOs in 2004. Seippel (2002) reported that volunteers in Norwegian sport clubs contributed an average of 17.4 hours per week to 'instruction', the highest number of hours by any type of sport volunteer and more than twice that of the nearest other category. The ABS (2005a) data also revealed that apart from volunteer administration, coaching requires more involvement compared to other categories of sport volunteers. More than a quarter of coaches (27 per cent) were involved for between 40 to 52 weeks per year whereas most sport volunteers tend to participate mainly on a seasonal basis. The ABS (2001b) also found that in terms of overall volunteering participation rates, coaching/refereeing/judging accounted for 22 per cent of all volunteer involvement though respondents could indicate more than one activity. Males (29 per cent) were more likely to be involved in these activities than were females (16 per cent).

Trends and issues in volunteer sport coaching

The literature suggests there are some common issues of concern for volunteer coaches in a number of countries. These include declining numbers, ethics, education and development, coaching of juniors and a lack of career pathways for coaches. However, while it is generally acknowledged that coaches are a vital element in sport programme delivery, understanding more about the nature and impact of coaching is hampered by a lack of comprehensive data on coaches in some jurisdictions. A report prepared for Sports Coach UK (2004) asserted that prior to their report there had been little systematic data collected on the number and profile of coaches in the UK. Furthermore, inconsistent data collection practices were problematic and hampered the opportunity to compare coach related data between different sports and geographical areas. The report suggested that the following main problems were encountered during the NGB data collection process:

- overall lack of information on coaches stored by NGBs resulting in incomplete responses to the surveys distributed;
- variations in storing data made it difficult for NGBs to report on coach profile information;

- variations in the types of data collected and associated difficulties in providing information in the form requested;
- a general lack of resources in NGBs to complete the survey;
- reluctance to provide information due to concerns over accuracy.

(Sports Coach UK, 2004: 17)

Coach recruitment and retention

Like other areas of sport volunteering, coaching also suffers from recruitment and retention problems. The ASC (2003, 2004c) reported that Australia recorded a 9.6 per cent reduction in the number of accredited coaches from 2003 to 2004 and this followed a 7.2 per cent fall in the previous year. However, Sports Coach UK (2005: no page) reported that data in the UK suggest that 'the provision and take-up of coaching opportunities has increased significantly in recent years' although coach drop out rates continue to be a problem. Approximately 7 per cent (3.4 million people) of the UK adult population had previously coached but were no longer involved. Insufficient time (38 per cent) was the most common factor for not continuing followed by moving away from the club where they had coached (26 per cent). Sports Coach UK (2004) reported that there was no particular factor that would encourage more of the adult population to take up coaching. Approximately 5 per cent of the population would be more likely to participate if their children were involved, 4 per cent if there was some form of financial incentive and 3 per cent would coach if they were asked to or if courses were more easily available. Sports Coach UK (2005: no page) argued that 'recruiting new coaches is less of an issue than up-skilling and professionalising the existing ones (though this is likely to vary between sports)'. It was further reported that anecdotal evidence from a majority of NGBs indicated that the main challenges in this area were encouraging new coaches to pursue coaching qualifications and encouraging Level 1 coaches to take additional qualifications and thus increase their commitment. These suggestions are consistent with data from Australia. The ASC (2001b: 1) reported that as of 'May 2001, 89% of accredited coaches were Level 1, 10% were Level 2, and 1% were Level 3. These figures indicate a "log jam" of coaches at the lowest level of accreditation'. According to Raedeke (2004: 333) coach drop out also appears to be an issue in the US as 'a substantial number of individuals leave the coaching ranks' each year. For example approximately 35 per cent of coaches with 'USA Swimming' discontinue their involvement annually.

Although the NCAS in Australia was initiated, among other reasons, to increase the number of coaches and develop more structured options for coaching careers including pathways from voluntary to paid positions, the available evidence questions the extent to which these goals have been achieved (ASC, 2003; Phillips, 2000). For example, despite the regular involvement of more than one-quarter of the Australian population in some form of sport and physical activity in 2004 (ABS, 2005a), only 1 per cent of the population recorded their primary occupation in sport and recreation in 2001 (ABS, 2003). Of these, only 2,878 were sports coaches (ABS, 2005b). However, the ASC (2001a) reported that there were more than 93,000 coaches currently accredited with national sports associations and more than 200,000 coaches had qualified through the NCAS since its inception.

Coaching ethics

While appropriate ethical standards are essential for all sport volunteers, they are especially important for sport coaches given the very direct relationships established between coaches, teams and athletes. This is also the case given that many of the highly publicized sexual misconduct problems associated with children and adolescents in sport have involved coaches (Brackenridge, 2002). As suggested by the ASC (2005e: no page), coping 'with ethical issues is becoming a regular part of a coach's duties'. Ethical dilemmas extend beyond sexual misconduct and may also include areas such as: sportsmanship and respect for officials; drug use; cheating and bullying; eating disorders; abuse of power; other forms of harassment; and injury management. The ASC argued that coaches must operate with integrity in the relationships with whom they interact. The coaches' code of ethics developed by SPARC (2005e) contains the following key points:

- respect the rights, dignity and worth of every athlete as a human being;
- maintain high standards of integrity;
- be a positive role model and act in a way that projects a positive image of coaching;
- be professional and accept responsibility for your actions in such areas as language, punctuality, presentation, control, courtesy, respect and honesty;
- do not initiate a sexual relationship with an athlete or respond to an athlete seeking a sexual relationship;
- commit to providing a quality service to athletes;
- provide a safe environment for training and competition;
- protect athletes from any form of personal abuse.

VSOs also have a responsibility to deal with their coaches in an ethical manner. SPARC (2005e) urged VSOs to treat coaches with respect and openness, provide access to self-improvement opportunities and to match coaches to a level of coaching commensurate with their ability. Importantly, VSOs must ensure that they do not create an organizational culture in which winning is emphasized over all other elements of the sport experience. Stewart and Taylor (2000) argued that if a coach feels that their most important role is to produce a winning team, this may result in conflict with the fun element of motivation for many participants.

Coaching career pathways

While for many 'coaching can be a very consuming, demanding and frustrating experience' (Raedeke, 2004: 333), for others it is an extremely rewarding experience and an area in which many would like to build some form of career (paid or unpaid). Coaches, more so than most other types of sport leaders, have the opportunity for a structured long-term career that can lead beyond the community level to paid involvement. The principles of the sport pyramid model applied to athletes are also relevant to sport coaches. The status of any nation as a high performing elite sport nation requires sufficient numbers of beginner coaches at the base of the pyramid in order to sustain an appropriate number of coaches who are subsequently able to negotiate the transitions to the elite level. However, the transitions are problematic for coaches because the key steps and pathways involved are less well understood than those for athletes. SPARC (2004: 4) concluded that 'clearly defined coaching career paths do not exist'.

Coaching junior sport

One of the key roles for volunteer coaches is working with young people. Coaches can act as powerful agents of socialization and have the potential to nurture a lifelong involvement in sport and physical activity or, on the other hand, turn children away from sport and towards alternative forms of leisure. Negative outcomes from sport can include undue stress, low levels of moral reasoning, overemphasis on winning, poor self-esteem, cheating, internalization of adult norms and lack of respect for others (McCallister et al., 2000). However, sport itself does not generate either positive or negative outcomes; those are largely dependent on the nature of the leadership, including coaching, encountered by participants. McEwin and Dickinson (1996: 218) suggested that coaches can shape the quality of adolescents' experiences in sport and can create 'negative reactions for life' when harmony, teamwork, safety and mutual respect are not incorporated as central features of the programme. In a study of 221 female athletes from a rural high school, the most favoured coaches were described in terms such as fun, nice, listened to and understood players, encouraging and pushing the team to do its best. Least favourite coaches were described as mean, rude, unfair, not encouraging, negative and too strict (Stewart and Taylor, 2000). Lee et al. (2000) found in a study of youth sport participants that the most important values were enjoyment and personal achievement and the least important was winning. This result was consistent across gender, age, sport type and level of performance subgroups. However, adults and children often have different views about sport and many criticisms of sport have focused on the impact of adult values on children (Wiersma and Sherman, 2005). For example, Martin *et al.* (2001) found that children, more so than parents, preferred coaches who allowed time for the athletes to develop team spirit and friendships, were able to perform the skills and kept athletes active during training.

There have been concerns about the quality of leadership within the sport system and nature of 'qualifications' for sport coaches, especially those working in junior sport, for a considerable period of time. A number of authors (e.g. Yeager, 1979; Martens, 1978) were extremely critical of the behaviour of coaches and Quain (1989) suggested that given the lack of training of many coaches and officials involved with sport, it is surprising that there are any positive outcomes for youth sport participants. McCallister *et al.* (2000) found that the great majority of coaches had no formal training and Clark (2000: 55–56) argued that in the US 'the majority of coaches are people whose only credentials are being parents, liking children, or having an interest in sport'. Wiersma and Sherman (2005) reported that research consistently found that coaching behaviours influence the quality of youth sport participation. Trained coaches have more positive influences on the elements of enjoyment, social cohesion and development of self-esteem of members of their teams than untrained coaches. Coaches who have been trained in supportiveness and instructional effectiveness have been evaluated more positively by their players and players also reported that they had more fun in the team (Smoll *et al.*, 1993). Positive outcomes for sport participants are most likely to occur in the presence of appropriate supervision and leadership (Coalter *et al.*, 2000). It appears that positive impacts for sport participants are likely to occur when sport is supervised by trained quality coaches and officials, with an appropriate orientation towards participation rather than 'win at all costs'. However, according to Clark (2000) most coaches in the US probably base their approach on observations of the behaviour of others including their own experiences as a participant. Such actions may result in liability exposure for both coaches and VSOs and:

> At best, the aspiring coach is ill-prepared . . . but finds a way to muddle through without doing too much damage. At worst, the person makes poor decisions or acts inappropriately. As a result, athletes and coaches drop out, game officials are needlessly abused . . . and parents are forced to look elsewhere for their children's recreation and instruction . . . .
> (Clark, 2000: 56)

Coach education programmes

Volunteer coaches must accept the responsibility for providing positive sport experiences and equally, VSOs must 'ensure that coaches are prepared and able to do so' (Wiersma and Sherman, 2005: 337). An important part of becoming prepared for the coaching role is appropriate education. However, the problematic nature of compulsory training and certification in the nonprofit sector and associated impacts on volunteer recruitment and retention were noted in Chapter 1. Wiersma and Sherman (2005: 325) reported that in the US 'most of the 2.5–3 million coaches of nonschool-based youth sport teams have no formal training or education in developmentally appropriate coaching practices'. Furthermore, they argued that the lack of training for youth sport coaches reflects a common view that anyone can coach. Despite these concerns there is little doubt there are increasing expectations by VSOs, sport participants and the public, that coaches should acquire qualifications and become accredited.

The importance of appropriate training for coaches has been recognized in a number of countries where longstanding comprehensive coach education policies and programmes have been developed. The value attached to coach education is further evident in the number of countries that in recent years have evaluated these programmes and/or developed new policies and approaches in coach education. SPARC (2004) recently released a national coaching strategy that argued that because New Zealand could not compete with other countries on the basis of the level of funding support for sport or the sheer numbers of sport participants, coaching quality was the key to international success: 'The quality of our coaching, therefore, must be a significant point of difference when compared to the rest of the world' (SPARC, 2004: 3). SPARC identified a number of problems with the coaching environment in New Zealand. These included:

- inconsistent standards and a lack of recognition and status for coaches;
- a lack of clearly defined coaching career pathways;
- variable quality in coach development, education, leadership and performance;
- insufficient access by coaches to research advice;
- a lack of structured networking opportunities and support structures;

SPARC consulted widely with coaches to develop a strategy to create a world-class coaching environment in New Zealand. The resulting New Zealand Coaching Strategy 2004 has parallels with the National Officiating Strategy (see Chapter 9) and focused on three main objectives:

- increase and improve both the quality and quantity of time for coaches to focus on coaching and coach education;
- increase the recognition and status of coaches to ensure they are valued and that coaching is seen as rewarding;
- continually improve the quality of the coach education process and ensure that there are ongoing pathways for coach development.

Importantly SPARC also developed a range of key implementation principles for the strategy, one of which was 'simplicity'. SPARC was conscious of the time pressures on volunteers and stated that 'all outcomes resulting from this strategy will be simple in their design and easy to administer and maintain' (2004: 8).

A report into sports coaching in the UK was part of a broader 'initiative to bring about significant improvements in sports coaching provision in the UK' (Sports Coach UK, 2004: 1). The report found that around 38 per cent (420,000) of coaches in the UK 'claim to hold a formal qualification in the sport that they coach' whereas sport NGBs recognized approximately 400,000 qualified coaches. This discrepancy is likely due to school providers not being included in the NGB figures. Male coaches were four times more likely than females to hold a coaching qualification. The report also indicated that during 2001/2002 around 31,000 coaches and teachers attended Sports Coach UK programmes and a further 15,570 were involved in workshops conducted by 'Premier Coaching Centres'.

Of the 595,000 Australians who were involved as a coach, instructor or teacher in sport during 2004, 328,000 (55 per cent) had a coaching qualification (ABS, 2005a). While this figure ranked third behind medical support (93 per cent) and referees/umpires (57 per cent) it was well ahead of the next category, committee member or administrator (30 per cent). Coaches, even at the volunteer entry level, require a coaching qualification and most coach education programmes involve a series of steps consistent with the levels recognized in the sport pyramid structure. For example, the NCAS incorporates four tiers. In the first stage, coaches participate in an initial orientation to coaching. This is a non-accredited experience focusing on children's and youth sport requiring a commitment of 4–6 hours. Coaches can then move on to Level 1, 2 or 3 qualifications that are analogous to the pyramid structure. Level 1, aimed at beginner coaches, requires 14.5 hours of instruction on coaching principles and sport-specific issues and 30 hours of coaching practice. Accreditation normally requires three months. Level 2, which targets intermediate coaches, involves 65.6 hours of instruction on coaching principles and sport-specific matters plus 60 hours of coaching practice. Accreditation normally takes about six months. Level 3 involves a total of 100 hours of instruction on coaching theory and practice together with 100 hours of coaching practice. Accreditation normally takes about 18 months. This model is typical of coaching education programmes in a number of other countries. SPARC has a similar system beginning with Level 0 progressing through to Level 3. Level 0 involves basic coaching concepts such as the role of the coach, sport for everyone, communication, skill teaching and learning, sport safety and planning. In the US, coach education programmes are provided through a range of organizations. According to Wiersma and Sherman (2005) these programmes cover areas such as: medical; legal; growth, development and learning; training, conditioning and nutrition; social and psychological aspects of coaching; coaching techniques; teaching and administration; and professional preparation and development.

Coaches operate within sport systems that reflect certain values. At the risk of over generalizing, many sport delivery systems have the twin goals of participation and performance. However, it appears that most coach education programmes have tended to reflect mainly the latter and emphasize sports science with minimal coverage of broader socio-emotional aspects of sport participation, especially those relevant to children. Jones (2000) argued that the education of coaches has evolved along developmental lines focusing on the bio-scientific principles of athlete development. SPARC (2004: 5) suggested that one issue that needed to be addressed in New Zealand was the 'emphasis on the scientific approach to coaching rather than the practice of coaching'. The focus on sport science tends to reflect an instrumental/functionalist view of sport, with an unstated performance focus. While there is some rhetoric in support of and policies aimed at increasing sport participation at the community level, they also frequently tend to reflect an underlying performance objective. This approach focuses on keeping the base as broad as possible in order to ensure the largest number of potential champions flow through to the top, rather than emphasizing the non-instrumental benefits of sport participation (i.e. fun, sport as an important goal in itself or as a form of leisure). However, McEwin and Dickinson (1996) argued that sport participation is usually a positive experience when coaches are knowledgeable about the developmental aspects of adolescents and perhaps more so than technical knowledge of the game and of sport science. Reinforcing this point Quinn and Carr (1998) advocated that a new national youth coaching education programme for soccer (football) in the US would be based on a child development perspective as opposed to teaching specific technical aspects of the game. The underlying philosophy was 'the game in the child' rather than 'the child in the game'.

Coach education programme evaluation

Although a number of coach education and development programmes have been in operation for considerable periods of time, it is not clear how effective such programmes are in modifying coach behaviour, encouraging long-term engagement in coaching or helping to establish career pathways to assist coaches with the desire to make the transition from the base to elite levels. While Woodman (1994 cited in ASC, 2001a) asserted that NCAS accreditation in Australia leads to better coaching, enhanced enjoyment for coaches and athletes, a decreased risk of litigation, better sports knowledge and increased competence and confidence as a coach, the ASC (2001a: 7) concluded that 'there was very little evidence that sustains these claims'. One problem with large scale education programmes is that not all coaches are the same nor will they return to the same type of contexts. Furthermore, some research has indicated that there may be variations in course delivery quality and content in large scale coach education programmes. Gilbert and Trudel (1999) when testing a procedure for evaluating coaching courses in Canada found that the course was not delivered as designed, no new knowledge was gained and that there was very little change in the coach's instructional behaviours after the course. However, in other jurisdictions there is some evidence supporting coach education programmes. In the UK, the standard of coaching was generally perceived to be satisfactory with 81 per cent of those who had received coaching indicated that the standard was 'good' (Sports Coach UK, 2004). The ASC (2001a: 2) reported that an evaluation of the NCAS found 'a general perception that the NCAS is effective and is raising the standard of coaching in Australia'. More specifically the evaluation study found that accreditation courses:

- in general, met the immediate needs of coaches;
- provide a range of benefits to coaches, particularly the facilitation of networking and the exchange of ideas and knowledge;
- provide skills that are in excess of those obtained through playing and occupational experiences.

Major recommendations emerging from the report included the development of post-course education opportunities, assessment and mentoring programmes and the establishment of formal peer networks. These recommendations were consistent with those suggested by Wiersma and Sherman (2005: 336) who found that while US coaches 'recognized the value of formal coaching education . . . participants also recommended less formal approaches to preparation, such as mentoring between veteran and novice coaches, [and] roundtable discussions in which coaches have an opportunity to discuss and brainstorm'. The ASC (2001b) also identified a number of perceived barriers to accreditation including costs, geographical location of potential attendees, other personal commitments such as family and work and the perceived difficulty gap between accreditation levels.

Concluding comments

Coaches play a significant role in the provision of quality sport experiences and hence help shape the values and attitudes towards sport and participation patterns of those with whom they interact, especially children. To do so effectively coaches must adopt appropriate ethical standards and act as suitable role models. If sport is not enjoyable, young people will not continue to participate, nor are they likely to develop an appropriate attitude towards sport and physical activity that may encourage lifelong participation. Children commonly report 'to have fun' as the most important reason for involvement in sport, yet the sport system, mainly as manifested through sport coaches, frequently fails to deliver this goal in a consistent and comprehensive manner. It is likely that the dominance of the sport experience by adult values is a major contributing factor. While coach education programmes can result in positive outcomes for coaches and sport participants, the issue of certification and accreditation remains problematic in the nonprofit sport sector. The need to formalize and 'professionalize' the coaching qualifications of those involved in sport coaching is acknowledged. However, this process should not impact on the basic enjoyment of participants nor be so onerous that it acts as a disincentive for volunteers, especially young volunteer coaches.

Chapter 11

Sport event volunteers

International multi-sport events such as the Olympic, Paralympic and Commonwealth Games rely on significant numbers of volunteers to deliver core event services. Without their efforts, organizations such as the IOC and the CGF could not afford to sustain the scale and scope of these global events (Green and Chalip, 2004). Similarly, national and state/provincial event organizers and VSOs utilize the knowledge and skills of event volunteers to administer competitions, liaise with visiting teams, work with media and security organizations, manage hospitality and catering services, and provide numerous other services for athletes, sponsors, spectators and other organizations associated with sport events. The purpose of this chapter is to explore the importance and significance of sport event volunteers, and the unique management environment of sport events that involve large numbers of volunteers. The chapter comprises four parts: first, sport events, the organizations that manage them and the scope of sport event volunteering; second, the roles of event volunteers; third, the unique aspects of sport event volunteers and the nature of the sport event volunteer experience; and fourth, the implications for working with sport event volunteers.

Sport events and volunteers

The size and level of sophistication of sport events can vary enormously. Sport events can be 'held annually or more frequently, conducted on a single day or over a number of days, staged in a single venue or multiple venues, focused on one sport or recreation activity or involve a variety of activities' and can be conducted for participants of differing age groups or abilities (ASC, 2000a: 3). Arthur (2004: 322) argued that an all-encompassing definition of a special event 'has proved difficult to achieve, largely due to the scope of events in existence'. For the purpose of this chapter sport events are defined as any event where sporting activity or competition is the focus. These include finals of sporting competitions, multi-sport events such as the Olympic or Commonwealth Games, or single-sport state/provincial, national or international level championships. Such a definition excludes events such as parades, fairs and other community activities. Additionally, the focus of the chapter is on the role of volunteers within sport events, thus the discussion focuses on those events that require a significant volunteer labour force.

It is necessary to also make a distinction between sport event organizations and VSOs. Sport event organizations such as the IOC or the CGF exist primarily to facilitate multi-sport events whereas VSOs exist to govern and manage the affairs of a discrete membership engaged in regular sporting activity or competition. While both types of organizations rely on volunteers to sustain their operations and deliver core services, the nature of the volunteer experience and the relationships between organizations and volunteers differ. These differences and the implications for the management of volunteers within the context of sport events are the focus of this chapter.

The scale of volunteer involvement in major sport events is significant. Volunteer numbers for the 2000 and 2004 summer Olympic Games exceeded 40,000 and 45,000, respectively, while the 2006 Commonwealth Games in Melbourne, Australia, and the 2006 Asian Games in Doha, Qatar, each utilized more than 15,000 volunteers. Single-sport events such as the 2007 Rugby World Cup (3,000 volunteers) and the 2007 ICC Cricket World Cup (3,500 volunteers) will also depend on considerable numbers of volunteers even though many of the competitors and their associated staff are professionals. Ironically, major sport events are not financially sustainable without the use of volunteer labour yet many competitors and event organizers are paid high salaries.

Solberg (2003) explored the economic contribution of volunteers to major sport events, in particular the value of volunteer work at the 1999 World Ice Hockey Championship. This was a two-week event with 16 national teams playing 49 matches, in front of more than 175,000 spectators. The 800 volunteers involved with the event worked more than 71,000 hours, the majority during the event period. Most volunteers took paid leave or used their leisure time to volunteer at the event, with the result that the event had little impact on the displacement of goods and services in the formal economy. The study concluded that the services provided by volunteers had a high market value. Solberg (2003: 24) also found that there was 'a net increase in people's motivation to work with other events and other kinds of voluntary work' and that, overall, volunteer involvement in the event did not adversely affect the supply of volunteers for other forms of sporting activity.

Sport events such as Olympic Games or World Cup tournaments in major sporting codes and often referred to as 'mega' or 'hallmark' events are supported by governments and communities both directly (e.g. finance) and indirectly (e.g. sport infrastructure) for the so-called legacies they create. These benefits may be 'economic, social, physical, cultural, technical or psychological in nature' (Ritchie, 2001: 156). The most obvious legacies are the physical infrastructure created to host such events such as new stadia, improved public transport systems and public housing. Economic benefits from increased tourism activity and capacity to host further events are also common reasons cited to support the public funding and support for hosting sport events. Ritchie (2001: 156) argued that some of the most valuable benefits of hosting major events may be psychological or social in nature and cited the example of the 1998 winter Olympics in Calgary, Canada, which enjoyed an 'enhanced international awareness/image of the city'. In addition, 'the strengthened social structure related to the strengthening of community volunteerism were regarded as perhaps the most valuable of all the legacies left behind by this highly successful event' (Ritchie, 2001: 156). This legacy has provided the city of Calgary with momentum to build 'strong social networks that have inspired the desire and confidence to pursue the hosting of more mega-events' (Ritchie, 2001: 160). This overwhelmingly positive view is balanced by critics such as Mules (1998: 42) who found that unless allied sectors that benefit as a result of major events, such as tourism, are encouraged to contribute to the costs of hosting events, 'it is difficult to avoid the conclusion that the taxpayer is generally the loser in the hosting of major sporting events'. Sandy *et al.* (2004: 292) argued that 'public sector support for major sporting events is a highly contentious issue . . . [and that] . . . economic theory casts doubt on the likelihood of a substantial windfall for the host city for such events'. In addition, there has been very little research focused on the long-term impacts of large scale sport events in supposed legacies such as maintaining or improving volunteer participation rates in VSOs.

Sport event volunteer roles

Gladden *et al.* (1998) identified the following critical sport event management functions: finance and budgeting, risk management and insurance, tournament operations, registration, marketing and volunteer management. Within the context of a specific sport event, volunteers may be involved in any of these areas. Gladden *et al.* (1998: 340) conceptualized volunteer management for sport events as comprising two areas: '(1) working with event organizers and staff to determine the areas and quantity of volunteers that are needed, and (2) soliciting, training, and managing the volunteers'. The specific issues associated with recruiting, training and managing sport event volunteers are explored later in this chapter. Sport event volunteers may be involved in various areas of event management and operations, including:

- team management and liaison;
- media roles;
- catering and hospitality;
- marketing;

- venue management;
- crowd control;
- finance and budgeting;
- risk management;
- first aid provision;
- event operations;
- registration;
- volunteer supervision and management.

These diverse roles require a range of skills, experiences, knowledge and, in some cases, accreditation or specialized training. The degree of complexity of these roles will vary according to the type, duration and size of the event, and the anticipated number of participants and spectators. Some roles require very little preparation while others, such as venue management or team liaison, may require volunteers to be involved for long lead times prior to the event period.

Most studies of sport event volunteers provide a brief description of the demographic profile of groups of volunteers, with little analysis or critical examination of the implications for volunteer management. In addition comparisons with non-event volunteer characteristics are rarely reported. Treuren and Monga (2002a) examined the demographic characteristics of volunteers from four events and found that men and women had higher propensity to volunteer depending upon the nature of the event. They also found that sport event volunteers, like most sport volunteers, are more likely than the general population to be highly educated and come from professional occupations. However, they concluded that 'special event volunteers can have significantly different demographic features to that suggested by the volunteering literature' (Treuren and Monga, 2002a: 296).

Issues related to sport event volunteers

Much of the research into volunteer motivation, satisfaction, commitment, performance and retention has been undertaken in the context of sport events and organizations with paid staff in which the programme management approach is the dominant volunteer management paradigm (see Chapter 7). The episodic nature of volunteering for sport events has a number of implications for these elements of volunteering.

Volunteer motivation

In one of the first published studies of volunteer motivations within a sport event context, Andrew (1996: 24) concluded that 'individuals will be attracted by and expect different material and personal incentives when volunteering for a cause'. This implies that sport event managers need to be cognizant of the variety of motivations that might exist among their volunteer labour force and hence should utilize a diversity of management techniques to sustain these motivations over the duration of an event.

Farrell *et al.* (1998: 288–289) argued that sport event organizers should understand volunteer motives in order to 'respond effectively to management needs in the areas of recruitment, retention, and daily operations'. In addition, if event organizers managed volunteer experiences appropriately, such investment would pay dividends for the 'maintenance of a strong volunteer base in the community for future events' (Farrell *et al.*, 1998: 289). The results of their study suggested that the motivation of sport event volunteers differed from sport volunteers in other settings and sport event volunteers could be grouped into four categories: purposive, solidary, external traditions, and commitments. The first two of these motivations are similar to the incentives identified by Knoke and Prensky (1984) discussed in Chapter 7. Purposive motivation is based on a desire to do something useful and contribute to a society or community, while solidary motivation was based on the need for social interaction, group identification and networking. These two categories matched those originally proposed by Caldwell and Andereck (1994) as incentives for volunteering. The additional factors identified in the study, external traditions (an emphasis on extrinsic motivations) and commitments (expectations from others for volunteering) were the lowest ranked in terms of importance to event volunteers. In other words, the nature of sport events and the volunteer experiences they provide attracted individuals for different reasons than those that are important to the longer-term volunteer roles typical of VSOs. Slaughter (2002) supported these findings but argued that the motivations of sport event volunteers may change over time. Sport event volunteers involved on a long-term basis tend to volunteer their time in order to give something back to the community rather than a need for social interaction or networking, which may have been part of the initial motivation to be involved in a sport event.

The uniqueness of the event and affinity with the sport are important reasons volunteers continue an association with a sport event over a long period of time. Coyne and Coyne (2001) found initial volunteer motivations were based on identifiable personal rewards but these changed over time as volunteers remained involved in successive events. It would appear that sport event volunteer motives are related to the length of time they have been associated with a particular event.

Ralston *et al.* (2004: 13) investigated the expectations of volunteers in the lead up to the 2002 Manchester Commonwealth Games, an event that utilized more than 10,500 volunteers, 'the largest volunteer workforce in the UK in recent decades'. Ralston *et al.* (2004: 15) reported that sport event volunteering 'tends to be sporadic and episodic and is highly dependent on the availability of tangible and intangible incentives and awards to attract and motivate volunteers'. Other factors identified by Ralston *et al.* (2004) that influence volunteer motivations included:

- a feeling of connectedness with something special;
- an empathy with the spirit or philosophy of the event;
- general commitment as local and national citizens;
- support for an event that leads to the development and image of a local community, region or nation;
- volunteers' expectations of the experience itself.

Ralston *et al.* (2004) found that 2002 Manchester Commonwealth Games volunteers were motivated by three factors: altruism, involvement and the uniqueness of the event per se. These factors have a direct impact on how volunteers should be recruited and trained, and in shaping volunteer expectations of the particular roles, they may play in an event. A study by Reeser *et al.* (2005) of the motivations of polyclinic volunteers (medical and allied health professionals) at the 2002 Salt Lake City winter Olympic Games yielded similar results to Ralston. Despite the specialized nature of their roles, the highest ranking motivating factors for polyclinic volunteers were a sense of altruism, wanting to be involved in working with a variety of people and elite athletes, and to feel part of a unique event. Reeser *et al.* (2005) concluded that polyclinic volunteers were motivated by a complex process they described as enlightened self-interest, where volunteer motives were not solely altruistic but based on a sense of reciprocity, with identifiable benefits accruing not just to the event organizers and participants but to the volunteers themselves.

In summary, from the relatively small number of studies conducted on the motivations of sport event volunteers several conclusions can be made: first, the variety of motivations held by sport event volunteers suggest they should not be treated as a homogeneous group; second, sport event volunteers tend to be motivated for reasons that differ from volunteers involved in VSOs on an ongoing basis; and third, these motivations may change over time for volunteers involved repeatedly in the same event.

Volunteer satisfaction

The concept and determinants of volunteer satisfaction were the focus of a study by Elstad (1997) who investigated volunteers involved with the 1994 winter Olympic Games in Lillehammer. Respondents in the study indicated a high level of satisfaction with their volunteer experience. Their satisfaction was based on the opportunity to expand their personal network, to be part of the event, and to achieve a desired level of job competence. Farrell *et al.* (1998) found that volunteer satisfaction was related to the level of communication between volunteers that was facilitated by the event organizers, and the recognition afforded individual volunteer efforts. Importantly, Farrell *et al.* (1998: 298) concluded that 'volunteer satisfaction with the experience overall is not only a function of fulfilling their expectations, but is also related to their satisfaction with the facilities and the organization of the event'. In other words, the way sport event volunteers are managed has a direct bearing on their level of satisfaction. Reeser *et al.* (2005) supported this view and concluded that feedback on performance and recognition of volunteer efforts by event managers has a significant effect on the level of volunteer satisfaction.

Volunteer commitment, performance and retention

While the reported studies of volunteer motives, expectations and satisfaction go some way to explaining the nature of the volunteer experience within the context of sport events, they do not explain the behaviour of sport event volunteers. Cuskelly *et al.* (2004) investigated the behavioural dependability of sport event volunteers in a number of sport event contexts. Behavioural dependability was defined as the extent to which the performance and attendance of sport event volunteers met or exceeded the expectations of event organizers. Using the theory of planned behaviour as a framework, the authors argued that the duration of an event and subsequent expectations placed upon volunteers by event organizers as well as support from family and friends of event volunteers were important determinants of the behavioural dependability of sport event volunteers. Cuskelly *et al.* (2004: 87) concluded that 'understanding and influencing the behaviour of major event volunteers is more complicated than ensuring that the motives of volunteers are satisfied by event organizers'. Event managers should not ignore the likelihood that sport event volunteers will maintain their intrinsic motivation through 'enjoyment of the activity of volunteering, interacting socially with other volunteers and event participants, and contributing to the larger social good', elements that are largely outside the control of sport event organizers (Cuskelly *et al.*, 2004: 87).

Working with sport event volunteers

Differences between sport event and VSO volunteers' motivation, satisfaction and commitment have several implications for sport event volunteer performance and retention. These factors require them to be managed in slightly different ways than volunteers in ongoing roles within VSOs. As discussed in Chapter 7, traditional HRM is based on the assumption that the motives, needs and interests of volunteers can be matched with the strategic and operational requirements of VSOs. The same logic can be applied to the context of sport events, except there are differences in the timeframes over which the HRM processes can be applied. A further assumption of the HRM approach to managing volunteers is that the commitment, satisfaction and ultimately the performance and retention of sport event volunteers are logical outcomes of appropriately deployed HRM practices. The differences in volunteer motives and the antecedents of satisfaction and commitment require HRM processes such as recruitment, selection, orientation, training, development, performance management, recognition and reward of volunteers to be adapted for the strategic and operational contexts of particular sport events.

As discussed earlier, Farrell *et al.* (1998) argued that the way sport event volunteers are managed has a direct bearing on their level of satisfaction. Specifically, event managers need to focus on providing volunteers with 'positive experiences during the event, particularly in the areas of operations and facilities' (Farrell *et al.*, 1998: 298). These areas are generally under the control of event managers so it is important they devote effort to those aspects of the volunteer experience that will directly impact on volunteer satisfaction and the likelihood of volunteers returning for subsequent events.

The success of most sport events relies on recruiting adequate numbers of appropriately motivated and skilled volunteers. Pegg (2002: 266) argued that 'the success of future voluntary action will depend upon organizations enhancing volunteer participation' and that this can be achieved by 'attracting and recruiting new volunteers, supporting and training them and importantly, by channelling the many different values, motivations and contributions of volunteers such that they are personally satisfied with their participation'. Pegg (2002) investigated how to match sport event volunteer motivations with elements of the volunteer experience by using the six elements of the Volunteer Job Satisfaction Scale: contingent rewards, nature of supervision, operating conditions, co-workers, nature of the work itself, and communication. From a traditional HRM perspective, sport event managers may be able to use the scale to identify volunteers' preferences in order to assist matching individuals' needs and expectations with the most appropriate volunteer roles. For example, the scale could be administered to volunteers and the results used to reassign volunteers to particular roles that offer them more attractive rewards, better role design or improved opportunities to work with other volunteers or in other work settings.

An important part of the HRM process is the induction of volunteers into the roles and responsibilities of specific volunteer positions at a sport event. The induction process is particularly important in the context of sport events that share the characteristics of pulsating organizations, where volunteer numbers increase substantially in the lead up to an event, peak and then decrease rapidly (Hanlon and Cuskelly, 2002). Induction in most organizations with a stable workforce tends to occur on an individual basis, whereas 'induction is more likely to be performed on a group basis at pulsating major sport event organizations, due to the influx of personnel over a limited time' (Hanlon and Cuskelly, 2002: 232). In order to manage the group induction process Hanlon and Cuskelly (2002) recommended the use of comprehensive induction manuals, group induction sessions involving presentations and training elements, and a range of specific checklists, venue tours and documentation to facilitate volunteers' understanding of sport event operations and the specific roles of newly appointed volunteers.

It is commonly acknowledged that high levels of personnel turnover are normally associated with poor organizational performance, ineffectiveness and instability in the workforce. High turnover rates also impose additional recruitment and training costs on organizations. Retention of sport event volunteers in the lead up to major sport events, during events and between the staging of a series of events, present sport event organizations with some significant challenges. Hanlon and Jago (2004) asserted that specific retention strategies should be employed by sport event organizations to maximize their retention of volunteers. Volunteer departures in the lead up stage to an event can threaten its viability as the preparatory work in event planning, staff and volunteer training, and development of operational systems is largely dependent on a stable workforce. Volunteer departures and low levels of behavioural dependability during the staging of an event are even more problematic for event operations. For seasonal sport events that depend on core volunteers returning each year, higher volunteer retention rates minimizes the time and financial costs required to recruit and train a new volunteer labour pool each year.

The transitory nature of major sport events with distinct operating stages requires event managers to utilize a variety of retention strategies at each of the pre-, during and post-event stages. Hanlon and Jago (2004) recommended a number of volunteer retention strategies for sport event organizers for each of these stages. In the pre-event stage, organizers should emphasize the status of the event, ensure the timing of the event suits the majority of volunteers (although this may be impractical), implement recognition schemes, and develop a sense of ownership among volunteers by involving them in event planning and other decisions. During the event, particularly events of more than several days duration, investing time in debriefing volunteers on issues associated with their roles and the efficacy of the support provided to them was recommended. In the immediate post-event period social functions designed to thank volunteers and recognize them for their efforts were considered effective. Post-event functions also present an opportunity to conduct debriefing sessions to gather feedback from volunteers regarding event operations and support provided to volunteers. In addition, organizers of seasonal sport events should attempt to maintain regular contact with their volunteer workforce through such things as sending birthday cards, event newsletters, surveying their requirements for subsequent events or promoting other volunteer opportunities.

Treuren and Monga (2002b) argued that the majority of volunteers involved in special events (including sport events) run on a regular or annual basis are repeat volunteers. In addition, they asserted that these volunteers are sourced from organizations related to the event organization, through the social networks of previous volunteers, or from prior participants. This suggests that 'a combination of targeted recruitment and planned training' may substantially increase the effectiveness and efficiency of volunteer recruitment efforts for sport events (Treuren and Monga, 2002b: 226). In addition, sport event organizers should recognize that if the majority of their volunteers are repeat volunteers or that their involvement is part of a long-term 'career' in volunteering at sport events, then the typical sport event volunteer will be familiar with many of volunteer management practices utilized previously. This suggests that organizers of sport events that are held on a regular or annual basis need to be innovative in how they manage volunteers to avoid dissatisfaction with volunteer management and support practices.

Many sport events are also highly commodified, generating significant revenues from the sale of broadcast rights, tickets and merchandise. Despite often high revenues, these events are dependent on large numbers of volunteers to fulfil key roles as officials, administrators, team and athlete support personnel and, in some cases, undertake significant responsibilities in ensuring the safety of event participants and spectators. Volunteers in these roles have been described as being involved in 'serious leisure' – leisure that takes place in a defined social world, with identifiable social contacts, within lifestyles that accommodate the leisure activity, in association with a variety of small groups, and in some cases focuses on a collective activity (Stebbins, 1996). Sustained involvement in volunteering roles associated with serious leisure pursuits have been defined as 'career volunteering' where volunteers seek satisfaction through contributing to their own wellbeing or that of the general community (Stebbins, 1996). Harrington et al. (2000: 445) identified volunteers at motorsport events as taking part in 'the collective provision of a mutually-valued phenomenon, the motorsport race' where their volunteer involvement 'makes possible the spectator sport/entertainment that corporate stakeholders invest in and control to profitable advantage'. The rewards that volunteers receive from their involvement assist them to sustain their 'career' as a volunteer at the events. However, the study by Harrington et al. (2000: 445) found that career volunteers with specialist skills that organizers rely on to conduct motorsport events 'resent the treatment and lack of appreciation they are afforded by organizers'. This can be addressed through better volunteer management practices that focus on providing better recognition and organizational support to sport event volunteers. However, sport events of this type that become dominated by corporate interests run the risk of exacerbating the 'contrast between the economic and social interests of the various sets of members in motorsport . . . [that] . . . will lead to a less willing and less available volunteer base in the future' (Harrington et al., 2000: 445).

The issues of working with and managing sport event volunteers should also be considered in light of the quality and capability of sport event organizations. In an analysis of the UK event management industry, Harris (2004: 108) contended that 'there remains little coordination, coherence, or understanding about what is required to be fully professionalized'. While this view relates to the wider event management industry, it could be said that while there are many examples of successful sport events involving large numbers of volunteers, the major sport event industry is in its infancy. Consequently, there remains much to be learnt about how best to work with and manage volunteers in the context of sport events, and how volunteer management practices should be adapted according to the scale, nature, duration and purpose of specific sport events as well as the expectations and motives of volunteers. This lack of detailed theoretical and applied knowledge of sport event volunteers was highlighted in a review of reported event management research by Harris *et al.* (2001) who noted that only 4.2 per cent of Australian articles and 3 per cent of articles published internationally focused primarily on the issue of volunteers in events. The study of volunteering within the context of sport events offers many opportunities for both conceptual and empirical research.

Concluding comments

Volunteers are fundamental to the success of international multi-sport events such as the Olympic, Paralympic and Commonwealth Games as well as sport events at the local, state/provincial and national level. Sport event organizers rely on the knowledge and skills of event volunteers to administer competitions, liaise with visiting teams, work with media and security organizations, manage hospitality and catering services, and provide services for athletes, sponsors, spectators and other event stakeholders. The scale of volunteer involvement in sport events is significant, enabling major sport events to create the potential for a range of economic, social, physical, cultural, technological and psychological legacies. The unique environment of sport events, in particular their episodic nature and the increasing commodification of major sport events, has a number of implications for volunteer motivation, satisfaction, commitment, performance and retention. Consequently these differences in volunteer motives and the antecedents of satisfaction and commitment require volunteer management practices to be adapted to particular sport event contexts.

Chapter 12

Future challenges in working with sport volunteers

Volunteers and VSOs are at the core of the sport system to the extent that most organized sport participants have had and will continue to have significant contact with sport volunteers through the course of their involvement in sport. Sport NGBs, governments at all levels and local communities are reliant on a vibrant and effective network of volunteers and VSOs to establish, develop, coordinate and sustain the delivery of a diverse range of sport experiences for individuals with a wide array of motives, abilities and preferences for participation in organized sport. It is almost inconceivable to visualize sport in the past, present or future without volunteers and VSOs. Despite its significance and importance within sport systems, the capacity and sustainability of the voluntary sport sector is facing increasing challenges, not least from difficulties in the recruitment and retention of volunteers. These difficulties are linked in some ways to what Houlihan and White (2002) described as deep structural changes impacting on the development of sport such as equity issues, commercialization of sport, and contract-based relationships between government and sport NGBs. There is an increasing level of reliance on the voluntary sport sector as government reduces its level of direct service provision.

The purpose of this chapter is to outline significant challenges that lie ahead for sport volunteers and VSOs, discuss management practices that may stabilize or improve rates of volunteer recruitment and retention, and consider future directions for research on sport volunteers. Issues identified in the preceding chapters including the recent foci of government policy, equity issues, the roles of NGBs and professional staff, and the demands of changing legislation are discussed in relation to the pressures faced by sport volunteers. A case is made for refocusing volunteer management practices on the nature of sport volunteers' involvement and motives rather than the human resource requirements of the wider sport system. At the same time the need for change is discussed in relation to VSOs maintaining a high degree of relevance to their respective communities and the strategic directions of NGBs within a rapidly evolving and increasingly commercialized sport system.

Two overriding concerns for sport volunteers and VSOs are the increasing complexity of volunteer work and the pressures of insufficient numbers of people willing to volunteer. Research in Australia (Cuskelly *et al.*, 1998), Belgium (Verhoeven *et al.*, 1999), Norway (Enjolras, 2002; Seippel, 2002), Greece (Papadimitriou, 2002), and the UK (LIRC, 2003) indicates that the increasing complexity of volunteer work is widespread. Nichols *et al.* (2005: 36) argued that since voluntary sport clubs were first established in the mid-nineteenth century 'the competition for leisure time, enthusiasm, and expenditure has increased enormously'. The LIRC (2003) identified a range of issues that it labelled drivers for change in the voluntary sport sector. These were introduced and discussed in earlier chapters and included a more competitive leisure market, increasing service quality expectations for VSOs and responding to changing conditions in the external environment government funding, NGB strategic plans, technology and the risks of litigation. Nichols *et al.* (2005) observed that these drivers for change are placing demands on volunteers to develop improved and specialized skills during a period when volunteers and VSOs are reporting that fewer people are doing the work that needs to be done.

Government policy and funding in relation to VSOs

Over the past decade government has generally reduced its direct involvement in the delivery of social services such as sport. Simultaneously, government has recognized the importance of the sport system and, by implication, volunteers and VSOs in achieving sport policy goals. Among the high priority policy goals are increasing levels of mass participation and excellence in organized sport with the intention of engaging sport more directly in community development initiatives such as those identified in the Value of Sport Monitor (Sport England, 2005f). Government interest in sport has moved beyond merely considering sport as an activity per se, to viewing sport as a vehicle for achieving measurable outcomes for individuals, communities and society generally. A collaborative effort by Sport England, UK Sport and more recently the ASC, the Value of Sport Monitor aims to build an evidence base for the benefits of sport in relation to:

- crime reduction and community safety;
- economic impact and regeneration of local communities;
- social capacity and cohesion;
- psychological health and wellbeing;
- education and lifelong learning;
- sustainability and improved environmental quality.

As discussed in Chapter 4, Houlihan and White (2002) argued there has been a fundamental shift in government policy and funding programmes from one of deference to sport to more contract-based partnership arrangements in which government views sport funding as an investment and VSOs as a vehicle to achieve policy outcomes. Government is placing increased expectations on NGBs in particular, but on VSOs and sport volunteers as well, to deliver measurable community benefits at a time when volunteer recruitment and retention appear to be increasingly problematic.

A challenge for government is to move beyond sport policy in a broad sense and develop policy that recognizes the specific role of volunteers. Sport England (2005c) identified this as a challenge and has responded with the development of its Policy on Volunteers in Sport. Consistent with government sport policy, the volunteers in sport policy initiative recognize volunteers as one of the key facilitators of change required to achieve increased participation in sport and physical activity. Sport England's 13-point plan, contained in the policy, is based largely on increased levels of coordination and partnerships between several government departments and non-government organizations, development of accredited training for the volunteer workforce, developing pathways into volunteering for young people, researching and disseminating good practice, and encouraging better support for volunteers. Sport England's club development programme, Running Sport, is designed to assist VSOs across a range of matters including volunteer management, development planning, finance, inclusivity and partnerships.

Reducing the complexity of funding programmes is also likely to assist the development of VSOs that seek government funding assistance. Until the release of its National Framework for Sport (Sport England, 2004a) in which funding was reduced to two streams, sport funding in England was delivered through a diverse array of 75 programmes. In some cases VSOs received funding indirectly through their NGB or directly through government programmes such as the UK National Lottery or local government authorities. Whatever the source of funding, VSOs and the volunteers that run them are subject to more accountability and compliance measures, partly due to a large number of funding programmes. Having access to a large number of programmes may be a deterrent to VSOs because of the complexity of meeting the differing grant application processes and compliance standards required by separate funding programmes. Reducing the number of funding programmes may not reduce the total funds available to VSOs but may contribute to a better understanding of government policy goals and the funding mechanisms used to achieve these goals in partnership with VSOs.

Among the most significant challenges confronting VSOs and sport volunteers is responding to the demands of government policy and funding programmes without losing sight of the values and motives that encourage the involvement and interests of volunteers. The underlying problem is that government increasingly views sport organizations as a means for delivering social and other community benefits, whereas the primary interest of most sport volunteers is to be involved in the sport activity itself or to be vicariously involved through their children's participation. Sport volunteers are more likely to be inclined to view abstract social benefits, such as the development of social capacity, community cohesion and crime reduction, as a by-product of their involvement in sport rather than its primary focus. As discussed in Chapter 4, the degree of alignment between the goals and means of government and VSOs has a bearing on the nature of their relationship. Direct government funding and other support such as club development programmes are an important means for VSOs and sport volunteers to achieve their goals. At the same time, sport volunteers and VSOs are important means for government in achieving its policy goals. Confrontational relationships are likely to emerge when VSOs and government fail to agree on their respective goals. Garrett (2003) found evidence of compliance and resistance to the conditions of grants awarded from Sport England's Lottery Fund in case studies of four voluntary sport clubs. Clubs that were compliant with funding conditions adopted a sport development focus and a willingness to re-orientate their core values to align with those of the funding agency. Resistant clubs were more concerned with survival and maintaining the status quo, fearing that current volunteers would leave the organization if it embraced significant change.

The processes of compliance and resistance to the conditions of government funding programmes in VSOs are complex and defy overgeneralization. However, contemporary/formal VSOs, discussed in Chapter 2, may be better positioned than traditional/informal VSOs to capitalize on funding and other forms of assistance provided by government such as VMPs. Contemporary/formal VSOs are proactive in identifying and resolving problems, focused on development and are receptive to external assistance. Because they share or are prepared to align their goals with government they are likely to be compliant with the conditions of funding programmes. However, relationships with government are likely to be complementary rather than cooperative. Although VSOs and government may share similar goals, they have differing means of achieving their goals. VSOs rely on volunteer labour whereas government uses funding programmes. In the future, VSOs and sport volunteers are likely to face a choice of either becoming more compliant with government policy and funding programmes and risk losing some of their autonomy, or maintaining their autonomy and risk losing access to government funding. Volunteers will be faced with decisions about the extent to which they are prepared to engage in government agendas for community change in order to access government funding and support for their respective VSOs. Contemporary/formal VSOs are likely to be led by and attract volunteers prepared to embrace changes necessary to advance government agendas. Whether VSOs remain relevant to their communities is open to question. A challenge for researchers is to explore and understand how the nature of different types of relationships between government and VSOs affect the values, attitudes and, ultimately, the behaviour of sport volunteers.

Equity and diversity

A particularly important area in which government policy is impacting upon sport volunteers is the goal of eliminating discrimination and harassment in sport. Member protection policies and guidelines for harassment-free sport are encouraging VSOs to be mindful of and address harassment and discrimination in the operation of their clubs. Houlihan and White (2002) argued that there has been greater acknowledgement of equity issues in sport but cautioned that there is a distinction between an increased presence of women in sport and a shift in power in a male-dominated policy area. Statistics on sport volunteers (see Table 2.4 on p. 23) reinforce this point. Sport volunteers are more likely to be male in Australia (60 per cent), Canada (64 per cent) and England (67 per cent). Increases in the number and range of programmes targeting women and girls have largely been brought about through focused government funding programmes, particularly in the UK. Whether such programmes are able to effect fundamental or long-term change in the beliefs and values held by individuals within VSOs is yet to be validated by research. VSOs, in particular those described in Chapter 2 as contemporary/formal sport organizations, while neither distrustful of nor hostile towards external agencies, are able to exploit external assistance for their own ends. Such organizations may be adept at preparing funding submissions, accounting for the appropriation of funds against performance measures and appearing compliant with funding programme objectives without making real changes to existing decision making structures and power relationships. In contrast, VSOs described as traditional/informal organizations are mistrustful of, and unlikely to seek, external assistance. The potential for fundamental change to take root in such organizations is limited to the extent that they refrain from preparing equity and diversity programme funding submissions.

There is a need for further research into the effectiveness and long-term change in the beliefs and values of sport volunteers within VSOs that access government funds aimed at addressing issues in equity and diversity. The motives of volunteers, particularly those in decision making roles, are an important consideration. The LIRC (2003: 78) found that 'they [volunteers] will accept new initiatives if they are consistent with their own motivations'. Achievement of harassment-free sport and putting an end to discrimination based on gender, age, race, religious beliefs or social class is unlikely to occur until the cultural diversity of local communities is reflected in the membership of VSOs. A challenge facing volunteers is the realignment of recruitment practices to ensure that such practices embrace diversity to ensure that VSOs are more comprehensively connected with their local community. This is a potentially greater challenge for volunteers who are members of more traditional/informal VSOs because of their resistance to change.

Young volunteers

Sport participation rates are generally much higher among younger age groups than middle-aged and older adults, yet sport volunteering is dominated by people aged 30 to 50 years. A further challenge for VSOs is to remain relevant to their communities by keeping in step with social change. The sport system generally and VSOs in particular provide an excellent opportunity to provide teenagers and young adults with their first volunteer experience in a formal organizational setting. The extent to which VSOs are amenable to the views and lifestyles of young people is likely to be related to how successfully they can meet the challenge of continuing to be relevant both locally and globally. Attracting young people to sport volunteering is an important factor in the continued development of social capital and cohesive, inclusive communities. However, differing lifestyles, attitudes and patterns of engagement in social institutions among the younger generation suggests that the involvement and motives of young people are different to many of the existing cohort of volunteers in VSOs.

Volunteers and NGBs

Over the past decade sport NGBs have been driven increasingly by strategic rather than operational concerns. As discussed in several chapters, NGBs have been subject to an array of external influences including:

- increasing engagement in commercial activities, risk management and avoiding litigation;
- recognizing and working towards government initiatives aimed at changing governance structures and improving management practices;
- compliance with government policy and funding requirements aimed at increasing participation numbers and performance standards at the elite level.

As sport NGBs formulate, implement and review their strategic plans the important roles of VSOs and sport volunteers are recognized. Sport volunteers and VSOs are sometimes regarded as the operational arm of NGBs with significant responsibilities for the roll out of programmes designed to improve the quality and safety of sport experiences, accreditation programmes and updated training for coaches and officials, data gathering for member registration systems and insurance purposes, and other significant operational tasks. Significant shifts in strategic direction or focus at the NGB level reverberate throughout the VSOs that constitute the organization at state/provincial and local levels. It is a significant challenge for NGBs to communicate, implement, monitor and control their strategic plans at the state/provincial level, let alone in local VSOs. As discussed in Chapter 6, most VSOs are separately constituted entities which, while affiliated with a NGB, are autonomous, have their own governance structures and in some cases their own strategic priorities and operational plans. Furthermore, few VSOs are made up of employees organized into particular functional units. In the absence of clear lines of accountability for performance outcomes from NGBs through to local VSOs, what incentives and sanctions can NGBs employ to ensure compliance with strategic plans among widely dispersed sport volunteers? From the perspective of sport volunteers, the challenge is one of deciding the extent to which they are prepared to act as an agent for the achievement of broad and more abstract system level organizational goals. Volunteers are more likely to engage in these processes if NGBs plan and implement strategies that are consistent with the values, motives and interests of sport volunteers and enable volunteers to perform their roles more effectively.

Volunteers and professional staff

One of the underlying themes of this book has been the increasing complexity of the operating environment for sport organizations. Volunteers can find it difficult to cope with the demands of managing contemporary sport organizations, particularly when pushed to be more professional in servicing the needs of members and participants. As discussed in Chapter 8, sport organizations are increasingly reliant on paid staff both to develop strategies and to manage their day to day operations. The move to employ paid staff has permeated sport NGBs as well as state/provincial VSOs and to a lesser extent well-resourced local sport clubs. The relationship between volunteers and paid staff can create a further layer of complexity because many of those employed in VSOs are directly responsible to voluntary boards or committees. While paid staff have brought many benefits to sport, their incorporation into management structures and decision making processes has made the management of VSOs more challenging. A substantial amount of research evidence supports this view and also suggests that the volunteer-professional relationship can be problematic. This increasingly important relationship depends on negotiations about the distribution of power and influence in decision making. The success of this relationship is crucial to the effective management of VSOs given the need for shared leadership in this context. To some extent volunteer-professional relationships in relation to the management of NGBs and VSOs has prompted governments to initiate management improvement and governance reform programmes.

Such programmes are aimed at improving the efficiency and effectiveness of management structures and decision making processes in sport in order to keep the focus on sport participation and international competitiveness in elite sport.

The future challenge for VSOs is to maximize the benefits of the working relationships between volunteers and professional staff. These working relationships are either direct or indirect. Direct working relationships develop when a VSO hires administration or development staff to work within the organization. In these settings the challenge is to manage the many relationships that develop at individual and group levels. The performance of volunteers and professional staff and the quality of their working relationships are likely to be hindered if organizational structures are not adapted to fully integrate professional staff. Indirect working relationships operate when professional staff such as coaching or officiating development officers provide arms-length advice, assistance, direction and support in a role not dissimilar to that of a consultant or contractor. The challenge in working with volunteers through such relationships is to ensure that the culture of VSOs is clearly understood and that the services provided are relevant to the organization and the needs and interests of the volunteers responsible for its day to day management.

Volunteers and legal issues

As societies have tended to become increasingly litigious there has been a concomitant rise in the legal pressures on VSOs and volunteers. Risk is an inherent component of sport participation and sport is likely to be an area of litigation given the increasing predilection to pursue individual rights through the courts. VSOs must also cope with heightened levels of expectations of standards and quality of service due to the professionalization of sport as well as those pressures exerted by government agencies due to more complex reporting, compliance and accountability requirements. This includes areas such as child protection, member protection, harassment-free sport, volunteer screening, privacy and data security.

VSOs, therefore, have had to develop more sophisticated management and legal structures that themselves are likely to attract more legal intervention due to potential variations in interpretation and application of rules and regulations. Much of the responsibility to deal with legal pressures falls to volunteer administrators as well as those working at the front line of service delivery such as coaches and officials. One mechanism to deal with legal complexity has been to require volunteers to become more qualified through training and development programmes. For many volunteers, though these expectations are inimical to the volunteer experience. Evidence suggests that concerns about possible legal liability and the demands of working within more legally complex environments have adverse effects on volunteer recruitment and retention. Although a number of jurisdictions have introduced legislative protective measures for volunteers, their impact is yet unknown. However, if national data on volunteer trends are used as a guide, civil liability protection legislation does not appear to have ameliorated the problems of recruitment and retention to any significant degree.

A major challenge for VSOs is to continue to offer meaningful sport experiences for members and participants that do not detract from the inherent qualities of sport and yet do so in ways that protect their members and volunteers from legal action. Volunteers must be informed of the potential risks they may incur from their involvement with a VSO and be prepared to accept all the responsibilities associated with their commitment. The challenge for professional staff working both directly and indirectly with VSOs is to find effective and efficient methods to support, train, advise and assist sport volunteers in a complex legal setting.

Working with sport volunteers: refocusing on important contextual factors

The evidence on participation rates among sport volunteers suggests that recruitment and retention are becoming more challenging for the sport system given the aggregate impact of the trends observed and described throughout the book. Volunteer retention is as important to VSOs and NGBs as it is to the wider sport system and governments. Many of the volunteers who remain in a sport for a more than several years are an important and integral component of the sport system infrastructure. Long-term volunteers provide a sense of stability and a point of reference to VSOs because they usually understand, influence and convey the culture of their organizations as well as how complex structures and systems (both formal and informal) operate in their sport. They are an important conduit for the implementation of the strategic plans of sport NGBs, government policy initiatives and legislative change. Equally, volunteers can constrain or inhibit these processes if they are unwilling to adapt to changing circumstances, systems and structures. Arguably, the most significant challenge for the sport system is to find ways to work with and manage sport volunteers while finding an appropriate balance between volunteer retention and systemic change across a vast array of VSOs.

Management approaches transferred from employee-focused HRM systems to complex and detailed VMPs designed from the perspective of organizational needs may not be the most appropriate way to work effectively with and retain sport volunteers. The values, motives and commitment of volunteers in member-based sport organizations in which the work of volunteers is intended to benefit themselves, their friends and family members as well as other community members, suggests that working effectively with sport volunteers requires a stronger focus on volunteers' needs and interests. The challenge is to find appropriate and effective ways of achieving a high degree of alignment between the interests of sport volunteers, the strategic intentions of NGBs, the policy initiatives of government and other external factors. A further challenge is to stay focused on the need for sport to change and develop in ways that will ensure its continued relevance to the communities and the nations that it serves.

Working with sport volunteers to confront these future challenges requires an understanding of four key contextual factors – attraction, involvement, motivation and support. VSOs and NGBs that position themselves to understand these factors are likely to better satisfy volunteers and may increase volunteer recruitment and retention levels. This represents a paradigm shift away from the HRM approach that dominates most VMPs and which is not well researched in terms of its effectiveness in satisfying or retaining sport volunteers. HRM practices need to be applied in a way that takes into account volunteer involvement and motivation rather than simply transferring traditional HRM practices from paid work organizations. The contextual factors in working with sport volunteers discussed below are based on the theories and available research evidence discussed in earlier chapters. This discussion is speculative and is therefore in need of research itself to test its efficacy in relation to volunteer satisfaction and retention as well as organizational and individual performance outcomes.

Attraction

From a VMP and HRM perspective the recruitment challenge is to identify and match individuals with specific skills to the volunteer tasks stipulated by the organization. However, sport volunteers tend to be relationship rather than task-orientated and are not likely to be attracted to a VSO by the work that needs to be done, particularly at the attraction stage. Doherty and Carron (2003) found significant relationships between task cohesion, intention to stay and volunteer effort suggesting that task-orientation may become more important after social cohesion has developed. From an organizational perspective it is important that club members and their associates are made aware that volunteers are needed to fill particular positions. However, a potential volunteer knowing about a vacant position and being attracted to taking up a position are two quite distinct processes. It can be difficult to attract volunteers to tasks that they consider as onerous, complex, stressful or overly time-consuming. Incentives and rewards such as financial payments are being used increasingly by VSOs where it is a constant challenge to attract volunteers to positions such as officiating. There is a need to better understand the initial stages of the social and cognitive processes that influence an individual's decision to consider whether they are attracted to the prospect of volunteering for a sport organization.

Involvement

An individual attracted to a volunteer position is soon faced with a decision about the degree and extent of their involvement both in terms of the position and the social networks within a VSO. The concepts of degree (core or peripheral) and extent (short or long term) of volunteer involvement were introduced in Chapter 2. Importantly, sport volunteers are unlikely to move rapidly from peripheral to core involvement in the initial stages of taking up a volunteer position. From an organizational perspective there is a high degree of uncertainty about the continued involvement of volunteers who have recently joined and who are involved peripherally in terms of their position and their social connections with other volunteers and VSO members. There is a tendency for volunteers to be self-protective to minimize the risk of becoming over-committed to a role that is complex, demanding or requires a significant amount of their time. For some volunteers their involvement may not progress beyond the periphery of a VSO. Their decision to volunteer, like all volunteers, is reversible and if involved peripherally they are not likely to experience high personal or social costs or a substantial loss of benefits if they decide to leave. Core volunteers are often more highly involved and face more significant personal and social consequences should they decide to leave a VSO.

Motivation

Through the processes of attraction and initial involvement, volunteers and those who work with them may not have given much consideration to what motivated their decision to volunteer initially or to continue volunteering. If questioned, those who work with volunteers and those who occupy leadership positions in VSOs are not likely to have discussed in any depth what motivates volunteers, even those volunteers whom they know quite well or whom they work with quite closely. A lack of consideration about motivation to volunteer from either a volunteer or an organizational perspective should not be interpreted as motivation being perceived as unimportant to the overall operation of VSOs. Sport volunteers are unlikely to continue to volunteer unless their organization and other volunteers understand what motivates them to continue their involvement and to complete the tasks for which they have volunteered. Equally, volunteers are not likely to achieve satisfaction in their roles unless they express their personal preferences and expectations to the organization and, in turn, the organization delivers on these expectations.

Volunteer motivation has been discussed in several chapters and in relation to a number of situational factors. In broad terms volunteers are motivated by a combination of altruism and self-interest, which is given expression through utilitarian, affective and normative incentives. An understanding of volunteer motivation is beneficial to volunteers and to those who work closely with volunteers. The seasonal nature of sport suggests that while volunteers may not give much consideration to their reasons for completing the tasks associated with their role on a day to day basis, there are critical decision points when volunteers tend to revisit their reasons for volunteering. These decision points are likely to occur around the beginning or end of a sport season or event and at times when VSOs are making plans for who will be approached to fill particular positions in subsequent sport seasons or events. Most VSOs conduct annual general meetings at which time volunteers are elected, appointed or invited to fill certain positions. VSOs, particularly those that do not engage in succession planning, can face particular challenges in attracting all but the most highly involved volunteers to annual general meetings.

Support

Volunteer motives vary among volunteer roles, within individuals and are also dependent upon the extent and degree of volunteer involvement in VSOs. The recognize-reward-retain approach common to many VMPs fails to recognize the complexity of volunteer motivation. Volunteer recognition and reward schemes are a tangible and often public acknowledgement that an organization supports and values its volunteers and the work that they do for the organization. However, a decision to become more involved or to discontinue as a volunteer rests largely with the individual volunteer. Although sport organizations have minimal control over such decisions, VSOs that develop a strong culture that values volunteers and derives momentum from their efforts and ideas are likely to provide the types of support that attract, involve and motivate sport volunteers. With the numerous demands faced by VSOs there is a tendency to become complacent about the organizational practices that attract, involve, motivate and support new and continuing volunteers. A study of local community rugby clubs (Cuskelly *et al.*, 2005) found an association between the extent to which volunteer support practices were utilized by volunteer managed rugby clubs and fewer problems with volunteer retention.

Concluding statement

This book has explored the characteristics and contributions of sport volunteers as well as the settings and roles in which they work and the issues associated with managing them. In doing so, a number of important issues have been identified and examined in light of current volunteer management theories and practice. Although sport volunteers and VSOs have attracted an increasing amount of research and attention from government policy makers, there are challenges ahead.

Volunteers and VSOs are the core of sport systems in many democratic nations and are essential to the continued development and delivery of sport, particularly at the local level. Sport volunteers are the first point of contact for the vast majority of organized sport participants as they enter the sport system. For the many participants for whom sport is a pastime rather than a profession, sport volunteers are arguably their only contact with the wider sport system. Sport volunteers are increasingly being recognized as agents for social change by governments irrespective of their political ideologies. Therefore it is not a question of whether volunteers have an important and significant role to play in the sport system. The challenge is how the sport system can adapt to a rapidly changing society while continuing to value the interests and motives of volunteers and deliver high-quality organized sport in many thousands of communities.

Much of what occurs in the sport system is influenced strongly by tradition and, consequently, there is a tendency for change to be incremental. In meeting the future challenges that face VSOs and sport volunteers there is a need for greater integration between theory and practice. Current research reveals that there is a good descriptive understanding of the characteristics of sport volunteers including their age, employment, gender, years and hours volunteered but little depth in understanding the attitudes and behaviour and sport volunteers. However, greater consistency in the collection, categorization and reporting of data, and similar methods for defining informal and formal sport volunteering and club membership, would facilitate more valid and frequent comparative analysis of international datasets and volunteer trends. Even though volunteer retention has been identified as an important and ongoing problem in the sport system, there is a dearth of theory or research that has accurately modelled and predicted volunteer performance, satisfaction or retention. Much of the body of knowledge that has been used in the nonprofit sector to design research and develop theory has been adapted from work organizations. Such organizations have a number of characteristics that fundamentally differentiate them from the nonprofit sector generally and VSOs in particular. Furthermore, much of volunteer literature is based on non-member voluntary organizations; again these organizations are markedly different to member-based VSOs common to the sport system.

In order to advance knowledge and current practice in working with sport volunteers there is a need for a more complete understanding of appropriate ways to respond to many of the tensions and pressures in the current sport system, particularly those which are impacting negatively on volunteer recruitment, retention and satisfaction. VSOs and by implication sport volunteers are being pressured by government, their respective NGBs, professional staff, the legal system and the expectations of sport participants to deliver more and higher quality sport experiences. There are also increasing expectations for VSOs to deliver benefits to the wider community in return for government investment. This is occurring at a time when there are increasing problems in attracting and retaining volunteers in sport. Collins and Nichols (2005) outlined a research agenda for volunteers in sport. They developed a framework that classified a large number of research issues as 'volunteers in sport in general, sports-related NGBs, and the sports clubs run by their members' (Collins and Nichols, 2005: 120).

The future wellbeing of the voluntary sport sector may depend upon finding the right balance on a number of issues: between individual experiences sought by volunteers and the imposition of VMPs; appropriate decision making control between professional staff and volunteers; between improving the individual work performance of volunteers and their attraction to volunteering; and renewal of the sport system without negatively impacting the stability of the many thousands of VSOs integral to the system. Therefore it is critical that the sport volunteer experience is positive and rewarding in order that more people may be retained as future volunteers across a diverse array of community settings. This book has aimed to assist those working with sport volunteers to facilitate such an outcome.

Bibliography

Abrams, J., Long, J., Talbot, M. and Welch, M. (1996) 'Organisational change in national governing bodies of sport', working papers from the School of Leisure and Sport Studies, Leeds: Leeds Metropolitan University.

ABS (1996) *Voluntary Work Australia, Cat. No. 4441.0*, Canberra: Commonwealth of Australia.

ABS (2001a) *Sports Industries, Australia 2000–01, Cat. No. 8686.0*, Canberra: Commonwealth of Australia.

ABS (2001b) *Voluntary Work, Australia, Cat. No. 4441.0*, Canberra: Commonwealth of Australia.

ABS (2002a) *Year Book Australia 2000: Income and Welfare Voluntary Work in 2000*, Canberra: Commonwealth of Australia.

ABS (2002b) *Social Capital and Social Wellbeing*, Canberra: Commonwealth of Australia.

ABS (2002c) *Involvement in Organised Sport and Physical Activity, Cat. No. 6285.0*, Canberra: Commonwealth of Australia.

ABS (2002d) *Sports Industries, Australia, 2000–01, Cat. No. 8686.0*, Canberra: Author.

ABS (2003) *Employment in Sport and Recreation, Australia, Cat. No. 4148.0*, Canberra: Author.

ABS (2005a) *Involvement in Organised Sport and Physical Activity 2004, Cat. No. 6285.0*, Canberra: Commonwealth of Australia.

ABS (2005b) *Year Book Australia: Culture and Recreation: Employment and Involvement in Sports and Physical Activities*, Canberra: Author.

Ajzen, I. (1988) *Attitudes, Personality, and Behaviour*, Milton Keynes: Open University Press.

Allison, M. (2002) Sport clubs in Scotland, Research Digest no. 59, Edinburgh: Sportscotland.

Amis, J. and Slack, T. (1996) 'The size-structure relationship in voluntary sport organizations', *Journal of Sport Management*, 10: 76–86.

Amis, J., Slack, T. and Berrett, T. (1995) 'The structural antecedents of conflict in voluntary sport organizations', *Leisure Studies*, 14: 1–16.

Amis, J., Slack, T. and Hinings, C.R. (2004) 'Strategic change and the role of interests, power and organizational capacity', *Journal of Sport Management*, 18: 158–198.

Andrew, J. (1996) 'Motivations and expectations of volunteers involved in a large scale sports event: a pilot study', *Australian Leisure*, 7(1): 21–25.

Anheier, H.K. (2005) *Nonprofit Organizations: Theory, Management, Policy*, Oxford: Routledge.

Anshell, M.H. and Weinberg, R.S. (1996) 'Coping with acute stress among American and Australian basketball referees', *Journal of Sport Behaviour*, 19: 180–203.

Arai, S.M. (1997) 'Volunteers within a changing society: the use of empowerment theory in understanding serious leisure', *World Leisure and Recreation*, 39(3): 19–22.

Arthur, D. (2004) 'Sport event and facility management', in J. Beech and S. Chadwick (eds), *The Business of Sport Management*, Harlow, Essex: Prentice Hall.

ARU (2004) *Annual Report 2003*, Sydney: Author.

ASC (2000a) *Active Australia Club/Association Management Program: Legal Issues and Risk Management*, Canberra: Author.

ASC (2000b) *Volunteer Management Program*, Canberra: Author.

ASC (2001a) *A Preliminary Investigation into the Effectiveness of the National Coach Accreditation Scheme*, Canberra: Author.

ASC (2001b) *Advancement in Sport Coaching and Officiating Accreditation*, Canberra: Author.

ASC (2003) *Annual Report 2002–2003*, Canberra: Author.

ASC (2004a) *Eligibility Criteria for the Recognition of National Sporting Organisations by the Australian Sports Commission 2004–05*, Canberra: Author.

ASC (2004b) *Problems and Issues in the Recruitment and Retention of Sports Officials*, Canberra: Author.

ASC (2004c) *Annual Report 2003–2004*, Canberra: Author.

ASC (2005a) *National Officiating Accreditation Scheme*, Canberra: Author. Online. Available www.ausport.gov.au/official/noas.asp (accessed 8 August 2005).

ASC (2005b) *Ethics in Sport – Legislation*, Canberra: Author. Online. Available www.ausport.gov.au/ethics/legischild.asp (accessed 21 July 2005).

ASC (2005c) *Governance and Management Improvement Program*. Online. Available www.ausport.gov.au/ibp/gmip.asp (accessed 28 November 2005).

ASC (2005d) *Officiating*, Canberra: Author. Online. Available www.ausport.gov.au/officials.asp (accessed 29 August 2005).

ASC (2005e) *Ethics in Sport – Coaches and Officials*. Online. Available www.ausport.gov.au/ethics/coachofficial.asp (accessed 23 November 2005).

Atchley, R.C. (1989) 'A continuity theory of aging', *The Gerontologist*, 29: 183–190.

Atchley, R.C. (1999) *Continuity and Adaptation in Aging: Creating Positive Experiences*, Baltimore: Johns Hopkins University Press.

Auld, C.J. (1997a) 'Professionalisation of Australian sport administration: the effects on organisational decision making', *The European Journal for Sport Management*, 4(2): 17–39.

Auld, C.J. (1997b) 'Centralisation and decision making: the influence of executive directors, presidents and board members', paper presented at the 3rd Annual Sport Management Association of Australia and New Zealand Conference, Auckland, November 1997.

Auld, C.J. (2004) 'Behavioural characteristics of student volunteers', *Australian Journal on Volunteering*, 9(2): 8–18.

Auld, C.J. and Cuskelly, G. (2001) 'Behavioural characteristics of volunteers: implications for community sport and recreation organisations', *Australian Parks and Leisure*, 4(2): 29–37.

Auld, C.J. and Godbey, G. (1998) 'Influence in Canadian national sport organisations: perceptions of professionals and volunteers', *The Journal of Sport Management*, 12(1): 20–38.

Badcock, B. (2002) *Making Sense of Cities: A Geographical Survey*, London: Arnold.

Becker, H.S. (1960) 'Notes on the concept of commitment', *American Sociological Review*, 66: 32–42.

Brackenridge, C. (2002) '"... so what?" Attitudes of the voluntary sector towards child protection in sports clubs', *Managing Leisure*, 7(2): 103–123.

Brackenridge, C., Bringer, J., Cockburn, C. *et al.* (2004) 'The Football Association's Child Protection in Football Research Project 2002–2006: rationale, design and first year results', *Managing Leisure*, 9: 30–46.

Bramham, P. (2001) 'Sports policy', in K. Hylton, P. Bramham, D. Jackson *et al.* (eds), *Sports Development: Policy, Process and Practice*, London: Routledge, pp. 7–18.

Bridgman, P. and Davis, G. (2000) *The Australian Policy Handbook*, 2nd edn, Crows Nest, NSW, Australia: Allen & Unwin.

Caldwell, L. and Andereck, K. (1994) 'Motives for initiating and continuing membership in a recreation-related voluntary association', *Leisure Studies*, 16: 33–44.

Centre for Philanthropy and Nonprofit Studies (2003) *Current Issues Information Sheet 2003/1*, Brisbane: Queensland University of Technology.

Centre for Sport and Law (2005) *Directors and Officers Liability*, St Catherines, Ontario: Author. Online. Available www.sportlaw.ca/directorOfficers.htm (accessed 6 October 2005).

Champion, W.T. (2000) *Sports Law in a Nutshell*, 2nd edn, St Paul, MN: West Group.

Charity Commission (2005) *The Charity Commission*, Taunton: Author. Online. Available www.charity-commission.gov.uk/ (accessed 7 October 2005).

Chelladurai, P. (1999) *Human Resource Management in Sport and Recreation*, Champaign, IL: Human Kinetics.

Chelladurai, P. and Haggerty, T.R. (1991) 'Differentiation in national sport organizations in Canada', *Canadian Journal of Sport Science*, 16(2): 117–125.

Clark, M.A. (2000) 'Who's coaching the coaches?', in J.R. Gerdy (ed.) *Sport in School: The Future of an Institution*, New York: Teachers College, Columbia University.

Clary, E.G. and Snyder, M. (1991) 'A functional analysis of altruism and prosocial behaviour: the case of volunteerism', in M. Clark (ed.), *Review of Personality and Social Psychology*, Newbury Park, CA: Sage, vol. 12: 119–148.

Clary, E.G. and Snyder, M. (1999) 'The motivations to volunteer: theoretical and practical considerations', *Current Directions in Psychological Science*, 8(5): 156–159.

Clary, E.G. Snyder, M. and Ridge, R. (1992) 'Volunteers' motivations: a functional strategy for the recruitment, placement and retention of volunteers', *Nonprofit Management and Leadership*, 2(4): 333–350.

Clary, E., Snyder, M. and Stukas, A. (1996) 'Volunteers' motivations: findings from a national survey', *Nonprofit and Voluntary Sector Quarterly*, 25(4): 485–505.

Cnaan, R.A. and Cascio, T.A. (1999) 'Performance and commitment: issues in management of volunteers in human service organisations', *Journal of Social Service Research*, 24(3–4): 1–37.

Cnaan, R. and Goldberg-Glen, R.S. (1991) 'Measuring motivation to volunteer in human services', *Journal of Applied Behavioral Science*, 27(3): 269–284.

Cnaan, R.A., Handy, F. and Wadsworth, M. (1996) 'Defining who is a volunteer: conceptual and empirical considerations', *Nonprofit and Voluntary Sector Quarterly*, 25(3): 364–383.

Coalter, F. (1990) 'Analysing leisure policy', in I. Henry (ed.), *Management and Planning in the Leisure Industries*, Basingstoke: Macmillan.

Coalter, F., Allison, M. and Taylor, J. (2000) *The Role of Sport in Regenerating Deprived Urban Areas*, Edinburgh: The Scottish Office Central Research Unit.

Cohen, J. and Arato, A. (1992) *Civil Society and Political Theory*, Cambridge, MA: MIT Press.

Cohen, A. and Lowenberg, G. (1990) 'A re-examination of the side-bet theory as applied to organizational commitment: a meta-analysis', *Human Relations*, 43(10): 1015–1050.

Coleman, R. (2002) 'Characteristics of volunteering in UK sport: lessons from cricket', *Managing Leisure*, 7(4): 220–238.

Collins, M. and Nichols, G. (2005) 'Summary – An Emerging Research Agenda', in G. Nichols and M. Collins (eds), *Volunteers in Sports Clubs*, Eastbourne: LSA.

Commonwealth of Australia (2001) *Backing Australia's Sporting Ability*, Canberra, Australia: Author.

Conn, J. (2003) 'Voluntary sport and recreation associations', in D.J. Cotton and J.T. Wolohan (eds) *Law for Recreation and Sport Managers*, 3rd edn, Kendall Hunt: Dubuque.

Corrigan, M.W. (2001) 'Social exchange theory, interpersonal communication motives and volunteerism: identifying motivation to volunteer and the rewards and costs involved', unpublished Master of Arts Thesis, West Virginia University.

Coyne, B.S. and Coyne, E.J. (2001) 'Getting, keeping and caring for unpaid volunteers for professional golf tournament events: a study of the recruitment/ retention of unpaid volunteers for staging large, mass-attended, high-profile Professional Golf Association (PGA) golf tournaments', *Human Resource Development International*, 4(2): 199–214.

Curtis, J.E., Baer, D.E. and Grabb, E.G. (2001) 'Nations of joiners: explaining voluntary association membership in democratic societies', *American Sociological Review*, 66(6): 783–805.

Cuskelly, G. (1995) 'The influence of committee functioning on the organisational commitment of volunteer administrators in sport', *Journal of Sport Behavior*, 18(4): 254–269.

Cuskelly, G. (2001) 'Declining volunteerism in sport: where is the evidence?', paper presented to the 7th Annual Conference of the Sport Management Association of Australia and New Zealand – 'Global Issues in Sport Management'. Victoria University of Technology, Melbourne, 1 December 2001.

Cuskelly, G. (2004) 'Volunteer retention in community sport organisations', *European Sport Management Quarterly*, 4: 59–76.

Cuskelly, G. (2005) 'Volunteer participation trends in Australian sport', in G. Nichols and M. Collins (eds), *Volunteers in Sports Clubs*, Eastbourne: Leisure Studies Association.

Cuskelly, G. and Boag, A. (2001) 'Organisational commitment as a predictor of committee member turnover among volunteer sport administrators: results of a time-lagged study', *Sport Management Review*, 4(1): 65–86.

Cuskelly, G. and Harrington, M. (1997) 'Volunteers and leisure: evidence of marginal and career voluntarism in sport', *World Leisure and Recreation*, 39(3): 11–18.

Cuskelly, G., Auld, C., Harrington, M. *et al.* (2004) 'Predicting the behavioral dependability of sport event volunteers', *Event Management: An International Journal*, 9(1): 73–89.

Cuskelly, G., McIntyre, N. and Boag, A. (1998) 'A longitudinal study of the development of organizational commitment amongst volunteer sport administrators', *Journal of Sport Management*, 12(3): 181–202.

Cuskelly, G., Taylor, T., Hoye, R., Darcy, S. (2005) *Volunteers in Community Rugby*, Sydney: ARU.

Daly, J. (1991) *Volunteers in South Australian sport: a Study Commissioned by the South Australian Department of Recreation and Sport and the Australian Sports Commission*, Adelaide: South Australian Department of Recreation and Sport.

Davies, J. (1998) 'The value of volunteers', *Australian Parks and Recreation*, 34(1): 33–35.

Davis, M.H., Hall, J.A. and Meyer, M. (2003) 'The first year: influences on the satisfaction, involvement and persistence of new community volunteers', *Personality and Social Psychology Bulletin*, 29(2): 248–260.

Davis-Smith, J. (1998) *The 1997 National Survey of Volunteering*, London: National Centre for Volunteering.

Deane, J.W. (1992) 'Sport management: a tertiary education perspective', *ACHPER National Journal*, Winter: 24–28.

Dekker, P. and Halman, L. (eds) (2003) *The Values of Volunteering: Cross-cultural Perspectives*, New York: Kluwer Academic/Plenum Publishers.

Department of Family and Community Services (2001) *Background Paper Strengthening Communities: Theory and Research*, Canberra: Commonwealth of Australia.

Dickson, N. (1999) *What is the Third Way?*, London: BBC. Online. Available www.news.bbc.co.uk/1/hi/uk_politics/458626.stm (accessed 1 October 2005).

Dietrich, J. (2005) 'Duty of care under the "Civil Liability Acts"' *Torts Law Journal*, 13: 17–40.

DiMaggio, P.J. and Powell, W.W. (1983) 'The iron cage revisited: institutional isomorphism and collective rationality in organizational fields', *American Sociological Review*, 48: 147–160.

Doherty, A.J. (1998) 'Managing our human resources: a review of organizational behaviour in sport', *Sport Management Review*, 1: 1–24.

Doherty, A. (2005) *A Profile of Community Sport Volunteers*, Ontario: Parks and Recreation Ontario and Sport Alliance of Ontario. Online. Available www.216.13.76.142/PROntario/PDF/reports/finalReport_phaseOne2005.pdf (accessed 6 July 2005).

Doherty, A.J. and Carron, A.V. (2003) 'Cohesion in volunteer sport executive committees', *Journal of Sport Management*, 17: 116–141.

Donovan, F. and Jackson, A.C. (1991) *Managing Human Service Organizations*, Sydney: Prentice Hall.

Dorsch, K., Riemer, H., Paskevich, D. *et al.* (2002) 'Differences in volunteer motives based on organization type and level of involvement', in 17th Annual North American Society for Sport Management conference, NASSM Abstracts, May 29–June 1, 28, Canmore, Alberta: North American Society for Sport Management.

Duley, L. (2005) *Good Sports: An Event Management Company Asks: What's the Liability Situation for the Organisers of Sporting Events?*, New Zealand: IDG Communications Ltd. Online. Available www.unlimited.co.nz/unlimited.nsf/toolkit/9DBA56F09BB943F4CC25703F001119E6 (accessed 5 October 2005).

Eady, J. (1993) *Practical Sports Development*, London: Longman.

Eburn, M. (2003) 'Protecting volunteers?', *The Australian Journal of Emergency Management*, 18(4): 7–11.

Eley, D. and Kirk, D. (2002) 'Developing citizenship through sport: the impact of a sport-based volunteer programme on youth sport leaders', *Sport, Education and Society*, 7(2): 151–167.

Elstad, B. (1997) 'Volunteer perception of learning and satisfaction in a mega-event: the case of the XVII Olympic Winter Games in Lillehammer', *Festival Management and Event Tourism*, 4: 75–83.

Elstad, B. (2003) 'Continuance commitment and reasons to quit: a study of volunteers at a jazz festival', *Event Management*, 8: 99–108.

Enjolras, B. (2002) 'The commercialization of voluntary sport organizations in Norway', *Nonprofit and Voluntary Sector Quarterly*, 31(3): 352–376.

Farrell, J.M., Johnston, M.E. and Twynam, G.D. (1998) 'Volunteer motivation, satisfaction, and management at an elite sporting competition', *Journal of Sport Management*, 12(4): 288–300.

Football Association (2003) *FA Learning Referees Department: Building on Our Successes*, London: The Football Association. Online. Available www.thefa.com/NR/rdonlyres/33FCD70E-2D50–462B-98B1–7939875B4AF8/30979/Ref_Building Success.pdf (accessed 25 November 2005).

Frisby, W. and Kikulis, L. (1996) 'Human Resource Management in Sport', in B.L. Parkhouse, *The Management of Sport: Its Foundation and Application*, 2nd edn, St Louis, MO: Mosby.

Garrett, R. (2003) 'The Response of Voluntary Sports Clubs to Sport England's Lottery Funding: Cases of Compliance, Change and Resistance', in G. Nichols (ed.) *Volunteers in Sport*, Eastbourne: Leisure Studies Association.

Gaskin, K. (1998) 'Vanishing volunteers: are young people losing interest in volunteering?', *Voluntary Action*, 1(1): 33–43.

Gibson, G. (1991) 'Managerial competencies of amateur sport general managers', Abstracts of the 6th Annual North American Society for Sport Management Conference, Ottawa: University of Ottawa.

Gilbert, W. and Trudel, P. (1999) 'An evaluation strategy for coach education programs', *Journal of Sport Behavior*, 22(2): 234–250.

Gillette, A. (1999) *A (Very) Short History of Volunteering*, Germany: United Nations Volunteers. Online. Available www.worldvolunteerweb.org/initiatives/stories/volunteers/history.htm (accessed 29 September 2005).

Gillette, A. (2001) 'From work camps to virtual aid', *The UNESCO Courier*, June: 22–23.

Gladden, J.M., McDonald, M.A. and Barr, C.A. (1998) 'Event management', in L.P. Masteralexis, C.A. Barr and M.A. Hums (eds), *Principles and Practice of Sport Management*, Gaithersburg, MD: Aspen.

Government of Canada (2001) *Towards a Canadian Sport Policy: Report on the National Summit for Sport*, Ottowa, Canada: Author.

Government of Canada (2002) *The Canadian Sport Policy*, Ottawa, Canada: Author.

Green, B.C. and Chalip, L. (2004) 'Paths to volunteer commitment: lessons from the Sydney Olympic Games', in R.A. Stebbins and M. Graham (eds), *Volunteering as Leisure/Leisure as Volunteering: An International Assessment*, Cambridge, MA: CABI.

Green, M. (2005) 'Integrating macro and meso-level approaches: a comparative analysis of elite sport development in Australia, Canada and the United Kingdom', *European Sport Management Quarterly*, 5(2): 143–166.

Grossman, J.B. and Furano, K. (2002) *Making the Most of Volunteers*, Washington, DC: Public/Private Ventures Brief. Online. Available www.ppv.org/ppv/publications/assets/152_publication.pdf (accessed 29 October 2005).

Grube, J. and Piliavin, J. (2000) 'Role identity, organizational experiences, and volunteer performance', *Personality and Social Psychology Bulletin*, 26(9): 1108–1119.

Hager, M.A. and Brudney, J.L. (2004) *Volunteer Management Practices and Retention of Volunteers*, Washington, DC: The Urban Institute.

Handy, F., Cnaan, R.A., Brudney, J.L. *et al.* (2000) 'Public perception of who is a volunteer: an examination of the net-cost approach from a cross-cultural perspective', *Voluntas*, 11(1): 45–65.

Hanlon, C. and Cuskelly, G. (2002) 'Pulsating major sport event organizations: a framework for inducting managerial personnel', *Event Management*, 7: 231–243.

Hanlon, C. and Jago, L. (2004) 'The challenge of retaining personnel in major sport event organizations', *Event Management*, 9: 39–49.

Harrington, M., Cuskelly, G. and Auld, C. (2000) 'Career volunteering in commodity-intensive serious leisure: motorsport events and their dependence on volunteers/amateurs', *Loisir et Societe/Society and Leisure*, 23(2): 419–430.

Harris, B., Jago, L., Allen, J. *et al.* (2001) 'Towards an Australian event research agenda: first steps', *Event Management*, 6: 213–221.

Harris, V. (2004) 'Event management: a new profession?', *Event Management*, 9: 103–109.

Healey, D. (2005) *Sport and the Law*, Sydney: UNSW Press.

Henry, I. and Spink, J. (1990) 'Planning for leisure: the commercial and public sectors', in I. Henry (ed.), *Management and Planning in the Leisure Industries*, Basingstoke: Macmillan.

Henry, I. and Theodoraki, E. (2000) 'Management, organizations and theory in the governance of sport', in J. Coakley and E. Dunning (eds), *Handbook of Sports Studies*, London: Sage.

Hibbins, R. (1996) 'Global Leisure', *Social Alternatives*, 15(1): 22–25.

Hillary Commission for Sport, Fitness and Leisure (1997) *Running Sport I: Recruiting and Retaining Volunteers*, Wellington, New Zealand: Author.

Hodgkinson, V.A. (2003) 'Volunteering in global perspective', in P. Dekker and P. Halman (eds), *The Values of Volunteering: Cross-cultural Perspectives*, New York: Kluwer Academic.

Hoggett, P. and Bishop, J. (1985) *The Social Organisation of Leisure: A Study of Groups in their Voluntary Sector Context*, London: Sports Council and Economic and Social Research Council.

Houlihan, B. (1997) *Sport, Policy and Politics*, London: Routledge.

Houlihan, B. (2001) 'Citizenship, civil society and the sport and recreation professions', *Managing Leisure*, (6): 1–14.

Houlihan, B. (2005) 'Public sector sport policy', *International Review for the Sociology of Sport*, 40(2): 163–185.

Houlihan, B. and White, A. (2002) *The Politics of Sports Development: Development of Sport or Development Through Sport*, London: Routledge.

Hoye, R. (2004) 'Leader-member exchanges and board performance of voluntary sport organisations', *Nonprofit Management and Leadership*, 15(1): 55–70.

Hoye, R. and Cuskelly, G. (2003a) 'Board power and performance in voluntary sport organizations', *European Sport Management Quarterly*, 3(2): 103–119.

Hoye, R. and Cuskelly, G. (2003b) 'Board-executive relationships within voluntary sport organizations', *Sport Management Review*, 6(1): 53–73.

Hoye, R. and Cuskelly, G. (2004a) 'Problems in recruiting and retaining sports officials: an exploratory study', *Australian Journal on Volunteering*, 9(2): 47–55.

Hoye, R. and Cuskelly, G. (2004b) 'Board member selection, orientation and evaluation: implications for board performance in member-benefit voluntary sport organisations', *Third Sector Review*, 10(1): 77–100.

Hoye, R. and Inglis, S. (2003) 'Governance of nonprofit leisure organisations', *Society and Leisure*, 26(2): 369–387.

Hoye, R., Smith, A., Westerbeek, H. *et al.* (2006) *Sport Management: Principles and Application*, Oxford: Elsevier Butterworth-Heinemann.

Hylton, K., Bramham, P., Jackson, D *et al.* (eds) (2001) *Sports Development: Policy, Process and Practice*, London: Routledge.

Independent Sector (2004) *Research: Value of Volunteer Time*, Washington, DC: Independent Sector. Online. Available www.independentsector.org/programs/research/volunteer_time.html (accessed 1 October 2005).

Inglis, S. (1997) 'Shared leadership in the governance of amateur sport: perceptions of executive directors and board members', *Avante*, 3(1): 14–33.

Institute for Volunteering Research (2005) *National Survey on Volunteering 1997*, London: Volunteering England. Online. Available www.ivr.org.uk/nationalsurvey. htm (accessed 1 September 2005).

Ironmonger, D. (2000) 'Measuring volunteering in economic terms', in J. Warburton and M. Oppenheimer (eds) *Volunteers and Volunteering*, Sydney: The Federation Press.

Jackson, D. and Nesti, M. (2001) 'Resources for sport', in K. Hylton, P. Bramham, D. Jackson *et al.* (eds), *Sports Development: Policy, Process and Practice*, London: Routledge.

Jacobs, J.A. (1997) 'How the new law will affect associations', *Association Management*, 49(8): 39–41.

Jago, L. and Dreery, M. (2002) 'The role of human resource practices in achieving quality enhancement and cost reduction: an investigation of volunteer use in tourism organisations', *International Journal of Contemporary Hospitality Management*, 14(5): 229–236.

Jarvie, G. (2003) 'Communitariansim, sport and social capital', *International Review for the Sociology of Sport*, 38(2): 139–153.

Johnson, D., Headley, B. and Jensen, B. (2005) *Policy Research Paper Number 26: Communities, Social Capital and Public Policy: Literature Review*, Canberra: Department of Family and Community Services.

Johnston, M.E., Twynam, G.D. and Farrell, J.M. (2000) 'Motivation and satisfaction of event volunteers for a major youth organization', *Leisure/Loisir*, 24(1–2): 161–177.

Jones, R.L. (2000) 'Developing an integrated coach education programme: the case for problem based learning', 2000 Pre-Olympic Congress, Sport Medicine and Physical Education International Congress on Sport Science, Abstracts. Online. Available www.ausport.gov.au/fulltext/2000/preoly/ (accessed 15 July 2005).

Kikulis, L.M. (2000) 'Continuity and change in governance and decision making in national sport organizations: institutional explanations', *Journal of Sport Management*, 14: 293–320.

Kikulis, L.M., Slack, T., Hinings, B. *et al.* (1989) 'A structural taxonomy of amateur sport organizations', *Journal of Sport Management*, 3: 129–150.

Kikulis, L.M., Slack, T. and Hinings, B. (1992) 'Institutionally specific design archetypes: a framework for understanding change in national sport organizations', *International Review for the Sociology of Sport*, 27: 343–367.

Kikulis, L.M., Slack, T. and Hinings, B. (1995a) 'Does decision making make a difference? Patterns of change within Canadian national sport organizations', *Journal of Sport Management*, 9: 273–299.

Kikulis, L.M., Slack, T. and Hinings, B. (1995b) 'Toward an understanding of the role of agency and choice in the changing structure of Canada's national sport organizations', *Journal of Sport Management*, 9: 135–152.

Kikulis, L.M., Slack, T. and Hinings, B. (1995c) 'Sector-specific patterns of organizational design change', *Journal of Management Studies*, 32(1): 67–100.

Knoke, D. and Prensky, D. (1984) 'What relevance do organization theories have for voluntary associations?', *Social Science Quarterly*, 65(1): 3–20.

Lee, M.J., Whitehead, J. and Blachin, N. (2000) 'The measurement of values in youth sport: development of the Youth Sport Values Questionnaire', *Journal of Sport and Exercise Psychology*, 22(4): 307–326.

Leiter, J. (2005) 'Structural isomorphism in Australian nonprofit organizations', *Voluntas*, 16: 1–31.

LIRC (2003) *Sports Volunteering in England 2002*, London: Sport England.

Lloyd, K. (1999) 'The relationship between place-centred and person-centred leisure attributes and quality of life', unpublished doctoral dissertation, Griffith University, Brisbane.

Lockstone, L., Jago, L. and Deery, M. (2002) 'The propensity to volunteer: the development of a conceptual model', *Journal of Hospitality and Tourism Management*, 9(2): 121–133.

Lynch, B. (2002) 'Volunteers 2000', in R. Cashman and K. Toohey, *The Contribution of the Higher Education Sector to the Sydney 2000 Olympic Games*, Sydney: Centre for Olympic Studies, pp. 84–96.

Lyons, M. and Fabiansson, C. (1998) 'Is volunteering declining in Australia?', *Australian Journal on Volunteering*, 3(2): 15–21.

McCallister, S., Blinde, E. and Kolenbrander, B. (2000) 'Problematic aspects of the role of the youth sport coach', *International Sports Journal*, 4(1): 9–26.

McDonald, C. and Warburton, J. (2003) 'Stability and change in nonprofit organizations: the volunteer contribution', *Voluntas*, 14: 381–399.

McEwin, C.K. and Dickinson, T.S. (1996) 'Placing young adolescents at risk in interscholastic sports programs', *The Clearing House*, 69(4): 217–221.

McGregor-Lowndes, M. and Edwards, S. (2004) 'Volunteer immunity and local government', *Local Government Law Journal*, 10(2): 53–72.

McGregor-Lowndes, M. and Nguyen, L. (2005) 'Volunteers and the new tort law reform', *Torts Law Journal* 13: 41–61.

Macintosh, D. and Whitson, D. (1990) *The Game Planners: Transforming Canada's Sport System*, Montreal: McGill-Queen's University Press.

McKay, J. (1990) 'Sport, leisure and social inequality in Australia', in D. Rowe and G. Lawrence (eds), *Sport and Leisure: Trends in Australian Popular Culture*, Sydney: Harcourt Brace Jovanovich.

Mahoney, J.W. (1998) 'Volunteer Protection Act: What does it mean for you?' *Nonprofit World*, 16(2): 36–37.

Martens, R. (1978) *Joy and Sadness in Children's Sport*, Champaign, IL: Human Kinetics.

Martin, S.B., Dale, G.A. and Jackson A.W. (2001) 'Youth coaching preferences of adolescent athletes and their parents', *Journal of Sport Behavior*, 24(2): 197–212.

Martinez, J.M. (2003) 'Liability and volunteer organisations: a survey of the law', *Nonprofit Management and Leadership*, 14(2): 151–169.

Meijs, L.C.P.M. and Hoogstad, E. (2001) 'New ways of managing volunteers: combining membership management and programme management', *Voluntary Action*, 3(3): 41–61.

Meijs, L.C.P.M. and Karr, L.B. (2004) 'Managing volunteers in different settings: membership and programme management', in R. Stebbins and M. Grahem (eds), *Volunteering as Leisure/Leisure as Volunteering*, Wallingford, Oxfordshire: CABI Publishers.

Meyer, J.P. and Allen, N.J. (1991) 'A three component conceptualization of organizational commitment', *Human Resource Management Review*, 1(1): 61–89.

Mowday, R.T., Porter, L.W. and Steers R.M. (1982) *Employee Organization Linkages*, San Francisco: Academic Press.

Mules, T. (1998) 'Taxpayer subsidies for major sporting events', *Sport Management Review*, 1: 25–43.

Najam, A. (2000) 'The four Cs of third sector-government relations: Cooperation, confrontation, complementarity, and co-optation', *Nonprofit Management and Leadership*, 10(4): 375–396.

National Centre for Culture and Recreation Statistics (2003) *Australia's Sports Volunteers 2000*, Commonwealth of Australia: ABS.

National Council for Voluntary Organisations (2005) *A Briefing on the Charities Bill*, London: Author. Online. Available www.askncvo.org.uk/asp/search/ncvo/main. aspx?siteID=1&sID=18&subSID=117&documentID=2393 (accessed 9 October 2005).

National Society for the Prevention of Cruelty to Children (1998) *Protecting Children: A Guide for Sportspeople*, 2nd edn, Headingley, Leeds: National Coaching Foundation.

Nichols, G. (2003) 'The tension between professionalization and volunteerism in English national governing bodies of sport', paper presented at the 6th Australia and New Zealand Association for Leisure Services Conference, Sydney, July 2003.

Nichols, G. (2005a) 'Stalwarts in sport', *World Leisure Journal*, 47(2): 31–37.

Nichols, G. (2005b) 'Issues arising from Sport England's survey of volunteers in sport 2002–3', in G. Nichols and M. Collins (eds), *Volunteers in Sports Clubs*, Eastbourne: Leisure Studies Association pp. 1–14.

Nichols, G., Gratton, C., Shibli, S. *et al.* (1998a) 'Local authority support to volunteers in sports clubs', *Managing Leisure*, 3: 119–127.

Nichols, G., Shibli, S. and Taylor, P. (1998b) 'Pressures that contribute to a change in the nature of the voluntary sector in British sport', *Vrijetijdstudies*, 16(2): 34–46.

Nichols, G., Taylor, P., James, M. *et al.* (2005) 'Pressures on the UK voluntary sport sector', *Voluntas*, 16(1): 33–50.

Noonan, D. (1998) 'The health care volunteer', *Hospitals and Health Networks*, 72(13): 124.

Oakley, B. and Green, M. (2001) 'Still playing the game at arm's length? The selective re-investment in British sport, 1995–2000', *Managing Leisure*, 6: 74–96.

OECD (2001) *The Wellbeing of Nations: The Role of Human and Social Capital, Education and Skills*, Paris: OECD Centre for Educational Research and Innovation.

Onyx, J. and Leonard, R. (2000) 'Women, volunteering and social capital', in J. Warburton and M. Oppenheimer (eds), *Volunteers and Volunteering*, Sydney: The Federation Press.

Onyx, J. and Bullen, P. (1997) 'Measuring social capital in five communities in NSW: an analysis', Centre for Australian Community Organisations and Management (CACOM) Working Paper Series No. 41, Sydney: University of Technology Sydney.

Oppenheimer, M. (2001) 'Rights and protection of volunteer workers', *Australian Journal on Volunteering*, 6(2): 139–144.

Oppenheimer, M. and Warburton, J. (2000) 'Introduction', in J. Warburton and M. Oppenheimer (eds), *Volunteers and Volunteering*, Sydney: The Federation Press.

Orchard, W. and Finch, C.F. (2002) 'Australia needs to follow New Zealand's lead on sports injuries', *Medical Journal of Australia*, 177(1): 38–39.

Papadimitriou, D. (1999) 'Voluntary boards of directors in Greek sport governing bodies', *European Journal for Sport Management*, 6: 78–103.

Papadimitriou, D. (2002) 'Amateur structures and their effect on performance: the case of Greek voluntary sports clubs', *Managing Leisure*, 7: 205–219.

Pearce, J.L. (1993) *Volunteers: The Organizational Behavior of Unpaid Workers*, London: Routledge.

Pegg, S. (2002) 'Satisfaction of volunteers involved in community events: implications for the event manager', in University of Technology, Sydney, Australian Centre for Event Management, Events and Place Making Conference Proceedings, 15–16 July 2002, Sydney: University of Technology, Sydney.

Penner, L.A. (2002) 'Dispositional and organizational influences on sustained volunteerism: an interactionist perspective', *Journal of Social Issues*, 58(3): 447–467.

Penner, L.A. (2004) 'Volunteerism and social problems: making things better or worse?' *Journal of Social Issues*, 60(3): 645–666.

Penner, L.A. and Finkelstein, M.A. (1998) 'Dispositional and structural determinants of volunteerism', *Journal of Personality and Social Psychology*, 74(2): 525–537.

Phillips, M.G. (2000) *From Sideline to Centrefield: A History of Sports Coaching in Australia*, Sydney: UNSW Press.

Phillips, S., Little, B. and Goodine, L. (2002) *Recruiting, Retaining, and Rewarding Volunteers: What Volunteers Have to Say*, Ontario: Canadian Centre for Philanthropy.

Pinnington, A. and Lafferty, G. (2003) *Human Resource Management in Australia*, Victoria, Australia: Oxford University Press.

Plowden, W. (2003) 'The compact: attempts to regulate relationships between government and the voluntary sector in England', *Nonprofit and Voluntary Sector Quarterly*, 32: 415–438.

Powell, J.L. and Edwards, M.M. (2002) *Policy Narratives of Aging: The Right Way, the Third Way or the Wrong Way?*, Athabasca, Canada: Athabasca University. Online. Available www.sociology.org/content/vol1006.001/powell-edwards.html (accessed 6 July 2005).

Putnam, R.D. (1993) *Making Democracy Work: Civic Traditions in Modern Italy*, Princeton, NJ: Princeton University Press.

Putnam, R.D. (2000) *Bowling Alone: The Collapse and Revival of American Community*, New York: Simon & Schuster.

Pybus, J. (2003) 'Cover me: insurance costs are rocketing and charities are feeling the pinch', *Guardian*, July 9: 4.

Quain, R.J. (1989) 'An overview of youth coaching certification programs', *Adolescence*, 24: 541–547.

Quinn, R.W. and Carr, D.B. (1998) 'The instructional design process in coaching education: the development of the U.S. soccer national youth coaching license', *Applied Research in Coaching and Athletics Annual*, 32–49.

Raedeke, T.D. (2004) 'Coach commitment and burnout: a one-year follow up', *Journal of Applied Sport Psychology*, 16: 333–349.

Rainey, D.W. (1995) 'Stress, burnout, and intention to terminate among umpires', *Journal of Sport Behavior*, 18: 312–323.

Rainey, D.W. (1999) 'Sources of stress, burnout, and intention to terminate among basketball referees', *Journal of Sport Behavior*, 22: 578–590.

Rainey, D.W. and Duggan, P. (1998) 'Assaults on basketball referees: a state-wide survey', *Journal of Sport Behavior*, 21: 113–120.

Rainey, D.W. and Hardy, L. (1999) 'Sources of stress, burnout and intention to terminate among rugby union referees', *Journal of Sports Sciences*, 17: 797–806.

Ralston, R., Downward, P. and Lumsdon, L. (2004) 'The expectations of volunteers prior to the XVII Commonwealth Games, 2002: a qualitative study', *Event Management*, 9: 13–26.

Reeser, J.C., Berg, R.L., Rhea, D *et al*. (2005) 'Motivation and satisfaction among polyclinic volunteers at the 2002 Winter Olympic and Paralympic Games', *British Journal of Sports Medicine*, 39(4): e20.

Ritchie, J.R.B. (2001) 'Turning 16 days into 16 years through Olympic legacies', *Event Management*, 6: 155–165.

Robinson, J. and Godbey, G. (1997) *Time for Life: The Surprising Ways Americans Use Their Time*, University Park: Pennsylvania State University Press.

Rugby Football Union (2005) *RFU 2005/06 – 2012/13 Strategic Plan*, Twickenham, Middlesex: The Rugby Football Union. Online. Available www.rfu.com/index.cfm/fuseaction/RFUHome.simple_Detail/StoryID/11011 (accessed 19 September 2005).

Salaman, G. (1980) 'The sociology of work: some themes and issues', in G. Esland and G. Salaman (eds), *The politics of work and occupations*, Milton Keynes: The Open University Press.

Salamon, L.M. and Anheier, H.K. (1998) 'Social origins of civil society: explaining the nonprofits sector cross-nationally', *Voluntas*, 9(3): 213–248.

Sam, M.P. and Jackson, S.J. (2004) 'Sport policy development in New Zealand', *International Review for the Sociology of Sport*, 39(2): 205–222.

Sandy, R., Sloane, P.J. and Rosentraub, M.S. (2004) *The Economics of Sport: An International Perspective*, New York: Palgrave.

Saxon-Harrold, S. (2001) 'Level of participation and promotion of volunteering around the world', Seminar on The Third Sector: Beyond Governance and the Market, Hong Kong SAR Government 25 July 2000.

Schmidt, C. and Stein, G.L. (1991) 'Sport commitment: a model integrating enjoyment, dropout and burnout', *Journal of Sport and Exercise Psychology*, 13: 254–265.

Seippel, O. (2002) 'Volunteers and professionals in Norwegian sport organizations', *Voluntas*, 13(3): 253–270.

Seippel, O. (2004) 'The world according to voluntary sport organizations', *International Review for the Sociology of Sport*, 39(2): 223–232.

Sessoms, H.D. (1991) 'On becoming a profession: requirements and strategies', *Journal of Park and Recreation Administration*, 8(4): 33–42.

Sievers, A.S. (1992) *Recent Developments in the Liability of Directors and Committee Members of Non-profit Organisations, Program on Nonprofit Corporations*, Brisbane: Queensland University of Technology.

Silverberg, K., Marshall, E. and Ellis, G. (2001) 'Development of a volunteer job satisfaction scale', *Journal of Park and Recreation Administration*, 2: 79–92.

Slack, T. (1985) 'The bureaucratization of a voluntary sport organization', *International Review for the Sociology of Sport*, 20: 145–165.

Slack, T. and Thibault, L. (1988) 'Values and beliefs: their role in the structuring of national sport organizations', *Arena Review*, 12(2): 140–155.

Slaughter, L. (2002) 'Motivations of long term volunteers at events', in University of Technology, Sydney, Australian Centre for Event Management, Events and Place Making Conference Proceedings, 15–16 July 2002, Sydney: University of Technology, Sydney.

Smith, D.H. (1981) 'Altruism, volunteers and volunteerism', *Journal of Voluntary Action Research*, 10(1): 21–36.

Smith, D.H. (1993) 'Public benefit and member benefit nonprofit, voluntary groups', *Nonprofit and Voluntary Sector Quarterly*, 22: 53–68.

Smith, D.H. (1999) *Grassroots Associations*, Thousand Oaks, CA: Sage.

Smith, D.H. and Shen, C. (1996) 'Factors characterizing the most effective non-profits managed by volunteers', *Nonprofit Management and Leadership*, 6: 271–289.

Smoll, F.L., Smith, R.E., Barnett, N.P. *et al.* (1993) 'Enhancement of children's self-esteem through social support training for youth sport coaches', *Journal of Applied Psychology*, 78(4): 602–610.

Solberg, H.A. (2003) 'Major sporting events: assessing the value of volunteers' work', *Managing Leisure*, 8: 17–27.

SPARC (2003a) *National Officiating Strategy*, Wellington, New Zealand: Author.

SPARC (2003b) *New Zealand's High Performance Sports Officials*, Wellington, New Zealand: Author.

SPARC (2004) 'Taking coaching into the future', *The New Zealand Coaching Strategy 2004*, Wellington, New Zealand: Author.

SPARC (2005a) *SPARC Facts*, Wellington, New Zealand: Author. Online. Available www.sparc.org.nz/research-policy/research-/sparc-facts-97–01 (accessed 7 July 2005).

SPARC (2005b) *Liability of Sport and Recreation Organisations in New Zealand*, Wellington, New Zealand: Author. Online. Available www.sparc.org.nz/research-policy/policy-/legal-liability (accessed 7 October 2005).

SPARC (2005c) *Business Improvement*, Wellington, New Zealand: Author. Online. Available www.sparc.org.nz/sport/business-improvement (accessed 14 November 2005).

SPARC (2005d) *Great Coaches Create Great Experiences in Sport*, Wellington, New Zealand: Author. Online. Available www.sparc.org.nz/sport/coaching/overview (accessed 23 November 2005).

Sport and Recreation New Zealand (2005e) *Coaches Code of Ethics*, Wellington, New Zealand: Author. Online. Available www.sparc.org.nz/filedownload?id=7d 68ae1f-8bc2-4add-bfgd-0c580d5455c4 (accessed 23 November 2005).

Sport and Recreation Victoria (2005) *Member Protection*, Melbourne: Government of Victoria. Online. Available www.sport.vic.gov.au (accessed 10 October 2005).

Sport Canada (2000) *Report on the Officials Roundtable*, Gatineau, Quebec: Sport Canada. Online. Available www.canadianheritage.gc.ca/progs/sc/pol/pcs-csp/ncs-of/tdm_e.cfm (accessed 12 September 2005).

Sport England (2000) *Active Communities: An Introduction*, London: Sport England.

Sport England (2004a) *The Framework for Sport England*, London: Sport England. Online. Available www.sportengland.org/national-framework-for-sport.pdf (accessed 5 July 2005).

Sport England (2004b) *Driving Up Participation: The Challenge for Sport*, London: Sport England. Online. Available www.sportengland.org/national-framework-for-sport.pdf (accessed 14 September 2005).

Sport England (2005a) *Tax Breaks for Community Amateur Sports Clubs*, London: Sport England. Online. Available www.sportengland.org/index/news_and_media/news_gs/news_tb.htm (accessed 5 July 2005).

Sport England (2005b) *Monitoring and Evaluation Toolkit – Section 6*, London: Sport England. Online. Available www.sportengland.org/monitoring_and_evaluation (accessed 5 July 2005).

Sport England (2005c) *Sport England's Policy on Volunteers in Sport*, London: Sport England. Online. Available. www.sportengland.org/text/se_volunteer_policy_april_2005.pdf (accessed 27 November 2005).

Sport England (2005d) *Volunteers: How Can I Recruit, Retain, Recognise and Reward Volunteers?*, London: Sport England. Online. Available www.sportengland.org/index/get_resources/developing_sport/clubs/running_sport.htm#downloads (accessed 19 October 2005).

Sport England (2005e) *Quest: Quest is the UK Quality Scheme for Sport and Leisure*, London: Sport England. Online. Available www.sportengland.org/index/get_resources/developing_sport/questuk.htm (accessed 14 November 2005).

Sport England (2005f) *The Value of Sport: Why We Need to Improve the Evidence Base for Sport*, London: Sport England. Online. Available www.sportengland.org/index/get_resources/vosm/about_vosm.htm (accessed 16 October 2005).

Sports Coach UK (2004) *Sport Coaching in the UK: Final Report*. Online. Available www.sportscoachuk.org/research/researchreports.htm#SCUK (accessed 28 November 2005).

Sports Coach UK (2005) *Research Updates*. Online. Available www.sportscoachuk.org/research/index.htm (accessed 28 November 2005).

Statistics Canada (1997) *National Survey of Giving, Volunteering and Participating*, Ottawa, Ontario: Author. Online. Available www.statcan.ca/english/Dli/Data/Ftp/nsgvp.htm (accessed 21 September 2005).

Statistics Canada (1998) *The Vitality of the Sport Sector in Canada*, Canada: Culture, Tourism and Centre for Education Statistics Division.

Statistics Canada (2000a) *Voluntary Organizations in Ontario in the 1990s*, Ottawa, Canada: Author.

Statistics Canada (2000b) *National Survey of Giving, Volunteering and Participating*, Ottawa, Canada: Author. Online. Available www.statcan.ca/english/Dli/Data/Ftp/nsgvp.htm (accessed 21 September 2005).

Statistics Canada (2000c) *Sport Participation in Canada 1998 Report*, Ottowa, Ontario: Culture, Tourism and Centre for Education Statistics Division.

Statistics Canada (2004a) *Cornerstones of Community: Highlights of the National Survey of Nonprofit and Voluntary Organizations*, Ottawa, Canada: Author.

Statistics Canada (2004b) *Sport Involvement by Sex 1998*. Online. Available www40.statcan.ca/l01/cst01/arts18.htm (accessed 14 November 2005).

Stebbins, R.A. (1996) 'Volunteering: a serious leisure perspective', *Nonprofit and Voluntary Sector Quarterly*, 25(2): 211–224.

Stewart, C. and Taylor, J. (2000) 'Why female athletes quit: implications for coach education', *The Physical Educator*, 57(4): 170–177.

Stewart, B., Nicholson, M., Smith, A. *et al.* (2004) *Australian Sport: Better by Design? The Evolution of Australian Sport Policy*, London: Routledge.

Stewart-Weekes, M. (1989) 'Planning, performance and power: new models for the management of Australian sports', *Proceedings of the Management and Sport Conference, Volume 2*, Canberra: Centre for Sports Studies, University of Canberra.

Stewart-Weekes, M. (1991) 'The 10 Commandments of Sports Management', *Sport Report*, 11(2): 18–19, 23.

Strigas, A.D. and Jackson Jr, E.N. (2003) 'Motivating volunteers to serve and succeed: design and results of a pilot study that explores demographics and motivational factors in sport volunteerism', *International Sports Journal*, 7(1): 111–123.

Taylor, A.H. and Daniel, J.V. (1987) 'Sources of stress in soccer officiating: an empirical study', in T. Reilly, A. Lees, K. Davids *et al.* (eds), *Science and Football: Proceedings of the first World Congress of Science and Football*, London: E and FN Spon.

Taylor, A.H. Daniel, J.V., Leith, L. *et al.* (1990) 'Perceived stress, psychological burnout and paths to turnover intentions among sport officials', *Journal of Applied Sport Psychology*, 2: 84–97.

Taylor, M. and Warburton, D. (2003) 'Legitimacy and the role of the UK third sector organizations in the policy process', *Voluntas*, 14(3): 321–338.

Taylor, P. (2004) 'Driving up participation: sport and volunteering', in Sport England (2004b) *Driving Up Participation: The Challenge for Sport*, London: Sport England.

Theodoraki, E.I. and Henry, I.P. (1994) 'Organisational structures and contexts in British national governing bodies of sport', *International Review for the Sociology of Sport*, 29: 243–263.

Thibault, L. (2004) 'Will volunteerism keep its place in public leisure?', paper presented to the World Leisure Congress Brisbane, 2004.

Thibault, L. and Babiak, K. (2005) 'Organizational changes in Canada's sport system: toward an athlete-centred approach', *European Sport Management Quarterly*, 5: 105–132.

Thibault, L., Slack, T. and Hinings, B. (1991) 'Professionalism, structures and systems: the impact of professional staff on voluntary sport organizations', *International Review for the Sociology of Sport*, 26: 83–97.

Treuren, G. and Monga, M. (2002a) *Are Special Event Volunteers Different from Non-SEO Volunteers? Demographic Characteristics of Volunteers in Four South Australian Special Event Organizations*, Sydney: Author. Online. Available www.business.uts.edu.au/acem/pdfs/Proceedings.pdf (accessed 27 November 2005).

Treuren, G. and Monga, M. (2002b) *Does the Observable Special Event Volunteer Career in Four South Australian Special Event Organizations Demonstrate the Existence of a Recruitment Niche?*, Sydney: Author. Online. Available www.business.uts.edu.au/acem/pdfs/Proceedings.pdf (accessed 27 November 2005).

Tung, Chee-hwa (2004) *2004 Policy Address by Chief Executive*. Online. Available www.info.gov.hk/gia/general/200401/07/0107001.htm (accessed 27 November 2005).

US Department of Labor (2004) *Volunteering in the United States, 2004*, Washington DC: Author. Online. Available www.bls.gov/news.release/volun.nr.nr0.htm (accessed 31 October 2005).

Verhoeven, M., Laporte, W., De Knop, P. *et al.* (1999) 'In search of macro-, meso-, and micro-sociological antecedents of conflict in voluntary sports federations and clubs with the Flemish situation as a case study', *European Journal for Sport Management*, 6: 62–77.

Volunteering Australia (2001) *National Standards for Involving Volunteers in Not For Profit Organisations*, 2nd edn, Melbourne: Volunteering Australia.

Volunteering Australia (2003a) *Running the Risk: Risk Management Tools for Volunteer Involving Organisations*, Melbourne: Author. Online. Available www.volunteering australia.org/publications/risk_man.html (accessed 27 November 2005).

Volunteering Australia (2003b) *Information Sheet: Volunteer Rights*, Melbourne: Author. Online. Available www.volunteeringaustralia.org/sheets/documents/VolunteerRightsandChecklist.pdf (accessed 3 November, 2005).

Volunteering Australia (2005) *Definitions and Principles of Volunteering*, Melbourne: Author. Online. Available www.volunteeringaustralia.org/sheets/definition.html (accessed 7 July 2005).

Volunteering England (2004) *Managing Volunteers: Screening and Police Checking*, London: Author. Online. Available www.volunteering.org.uk/missions.php?id=435 (accessed 27 November 2005).

Wann, D.L., Melnick, M.J., Russell, G.W. *et al.* (2001) *Sport Fans: The Psychology and Social Impact of Spectators*, New York: Routledge.

Warburton, J. and Mutch, A. (2000) 'Will people continue to volunteer in the next century?', in J. Warburton and M. Oppenheimer (eds), *Volunteers and Volunteering*, Leichhardt, NSW: Federation Press.

Watt, D. (2003) *Sports Management and Administration*, 2nd edn, London: Routledge.

Weaver, M. (2001) *Labour Chooses Third Way to Improve Failing Services*, Guardian Unlimited Monday 22 October, Manchester: Author. Online. Available www.guardian.co.uk/ppp/astory/0,10537,578824,00.html (accessed 6 July 2005).

White House (2002) *President Delivers State of the Union Address*, Washington, DC: Author. Online. Available www.whitehouse.gov/news/releases/2002/01/20020129–11.html (accessed 29 October 2005).

Whitson, D. (1986) 'Leisure and the state: theorising struggles over everyday life', in F. Coalter (1984), *Leisure: Politics, Planning and People*, Proceedings of the Leisure Studies Association Annual Conference Sussex (1984), London: LSA Publications.

Wiersma, L.D. and Sherman, C.P. (2005) 'Volunteer youth sport coaches' perspectives of coaching education/certification and parental codes of conduct', *Research Quarterly for Exercise and Sport*, 76(3): 324–338.

Wilson, J. (1988) *Politics and Leisure*, Boston, MA: Unwin Hyman.

Winniford, J.C., Carpenter, D.S. and Grider, C. (1997) 'Motivations of college student volunteers: a review', *NASPA Journal*, 34(2): 134–146.

Wood, S. (1999) 'Human resource management and performance', *International Journal of Management Reviews*, 1(4): 367–413.

Yeager, R. (1979) *Seasons of Shame: The New Violence in Sport*, New York: McGraw-Hill.

Index